WE WANNA BOOGIE

An Illustrated History Of The American Rockabilly Movement

By Randy McNutt

HHP Books
Hamilton, Ohio

The photographs in this book appear by courtesy of the following sources: Capitol Records, Sun Corp., MGM, Twentieth Century Fox, Hi Records, Columbia Records, Gannett Corp., Shad O'Shea, Steven Rosen, Mean Mountain Music, Randy McNutt, Rusty York.

Copyright © 1988 by Randy McNutt
All Rights Reserved

First Edition
Printed in the United States of America

Published by The Hamilton Hobby Press, P.O. Box 455, Fairfield, Ohio 45014-0455. This book was printed with the finest materials. The pages are made of acid-free paper. They will not turn yellow with age.

Library of Congress in Publication Data

McNutt, Randy.
   We Wanna Boogie.
   1. History of the American Rockabilly Movement.
International Standard Book Number: 0-940152-05-3

Library of Congress Catalog Number: 87-082602

Photographs in this book were taken by the author or a photographer designated by the publisher. All older photos, including family pictures, were supplied by the individual artists for use in this book. Several others, as noted throughout the book, came from the author's personal collection or from newspaper files. The author offers thanks to the artists and their families for supplying the photos and other materials for the project.

Photo, front cover: Gene Vincent and the Blue Caps, from the 1956 film *The Girl Can't Help It*. Courtesy Twentieth Century Fox.
Photo, back cover: Randy McNutt at the control board in the RCA Studio B, Nashville, Tennessee, 1987. Photo by Cheryl McNutt

Dedicated with love and appreciation to the memory of my father, Bill McNutt, who made music a part of our family life; to my mother, Kay McNutt; and to my devoted aunt and uncle, Claire and Vernon Hornung.

Table Of Contents

INTRODUCTION 9

PART ONE: THE MUSIC
Rocking Rebellion 11
Country Boogie Days 14
Origins of Rock 19
Blue Suede Songs 31

PART TWO: THE INDEPENDENTS
Where It All Began 45
The Rise of Sun 50
When King Was King 65
"Go, Cats, Go!" 76

PART THREE: THE ROCKERS
Elvis Presley: 'I Have To Move' 78
Buddy Holly: That Was The Day 84
Carl Perkins: Rocking Guitar Man 88
Gene Vincent: Be-Bop-A-Lula 97
Conway Twitty: Lonely Blues Boy 99
Jerry Lee Lewis: Mr. Puming Piano 103

PART FOUR: SIDEMEN AND SAGES
Dumpy 106
Looking For The Cool Spot 115
Even Cowboys Get The Blues 119
Requiem For A Bantamweight 125
Sugaree Revisited 129
Story Of The Rocker 134
All For A Song 139
Teen Rockabilly 144
No Regrets 151
Rockabilly Soul 157

PART FIVE: ALL-AMERICAN BOYS AND GIRLS
Wild, Wild Wimmen 185
All-American Boys 204

BIBLIOGRAPHY 283
INDEX 284

Introduction

THIS BOOK IS THE CULMINATION of many years of work. My purpose was to provide a historical overview — not a definitive exploration — of the American rockabilly movement. I did not want to compile lists of records, release dates, and other routine trivia, for they have been covered in numerous magazine articles. Nor did I attempt to write a source book for every rockabilly performer I could find. Such an attempt would be futile. There are simply too many artists. Instead, I had to arbitrarily seek out certain performers to write about and study. Some of them did not want to participate; others participated to varying degrees. This is why some artists are better represented in story and photographs.

Several years ago, I got the idea to present the history of the rockabilly movement through the oral histories of the performers themselves. The movement could be chronicled more effectively that way, I believed. I wanted to learn about the fringe artists, and to find out what they did and why they did it. I wanted their stories to tell about the forces behind the music. And I wanted my book to be a book about people.

So this book is a tribute to those thousands of rejected performers who never brushed fame's skirt or even cared. Interestingly, many of them are now minor cult heroes whose once-worthless records are valued at hundreds of dollars by collectors. Perhaps there is some justice in this world after all.

I did not want to list their records and prices, however. I only wanted to try to tell their stories. When I first entered the record business as an independent producer in 1969, I never thought I would end up taking a magical journey through the South in search of forgotten rockabillies. After working so hard, I wanted to make records, not write about them, but somewhere along the way I decided to start taking notes in conversations with the many interesting characters that I met in the business. In the late '60s, the rockabillies passed before us as specters. Many people knew little about them. They had trouble finding work.

I met Denzil "Dumpy" Rice about 1971. Now Dumpy is a talented piano man who can still play those boogie licks and do it creatively. I hired him to play on several records that I was making for Avco-Embassy Records and Fraternity Records. But I was as impressed with his past as I was his performances. Through his career I could trace the evolution of rockabilly. Dumpy Rice was still the quintessential rockabilly player.

People like Dumpy are what this book is about — a history of rockabilly as a pure American musical form, as told through the eyes of its practitioners. Other books have examined the careers of Elvis Presley, Jerry Lee Lewis, and other big-name performers. In this book, I wanted to seek out those who were neglected to varying degrees.

My goal was not always easy to attain, for rockabilly admirers often disagree on what constitutes a rockabilly artist and record. Many performers were really country artists who recorded one or two rockabilly records in the '50s to keep up with the times. Others were once rockabilly artists who changed to other styles of music. So in this book you will find artists who had questionable rockabilly ties, but are interesting nonetheless. For example, Cowboy Copas was a country singer. No doubt about that. But I wanted to write about him because rock 'n' roll affected his career.

In a few cases, you'll also find artists mentioned in this book who never cut a rockabilly record, but they did influence the genre in some way. In short, my rules were flexible. My purpose was to entertain.

I urge you to seek other books to learn more about Sun Records, the history of rock 'n' roll, and the life stories of rockabilly artists. It is a fascinating field. My research will continue.

Randy McNutt
Hamilton, Ohio
September, 1987

1

Rocking Rebellion

ROCKABILLY MUSIC IS ENJOYING a revival all over the world. The demand for appearances by the older artists is growing, particularly in Europe. The demand is not so strong in the United States, but interest remains high.

Record companies are hurrying to release old and new recordings of these artists. Original records are selling for inflated prices. The world seems to have gone rockabilly crazy.

Why is this happening now? Maybe the music is finally getting the attention it deserves, and finally being appreciated for its explosive simplicity. Or maybe people are just feeling more nostalgic. I like to think that rockabilly, after a long period of benign neglect, is becoming popular again because the music is good.

But what *is* rockabilly? One gropes for an explanation. The music is more of a feeling than a highly defined style. It is, for certain, a simple music, featuring an uncluttered rhythm track and emotional vocals. The music is a marriage or rhythm and blues and hillbilly, or country. Poor white young people started combining these elements in the early '50s, and the hybrid was destined to become a vehicle for social commentary.

And develop it did. Rockabilly enjoyed only about four good years, from 1954 to 1958, but it left a musical impression. In '58, Elvis Presley, the guru of rockabilly in those early days, had entered the U.S. Army and become something less than his musical form. Starting about this time, his music became the antithesis of rockabilly — uninspired, bland, commercial. The days of his recorded spontaneity were over, at least for a few years.

New artists arrived to continue Presley's rockabilly work, however. Out of Texas came Buddy Holly, a gentleman rockabilly who moved rock 'n' roll — the music could not be accepted with a partial hillbilly tag — into a textured direction. Holly experimented with his own harmonies and helped develop production techniques beyond the usual echo-covered records of the early days. No longer would a sea of echo sufficiently cover a vocalist's sins. People started thinking about what the singer was saying.

Rockabilly went on to experience three phases. Phase One was the early period,

1953-56, when all kinds of rockabillies warbled because they had a need. Cut off from country music's mainstream because of too much competition and not enough conformity of their own, the rockabillies independently forged a new music that reflected their values and tastes. They set the rules by having no rules; singers sang what they wanted, and thought about how the record would be accepted after it was being shipped. Many artists chose country songs or rhythm and blues songs. In the early to mid-'50s, black records were rarely played on white radio stations. White artists had to record the songs if white audiences were to hear them.

Phase One was a crude period in which the artists generally borrowed from other musical forms. Presley could record a bluegrass piece, "Blue Moon Of Kentucky," but he could not sing it as it was intended. He added the rockabilly production and feel.

As the music progressed, from 1956-58, the lyrics, melody and recording quality improved. This was Phase Two. The young people had adopted rock as their own music, and the rocking country boys were starting to compete with their city cousins for hits and record deals. With the adoption of the term rock 'n' roll after a few years, the new music took on a definite wide-angle approach: rock was all kinds of things, from R&B to country to pop. When the large record companies learned that they could make money — and a lot of it — in this new musical field, rockabilly was doomed. Fabian, Frankie Avalon, Bobby Rydell — these were but a few of the manufactured "pretty boy" stars, whose careers were built on Dick Clark and the great American dollar. Could such people as Ray "Caterpillar" Campi, Sleepy LaBeef, and Billy Lee Riley compete with such corporate foot soldiers? Obviously not.

Rockabilly soon matured into rock 'n' roll without so much as a sigh. And suddenly an entire industry was built around the new music. Professional rock songwriters, publishers, studio musicians, background vocalists, producers, promoters and more sprang up all over the nation.

Not that rockabilly was dead, however. It continued to exist, as it still exists today. But from 1958 to 1963, Phase Three, rockabilly was gradually assimilated into the bigger ocean of rock 'n' roll, where different kinds of music flourished under one name. Only a few singers and musicians were so devoted to pure rockabilly that they would uphold its old-fashioned traditions. As Roland Janes, the Memphis guitarist, told me: "Musicians wanted hit records. They could progress and write and perform what radio wanted because radio created the hits. Progression is the natural way of things."

Of course, rockabilly did not die. It simply went underground, in the small clubs of rural America. To those musicians who could be happy to practice it, rockabilly was a satisfying, emotional release. Like a cicada, rockabilly was only waiting for the right time to re-emerge.

So let us examine the three phases of rockabilly and its rich history. It is a history that will continue as long as there is music.

Country Boogie Days

COUNTRY BOOGIE FLOURISHED all over the South at the close of the Second World War. Hank Williams recorded some boogie numbers in the late 1940s, and many other artists did too. But some performers built careers on the boogie.

In Birmingham, Alabama, for instance, Sidney Louis Gunter incorporated the new style into his hillbilly music, and folks liked what they heard. Sid's nickname was Hardrock. Hardrock Gunter, they called him, although nobody knows exactly why. A popular story goes that he was loading instruments into his car one day when the trunk lid fell on his head. When he didn't flinch, a fellow musician remarked that Sid's head was as hard as a rock. Hardly original, but catchy nonetheless. The name stuck. At least that's what a King Records biography writer said on a promotion record label in 1955.

We mention Mr. Hardrock Gunter simply because he was typical of the early country boogie artists of the pre-rock era. Many of these performers were interim boogie men only, as fate would work it. They were too old to rock when rock 'n' roll finally came to be, but still too young to go sit on the front porch and fiddle the night away. So, they existed somehow in the twilight between rock and country music. Few lived to enjoy the recognition that came from either musical form.

Yet Gunter did, to a limited extent. In his own way perhaps, he was a pioneer of the rock music field and an explorer of the uncharted regions between hillbilly and rhythm and blues. He took the name Hardrock Gunter as a disc jockey on a Birmingham radio station, and continued to perform with his six-piece band, the Pebbles. In 1949, when America was starting to emerge from the seriousness of the war years, Gunter wrote "Birmingham Bounce," a happy boogie tune that used the word rockin'. By 1950, he had signed with Bama Records, and "Birmingham Bounce" was released. It was limited to only local hit status, however, and soon Red Foley recorded his version and sent the song to number one on the national country — or folk — charts. In the next few years all manner of singers cut the song, both white and black. Hardrock Gunter was a local hero and the author of a hit song. Then, in 1954, he went to the young Sun label in Memphis and recorded "Gonna Dance All Night," a song that actually revealed: "We're gonna rock and roll. . . ." But that record failed, and Gunter moved on to television to perform. Sun would have to wait a few more months before a young truck driver named Elvis Presley would change the world with his music.

Gunter's career always swayed between country and rock. In 1951, he recorded for Decca in Nashville, with one good pre-rockabilly record, "Boogie Woogie On Saturday Night," resulting from his sessions at the old Tulane Hotel studio. He later recorded a version of the Dominoes' R&B hit "Sixty Minute Man" and other songs, but none of those Decca recordings succeeded. Neither did subsequent ones for King, Starday and other labels.

Despite a lack of sales, Gunter was a part of a bigger picture, one that was starting to grow: the birth of rock 'n' roll. By the time it was in its infancy in the middle of the decade, Sidney Gunter was already thirty-seven years old, and socially far removed from the lyrical meaning of the new music he had helped to create. He quietly faded.

His contributions did not, however. Country boogie was indeed a precursor of rock. Boogie singers moaned, yelped, whined and *rocked* their way through rhythmic songs that usually lacked only a heavy beat to make them real rock 'n' roll. The same vocal style would be borrowed by the rockabillies in a few years. Boogie singers sounded similar to the early rockabilly artists, in fact, with such performers as the Delmore Brothers, Wayne Raney and Moon Mullican wailing right up to and after the birth of rock 'n' roll. The Delmores actually gave their music a name with their record "Hillbilly Boogie" in 1945.

Another interesting and talented artist, Wayne Raney, recorded many good country boogie numbers during his long career as a harmonica player, guitarist, and vocalist on various labels. He went to number one on the national charts for country in July, 1949, with "Why Don't You Haul Off And Love Me" on King Records, and he continued to record for the label into the early '50s. He also recorded with the Delmore Brothers for King.

By 1956, however, Raney saw the reality of rock 'n' roll, and cut "Shake, Baby, Shake," a wild rockabilly song, for Decca. It did nothing, though, and Wayne Raney became a footnote for music historians: another singer with a number one record of long ago.

Perhaps one of the most interesting aspects of country boogie was that many black artists recorded its songs at a time when some boogie performers were recording black songs. R&B singer Bull Moose Jackson cut "Why Don't You Haul Off And Love Me," Ivory Joe Hunter recorded Al Morgan's "Jealous Heart" and Ray Charles covered Bob Wills' "Roly Poly." Many of Hank Williams' songs were recorded by black artists, too.

By the mid-'50s, a new style, rockabilly, combined elements of R&B and country boogie. The new music emerged with such stars as Bill Haley and Elvis Presley. Actually, the country boogie movement was an early stirring in the soul of rock 'n' roll. It was rockabilly without the R&B flavor, and a true *hillbilly* boogie. Its style was adopted by such diverse artists as Little Jimmy Dickens ("Hillbilly Fever," 1950, Columbia Records) and Merrill Moore, the rocking country piano player who toured with his Saddle, Rock & Rhythm Boys in the early '50s. Merrill cut such hot — but generally unsuccessful — records as "Fly Right Boogie" (1954) and "Rock-Rockola" (1955) for Capitol Records. The latter was a tribute to the grand old jukebox.

Many people are surprised to learn that Tennessee Ernie Ford recorded some fine country boogie songs, including "Smokey Mountain Boogie" (1949), "Shotgun Boogie" (1950) and "I Don't Know" (1953), all for Capitol.

But one of the wildest pre-rockers was Rose Maddox, who performed with her brothers as The Maddox Brothers and Rose on the West coast. Her style was cut right from the rockabilly cloth. She was younger than many of the boogie artists — only twenty-nine when rock hit in 1955 — and she had dark hair and good looks. She cut "Hey, Little Dreamboat," a quintessential rockabilly number, for Columbia that year, and moaned her way through some of the wildest boogie-rockabilly tracks of the times. When the band broke up, she went into country music as a single performer, and enjoyed a solid recording career from 1959 to 1964.

For all their efforts, however, most of the country boogie artists did not transcend the rise of rockabilly. They were of the same family, yet different somehow. By 1956, the rockabilly singers had all but taken away the boogie's reason for being. Country music had become identified more with honky-tonk. The boogie performers were hopeless anachronisms who had to adjust or go hungry. Many of them drifted off to the automobile plants instead.

Rockabilly, indeed.

Red Foley

Hank Williams Sr.

Rose Maddox

Origins Of Rock

AS AMERICA PULLED ITSELF out from the gloom of the Second World War, some strange things were happening in the nation's record business. During the war, the record industry and most others had to make do with what was available. Shellac was in short supply, as were talent and, to some degree, even interest. Naturally, the smaller independent labels suffered the most, and many had to suspend operations. Then, in 1945, the restrictions of the war years were finally lifted. The boys were back home, and everybody suddenly wanted to have some fun again.

About this time, America was experiencing other changes, however. The boys may have been home again, but not all of them found happiness. The emotional turmoil created by the war caused divorce, family strife, labor trouble and other adjustment problems — all the result of a changing nation. Women had taken jobs during the war, and many wanted to continue to work. In those days, country music was profoundly affected by the changes, and the honky-tonk style grew in popularity. Honky-tonk music was, simply, an expression of the new reality. Alcoholism, divorce, sexual infidelity — these were the main themes of the honky-tonk performers.

Hank Williams started singing in the honky-tonks — usually tough little roadhouses — in the South in the early '40s. By the end of the decade, the honky-tonk style had started to dominate country music and Williams was well-known. The music had a distinct sound: steel guitar, drums, electric guitars, electric or acoustic bass and whining vocals. In fact, the honky-tonk singers did not care at all if they missed notes and moaned in a nasal tone, for they were there to express emotion. And, they did just that.

With the new realism of honky-tonk music came a decline in traditional country song topics and flavor. Goodbye mother, sweetheart and rural appreciation; hello cheatin', losin' and drinkin'. The soft, mountain-style of traditional country music was taken over by the loud, rhythmic honky-tonk music. The new stars were Ernest Tubb, Lefty Frizzell, Ray Price and Webb Pierce. Unfortunately, the stars were the only ones to enjoy significant success as the 1950s moved toward its halfway point, and as President Eisenhower brought American servicemen home from Korea. Country music was slumping badly; little room existed for new artists. The number of country radio stations was small by today's standards.

About this time, however, some younger performers began to experiment with their music. As early as 1950, many black artists had already rocked the rhythm and blues charts with a jumping blues style. Roy Brown had stirred interest in his record "Good Rockin' Tonight" in 1947, and Wynonie Harris cut the song again for King Records of Cincinnati in 1948. It was an R&B hit, but one of only many that would come onto the charts by various artists in the next few years. At the same time, country music spawned its own version of jump songs with hillbilly or country boogie. Moon Mullican and the Delmore Brothers — both on King — helped forge the new sound. They were essentially doing what other performers had tried in the mid-'40s — bring in some life to country music.

Then, in 1951, William John Clifton Haley, of Highland Park, Michigan, a Detriot suburb, cut "Rocket '88'," a former number one R&B hit by Jackie Brenston (and, coincidentally, produced by Sam Phillips, founder of Sun Records in Memphis). Bill Haley, a country performer with a dark curl hanging over his forehead, also recorded some other R&B songs for the Holiday label in those early years. Then he left that Philadelphia label for another in that city called Essex. He continued to record country and R&B songs, such as "Rock The Joint," but had little success. Then, in 1953, Haley finally cut himself what can arguably be called the first rock 'n' roll "hit": "Crazy, Man, Crazy." Actually, nobody knows where the name rock 'n' roll originated, but it had been used musically for decades. Whatever this new sound was, however, Haley had harnessed it for a popular record. Oddly enough, he rocked harder and with more feeling on a previous cut, "Rock The Joint," but he wasn't complaining. He finally had attention.

Next, came the contract. Decca Records liked his potential, so the label signed him in 1954. He released a record called "(We're Gonna) Rock Around The Clock," but it was largely ignored. He later hit the top ten with Ivory Joe Hunter's "Shake, Rattle and Roll." Haley's theme song, "Rock Around The Clock," didn't hit until 1955, when it was used as the theme song of a film called *Blackboard Jungle*. The song was not the product of some wild men in leather jackets, however. It was written by Tin Pan Alley composers Max

Freedman and Jimmy DeKnight.

Haley was an unlikey teenage hero. He was a walking, singing anachronism. His music was a coarse blend of country and R&B and saxophones and steel guitars. And, of course, of plaid jackets and baggy pants.

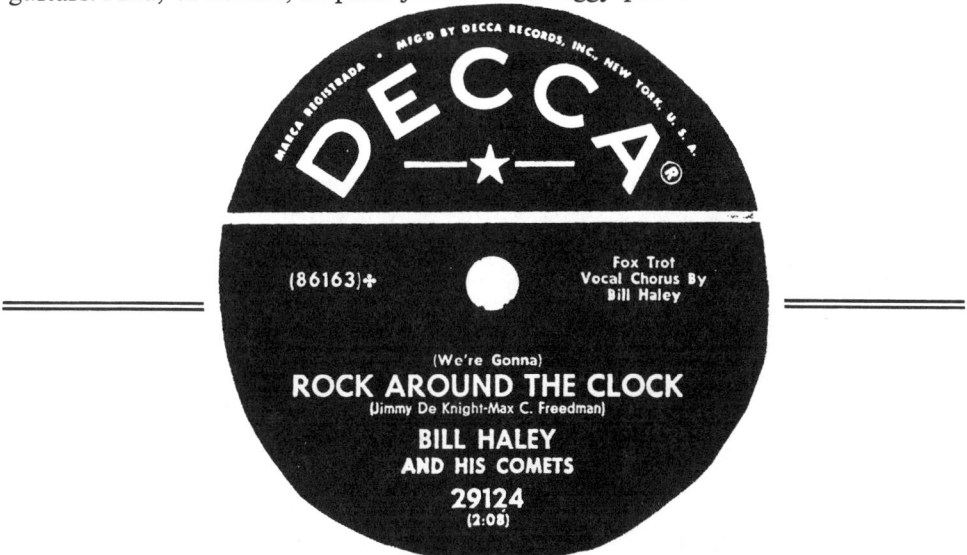

Despite his contributions and early successes, however, Haley will not be remembered as rockabilly's main leader. Perhaps that's because he was already too old (27 in 1954), too dumpy and too stiff on stage. It was Elvis Presley, a young truck driver from Memphis, who was destined to be favored by history. The story has been told so many times that it need not be repeated at length: Presley walked into Sam Phillips' Memphis Recording Service office one day, paid about $4.00 to record an acetate of a song for his mother, and left. Or, so the story goes, anyway. An office employee later brought Presley to Phillips' attention, saying the kid looked like he could be what the engineer was seeking. What Phillips wanted was a white kid who could sing like a black man. Here was this Presley kid. Only 19. Handsome. Dark. Why not?

Presley had charisma, a *feel*, that Haley did not. The young man joined guitarist Scotty Moore and bassist Bill Black to record "Blue Moon Of Kentucky," backed with "That's All Right," a song by blues man Arthur Crudup. Phillips released Sun number 209 in July, 1954. Soon, "That's All Right" was number one in the Memphis country music circles.

More releases followed throughout 1955, and Presley's reputation as a new musical phenomenon grew throughout the South. Late that year, Presley's contract was sold to RCA-Victor Records. By that time, he had added a drummer, D.J. Fontana, and established himself as some sort of rock meteor.

Presley then recorded "Heartbreak Hotel," a superior rockabilly piece, and others followed: "Hound Dog," "Don't Be Cruel," "Jailhouse Rock." But he slowly drifted from rockabilly's intensity to commercial rock's blandness. His later records seemed a part of a plan to be safe; to chart without danger of losing his place in contempory music.

By the end of the decade, Elvis had taken up the pop ballad and rockabilly was doomed.

Yet for one glorious period, roughly 1953 to 1963, rockabilly flourished. When the early rockabilly performers started attracting large crowds, a number of record executives watched with interest. Local record company owners took rough-edged singers into recording studios and cut all kinds of music. Often, the artists themselves would write and record a couple of their own songs, and then send the tapes off to a custom record label to get 500 or 1,000 copies of a single pressed on their own label or the pressing plant's special label. Starday Records of Houston did a big business this way, offering budding stars a a package deal: records shipped directly to them, for easy sale to nightclub audiences, friends and relatives. The artists were happy and Starday's Dixie label was busy.

The rockabilly movement of the 1950s was — and still is — essentially an elemental operation. From the sparse instrumentation to the no-frills record distribution, rockabilly seemed basic in every way. For every Buddy Holly and Gene Vincent, there were thousands of people like Orangie Ray Hubbard of Cincinnati, who recorded several local records and went to work in the factories. But music business irony strikes deep, and today many of those obscure local records are commanding higher prices from collectors than the hits.

And as in the '50s, the rockabilly movement remains extraordinarily close to its audiences. The old stars and nonstars can tour Europe and some parts of America to enthusiastic response, just as they did years ago. In 1986, for example, a balding school bus driver named Claiborne Joseph Cheramie left his home in Gretna, Louisiana, near New Orleans, to go to London, England, to perform for grateful crowds. His name may not be familiar to most people, but rockabilly admirers know him better as Joe Clay, a minor rockabilly star from the '50s and the rediscovery of London businessman Willie Jeffrey. Jeffrey appealed to disc jockeys throughout America to locate Clay, and later booked Clay into some London clubs for a concert tour.

Now, many of the early rockabilly stars regularly travel to Europe to perform because they seem to be more popular there than in the United States.

In concert, many performers sing their own songs because the nature of the movement encouraged them to do so in the '50s. This was due in part to the experimental approach of the music in those days. There were few role models in '54.

The charts were generally filled with pop singers; R&B artists remained practically unknown to many white audiences. So, if rockabilly singers were to croon about something, they were going to have to either borrow from country or R&B songs or write the material themselves. Many chose the latter alternative.

The rockabilly movement's lyrics were open to just about any subject of interest to listeners. In homes, schools and taverns throughout America, these slick-haired young vocalists sang songs that reflected their environment and social relationships. The songs, however ludicrous, were usually performed with such uncommon emotion that they took on the approach of honoring the subject. And, with the rockabilly singer's penchant for stuttering and warbling, his songs were incredible all the more to mid-'50s America. Just look at one such wild song, Gene Vincent's "Be-Bop-A-Lula," recorded, it seemed, in Mammoth Cave. Vincent moaned the lyrics in a sea of echo, singing about a girl named "Be-Bop-A-Lula" being his baby and the girl with the flying feet. This song was *not* an Eddie Fisher number. It was hot. But let's not forget other important compositions, including Carl Perkins' "Blue Suede Shoes." Do what you're going to do, he warned, but, cat, *don't* step on my blue suede shoes.

We will skip the usual sociological review and simply say that rockabilly's words, music and feeling reflected a changing American youth.

Rock 'n' roll had not yet developed a personality of its own in 1953 and '54. It was only a feeling, a seed of youthful rebellion and expression that would not create its own poets until later.

In fact, not until Elvis Presley's fourth single, "Baby Let's Play House," backed with "I'm Left, You're Right, She's Gone," did the local songwriters and musicians of Memphis begin to exercise more creative control over their recordings with Sam Phillips of Sun Records. The A-side was a song recorded earlier in 1955 by Arthur Gunter on Excello Records. The B-side was written by Bill Taylor and Sun sideman Stan Kesler. Presley's next release was a two-sided hit that went to number one on the country charts in September of that year and stayed on the charts for about forty weeks. The songs were "Mystery Train," originally cut for Sun as an R&B record in 1953 by Junior Parker, and "I Forgot To Remember To Forget," another original song by singer Charlie Feathers and Stan Kesler.

By 1956, rockabilly had moved from its dark age to a more enlightened one, using more original material and leaving the old songs behind more and more. Then, Phillips sold Presley's contract to RCA-Victor, and Sun took on numerous new rockabilly artists. Some, like Sonny Burgess, even wrote their own material.

Out of Arkansas came wild man Billy Lee Riley to sing "Flying Saucers Rock 'n' Roll" and "Red Hot." Riley sang of things that mattered to a teenager: his girl was so cool, she was red hot. To that, a taunting male chorus replied, "Your girl ain't doodly-squat. . . ." And, of course, there were also those odd flying saucers, little green men and rock 'n' roll. Yeah! Riley was so fascinated by saucers — so was America — that he called his band The Little Green Men.

Sun's list of artists would ultimately include Johnny Cash, Dickey Lee, Sonny Burgess, Charlie Rich, Jerry Lee Lewis and others. Many wrote their own songs. By 1956, the rockabillies were all over America, singing, waiting and recording.

Up until that time, singers were expected to sing, nothing more. They were to interpret. But how could a young, poor Southern white express the true meaning of something like "Lipstick And Candy And Rubbersole Shoes" by Julius LaRosa? No, if true sentiments were to be expressed, the rockabilly singer was going to have to write his own songs, unless a suitable one could be provided. And, with many rockabillies recording on low budgets and with small labels, often under crude conditions with little or no guidance, the original song was about the only way to get meaningful material.

In fact, that is how some of rockabilly's biggest hits were born, including "Peggy Sue" by Buddy Holly, a number three hit in 1957, and "Be-Bop-A-Lula," a number seven hit in 1956. That something so wild and sexy as "Lula" could also thrust itself to the top of the country charts seems unthinkable for us today, but its success in that market reflects the fluidity of the record business of the mid-'50s. After all, country music had given birth to rockabilly, and this strange new child would be welcomed — at least temporarily — by country stations. The border between country and rockabilly was a blurry one at best in those days, in fact, and many rockabilly hits jumped higher on the country charts than they did on the pop charts. For instance, from early 1956 to early 1958, Carl Perkins scored with three top ten and one top fifteen country hits on Sun, including "Blue Suede Shoes" (number two) and "Boppin' The Blues" (number nine). A Columbia single in 1956, "Pink Pedal Pushers," went to number seventeen. On the corresponding pop chart, however, only "Blue Suede Shoes" was a big national hit, jumping to number two. His succeeding records went no higher than number seventy on the pop charts in that period.

Other artists suffered a similar experience. That's one reason why the term "rockabilly hit" is a nebulous one today. Artists often talk about their "hit," when, in fact, it was only a regional one ("Sugaree" by Rusty York on Chess and "I've Got A Rocket In My Pocket" by Jimmy Lloyd on Roulette come to mind). Even Wanda Jackson, the undisputed queen of rockabilly, achieved only limited success in the early 1960s, when she hit with "Let's Have A Party" (number 37) on Capitol Records. That recording, a classic expression of teen lusting and wildness, did not even hit the national country charts, however.

Perhaps rockabilly performers and their obscure records are popular today because of their limited exposure in the past. But then, that is a part of rockabilly's appeal to us now: even the unknown singers can be big cult performers.

Life wasn't always that easy for the rockabillies. In fact, many were ignored for years until a wave of nostalgia swept them into the late 1970s. Many played in roadside taverns to earn a living in the early 1960s.

By 1963, anyway, the Beatles and the rock groups had practically killed the rockabilly movement in the United States. Audiences wanted to hear the hip new groups. The world seemed to forget rockabilly and its rural roots, and "Be-Bop-A-Lula" seemed as distant as Jupiter to most teenagers.

Those old sounds were revived somewhat in the late '60s, however, particularly in England. Buddy Holly, Bill Haley — they were all stars again, to a certain extent. Although Holly had died about a decade earlier, interest in him was rekindled. A movie, based on his life, followed in the 1970s.

From our perspective today, history has shown that rockabilly contributed not only a lot to general rock music but also gave much talent to the general pool of producers, engineers and record company executives. Many former rockabilly artists produce records (Jerry Fuller and Jimmy Bowen are two) and others write (Chip Taylor, Ray Pennington, Jean Chapel).

Now, the rockabilly movement is popular again as an oldies genre. It is still being recorded, wherever the simple ways of country and rock meet. But it remains essentially a musical footnote: about 10 great years of American music, when the world was a little simpler place, and the young person spoke up to say what mattered to him and her. It was said in such a special way.

Left, Bill Haley performing. Date unknown, but probably from early 1960s. Top, right, Haley singing with Ron Howard (left) and Anson Williams on the "Happy Days" television show in 1974.
Below, publicity photograph of Haley and the Comets from about 1956.

Bill Haley at the top of his career, mid-1950s.

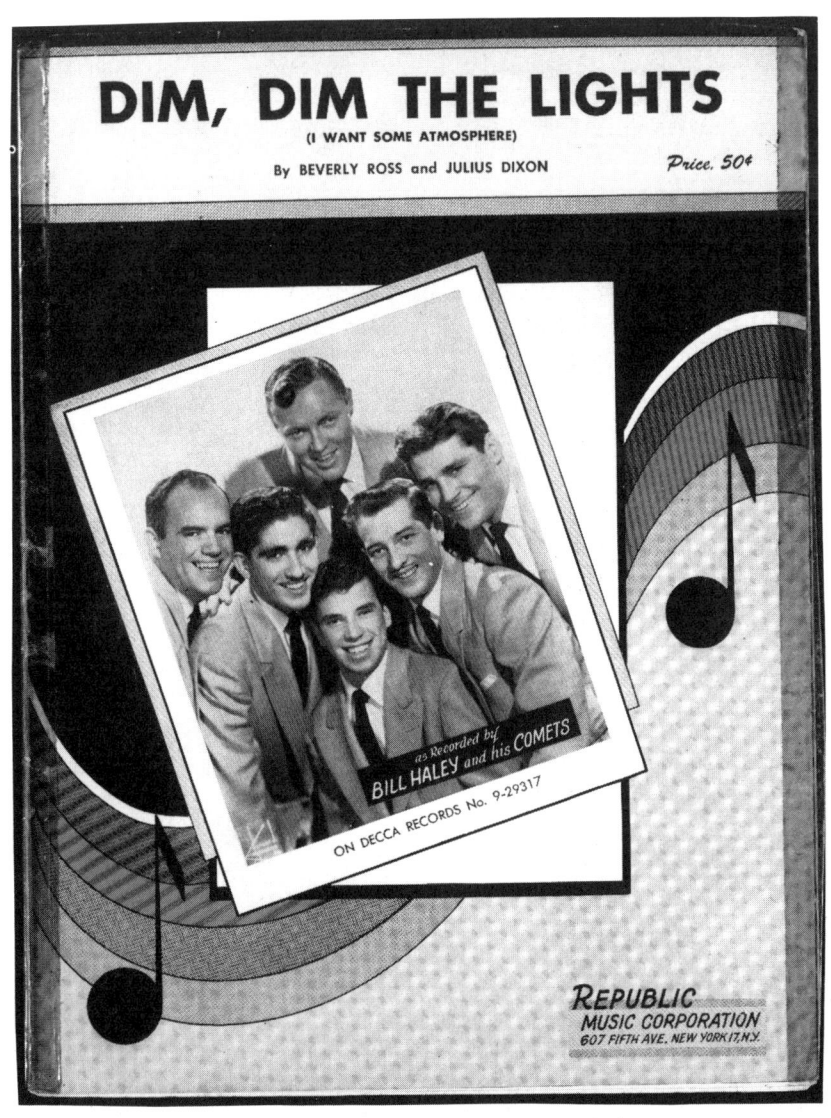

"See You Later, Alligator" hit the top ten in January, 1956, and started a new national greeting. Billy Haley was on his way.

Blue Suede Songs

WHAT MAKES ROCKABILLY SO INTERESTING is that it was doomed to extinction from the start. The genre may have started in the early 1950s, but it did not explode nationally until after Elvis Presley's recordings of 1954 and '55 gained in popularity. Crowds lined up to see the new wild man. As the imitators appeared, they — at least the more talented ones — brought with them a style peculiar to their own personalities and regions. The music's basic instrumentation evolved only slightly as the years progressed. Elvis added a drummer to his combo, consisting heretofore of rhythm guitarist Scotty Moore and string bassist Bill Black. The upright bass eventually gave way to the electric bass, and another Sun artist, Jerry Lee Lewis, showed the power of his famous pumping piano. Nevertheless, the rockabilly sound was always uncluttered and usually smothered with echo on the vocal tracks. The artists mainly sang live with the band in those days, before multi-track recording was popular.

By 1956, the record business was being shaken to its foundations. Small, independent labels were popping up all over the nation. The larger labels, being more conservative, had waited too long to jump into the rock market. They were now trying to make up that lost time by signing new young artists and leasing master tapes from the independent labels and producers.

Country music, meanwhile, entered a slump. Hank Williams was dead, and country seemed to wonder exactly what to do next. Rock or waltz? It is difficult to imagine such a time: established country stars like Cowboy Copas were rushing into the studio to record rockabilly music to improve their sagging recording careers. Staid country performers were trying rock; country stations were playing such bizarre records as "Blue Suede Shoes" and "Be-Bop-A-Lula."

The rockabilly boom sent country reeling. The market had been weak for some time, but then this new rock 'n' roll music — music some folks said was inspired by the devil — was *selling*. Country artists reacted differently to the crisis. Some, like the unknown Malcomb Yelvington of Memphis, thought they might as well adapt to the change by adding drums to their act and cutting a "rock" record. After all, they reasoned, the change was not *that* radical; they were essentially doing the old hillbilly boogie with more bottom to it. Other artists, however, especially the older, more established ones, reacted angrily, saying they would never compromise.

The popularity of rockabilly in a time of declining country music brought the inevitable friction. Johnny Cash — he was always country, really, despite a few youth-oriented songs and a label like Sun behind him — has said he was not welcomed in Nashville at first. Other country artists resented the new rockabillies, regarding them as wild men and women.

But after a little pressure from their record labels, many old-time country artists tried to go rock. Copas, the Grand Ole Opry star who hadn't had a major chart record since "Strange Little Girl" in 1951, recorded "Circle Rock" for Decca under his real name, Lloyd Copas. The record is highly prized by collectors today, but the disc did nothing to improve Cowboy's standing on the charts. Other artists recorded songs of a rockabilly nature, and others looked for songs with rockabilly in the titles. In 1956, Webb Pierce, one of the top country stars of that era, released "Teenage Boogie" on Decca. Don Reno and Red Smiley recorded "Country Boy Rock 'n' Roll" on King, Hank Snow cut "Hula Rock" for RCA-Victor and Bob Wills (yes, Bob Wills) brought out "So Let's Rock" on Decca. The trend continued in 1957, with "Rockin' And Rollin'" by Carson Robison, of all people, on MGM. Then came "Rock 'n' Roll Fever" by Cecil Campbell on MGM, and "Shake, Baby, Shake" by Wayne Raney, king of the country boogie, on Decca.

As youth became increasingly popular in our culture, and the rockabilly movement continued to grow, more country artists tried their efforts toward its name. In 1958, Tex Williams moaned "Let's Go Rockabilly" for Decca and Little Jimmy Dickens proclaimed "I Got A Hole In My Pocket" for Columbia. Dickens had already recorded some boogie numbers in the past, so he was not totally unfamiliar with rockabilly.

Other country performers recorded rockabilly and pseudorockabilly and country boogie masquerading as rockabilly. Justin Tubb, Johnny Horton, Skeets McDonald, Leon Payne, Carl Belew, Freddie Hart — many country performers flirted with rockabilly in the mixed-up '50s.

So let us examine why they would want to associate themselves with rock music. For one thing, the country market was in a recession at a time when rock was blooming. The days of the mass marketing of country stars had not yet fully arrived. The business was even more closed to outsiders, more clanish, than it is today. In the '50s, when rock almost seemed invincible to the country artists, many singers were eager to find a change. They wanted their records to sell a million copies, too. Later, in the 1970s, when country enjoyed a resurgence, many of those same artists said, yes, we were always country performers, but open to new things. And then, a few artists were simply identified wrongly as participants in the rock rebellion, when in fact they did nothing but try to keep working. Ferlin Husky, for example, was a smooth-singing country singer who first hit in the early months of 1955 with "I Feel Better All Over," a number fifteen hit on Capitol. That record launched a long list of big hits, including "The Wings Of A Dove" in 1960. Somehow, Husky was dubbed a rockabilly by some people in the music industry in the late '50s, although he insisted that the term was wrongly used. "Now Conway Twitty, *he* was what I'd call rockabilly," Husky told us one night in early 1986 in Franklin, Ohio. "Not me, though. I recorded under four names, including Terry Preston, after starting my career in 1948. I saw the rockabilly thing come and go, and through it all, I was a *country* artist. But when rock 'n' roll hit, you see, the writers put labels on me. Some people called me rockabilly. Country. Everything. I did do a variety of music, but, heck, I'm country. Elvis started that way, you know. So did I. I had records on the pop charts in those days, so writers had to call me something. But I never did call myself a rockabilly."

There really was not that much difference between many country and rockabilly performers. Both musical forms were clean, and rockabilly had, after all, come from the soul of country. So rockabilly artists could hide themselves in the cloak of a good country song, and vice versa. The big difference, beat notwithstanding, was the topic of the song. Country music had traditionally been the domain of rural whites of poor to modest means. Their songs reflected that constituency's problems and interests. Rockabilly, however, was primarily the music of young people, and therefore reflected a certain amount of rebellion against parental authority. The line of demarcation was the title and subject. While Warren Smith could croon a country ballad on one side of a Sun record, he could just as easily wail something like "Ubangi Stomp" on another side.

Some country singers sang both rockabilly and country. George Jones cut such rockabilly songs as "Rock It" and "Heartbreak Hotel" under the name Thumper Jones on the Starday label in Houston. Starday was a leader in the development of southwestern rockabilly music, using a number of well known local and national performers — including Sleepy LaBeef and Leon Payne — to record remakes of recent rockabilly hits for jukebox operators in Texas. Often the artists were listed, or they recorded under different names so they would not offend the country crowds. Leon Payne, for instance, recorded as Rock Rogers to protect his country image.

Some of the new rockabilly talent went on to become a part of the Nashville country music establishment of the late 1960s: Johnny Dee, singer of such songs as "Teenage Queen" and "Sittin' In The Balcony" for Colonial Records, was actually songwriter John D. Loudermilk, the author of such hits as "Then You Can Tell Me Goodbye," "Norman," "Sad Movies" and "Tobacco Road" (his Columbia version is classic rockabilly); rockabilly writer-singer Billy Swan became a top session player and a hit man himself with "I Can Help."

Other present-day country artists who once recorded as rockabillies include Mickey Gilley, Jerry Reed, Johnny Paycheck, Warner Mack, Roy Head, Mack Vickery and others. Of course, Jerry Lee Lewis was a top rockabilly singer, and a man possessed of the keyboard. He even made a movie, *High School Confidential*, in 1957, but not much happened after that. The spark was gone. Jerry Lee's movie finally opened in 1958, but he was hounded by scandal in the marriage of a cousin. He has remained successful in country music, however.

And rockabilly lives on, at least in altered form.

SENSATIONAL 45EP ALBUMS ON RCA VICTOR... only $1.49 each

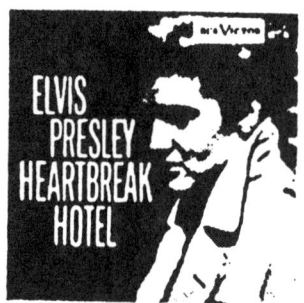

Little Jimmy Dickens

Bobby Lord

Carl Belew...

Ferlin Husky...

Hank Snow...

Justin Tubb...

Photos courtesy Mack Vickery Fan Club

"Those days seem like some kind of dream to me today," said Mack Vickery, the son of a sharecropper from Alabama. Vickery (left, and in center, at right) recorded for numerous labels, including Gone Records, before becoming a popular Nashville songwriter.

Van Trevor (left) and Gordon Terry (center) were country singers who dipped into the rockabilly song pool on occasion in the early 1960s; Charlie Walker (right) generally stayed faithful to his country roots.

Dorsey and Johnny Burnette were Memphis brothers who started their recording careers with The Rock And Roll Trio, but soon switched to solo performances. Although Dorsey never achieved as much success as Johnny, Dorsey was a smooth and outstanding vocalist. He also wrote songs, including his moderate hit "Hey Little One," later recorded by Glen Campbell. His biggest pop hit, "There Was A Tall Oak Tree," reached number twenty-three on Billboard's chart in early 1960 on the Era label. Dorsey Burnette died in 1979. He was forty-six years old. His son, Billy, is now a recording artist.

Even established country star Webb Pierce tried to jump into the rockabilly wave with "Teenage Boogie" on Decca in 1956.

Coming Soon!

JOHNNY CASH

RAY PRICE

JOHNNY CASH

SMILEY BURNETTE

SANFORD CLARK

**A Smash New Release!
Another Two Million Seller!**

SONNY JAMES SINGS

"First Date, First Love, First Kiss"
and
"Speak To Me"

On Capitol — Still Riding High
"Young Love"

Here Next Week
Sensational!

JERRY LEE LEWIS

JERRY LEE LEWIS & BAND

SID KING & THE FIVE STRINGS

THE FIVE STRINGS

Starring Tonight...

BILLY RILEY
& His Little Green Men!

JERRY REED

THE RANGERS QUARTET

TEX MASON

TOMMY MITCHELL

Plus The Big D Gang! & The "Search For Stars"!

GEORGIA ROCKABILLY MAN

Country singer Jerry Reed started his career as a rockabilly and country vocalist in the late 1950s. In the photograph above, Reed is shown in a familiar pose. The advertisement was for the "Big D Jamboree" in Dallas in 1957. Reed cut some good records for Capitol in those early days, including "Rockin' In Bagdad." Reed later swtiched to his own brand of upbeat country music and recorded numerous country hits for RCA Records in the 1970s. Two records, "Amos Moses" and "When You're Hot You're Hot," hit the pop charts, too.

Guest star time again,
THE GEORGIA GENTLEMAN
JERRY REED
with his Capitol recordings

SOME COUNTRY MUSIC STARS OF THE LATE FIFTIES

Faron Young

Connie Hall

Jimmy Wakely

Tommy Duncan

George Morgan

Mitchell Torok

Lawton Williams

Billy Walker

Gov. Jimmy Davis

Country singer Mickey Gilley was once a rockabilly-country performer. An early record was called "Call Me Shorty."

Even the legendary Bob Wills rubbed the rockabilly genie.

"Country" Johnny Mathis recorded for the D label of Texas in the late-1950s. He recorded a duet with Jimmy Fautheree, "My Little Baby," about 1958, but it was not a big national hit. The record was upbeat country and rockabilly. Mathis later practiced country music exclusively, and recorded for such labels as Little Darlin' and Hilltop. He also recorded some gospel records.

Country singer Warner Mack — born Warner McPherson — started his career as a rockabilly singer with two moderate national hits on Decca, "Is It Wrong (For Loving You)" and "Roc-A-Chicka." That was in 1957 and '58. "I'm not interested in seeing my name up in lights anymore," he told me in early 1987. "Now if somebody had $5,000 to pay me for an interview so that I could tell my experiences and the phoniness of the business, that's another matter. But I'm not interested in an interview."

JIMMIE SKINNER PRESENTS
A BIG COUNTRY MUSIC JUBILEE
SUNDAY, MAY 18, 1958

SHOWS AT 2 AND 5 P.M.

OPENING DAY—VERONA LAKE RANCH, VERONA, KY.

5 Miles West of Walton, Ky., on Route 16 (25 Miles from Cincinnati)

RECORDING ARTISTS IN PERSON

Direct from Grand Ol' Opry

GEORGE JONES (Mercury-Starday Records)—"Color of the Blues"

(Direct from Bristol, Va.)

STANLEY BROS. (Mercury-Starday Records)—"No School Bus in Heaven"

JIMMIE SKINNER (Mercury-Starday Records)—"What Makes a Man Wander" "I Found My Girl in the USA"

RAY LUNSFORD (Mercury-Starday Records)—"Carroll County Blues"—"Sheila"

CONNIE HALL (Mercury-Starday Records)—"I'm the Girl in the USA" "We've Got Things in Common"

RUSTY YORK (Mercury-King Records)— "Dixie Strut" (5-String Banjo) "Peggy Sue"

SKEETER DAVIS (RCA Victor Records)— "Lost to a Geisha Girl" "I Need You All the Time"

JIMMIE LLOYD (Roulette Records)—"You're Gone Baby" "I Got A Rocket in My Pocket"

DONNIE BOWSER (Fraternity Records)—"Stone Heart"—"I Love You Baby"

BOBBY GROVE (King Records)—"Mocking Bird Sings at Midnite"

RALPH BOWMAN (Excellent Records)—"Tragedy of School Bus 27"

and Many Others

Jimmie Skinner Will Celebrate His 7th Anniversary on WNOP (740 on Dial)

Also Sixth Anniversary of Jimmie Skinner Music Center

MANY FREE RECORDS AND ALBUMS GIVEN AWAY PLUS MANY DOOR PRIZES

Picnic Tables   Fishing   Kiddie Rides   Refreshment Stands

ADMISSION AT GATE 75c

Jones and vocalist Rusty York in 1959.

George Jones, one of the greatest country music singers of all time, once recorded rockabilly under the name Thumper Jones for the Starday label out of Houston, Tx. Of course, Jones also continued to record country music. He went on to set the exacting standards of what country music is all about today.

GEORGE "THUMPER"... JONES

2

Where It All Began

SO THIS IS A TALE of *three* cities: Nashville, Cincinnati, Memphis. They were chosen arbitrarily. Other cities produced good music, too, but these three recorded a large portion of rockabilly records made in the 1950s. Of the three cities, however, only Nashville remains a major force in America's record industry. Memphis is still somewhat active in the production and marketing of recordings, but not to the extent that the city was involved in the late '60s and early '70s. And Cincinnati seems practically dormant. With apologies to other cities with strong rockabilly ties, we will consider the rockabilly phenomenon as it occurred in three towns.

Let's begin with Nashville, Tennessee. Visitors walk by its famed Music Row and wonder why it all started *here.* They look for a golden Oz but find only an urban neighborhood laced with small brick houses, some low, flat buildings, and a couple of glass towers.

The heart of this twanging Southern Mecca — primarily the area around 16th and 17th avenues — remains as humble as its songs. Here, in remodeled kitchens and dining rooms in former single-family homes, the music business has hummed steadily over the last three decades, all the time cooking up hit records with homey flavor. All the while, Nashville has wrapped itself tightly in the banner of country music. For good reason too: the music drew people. They longed to see the Grand Ole Opry and, later, the Country Music Hall of Fame and Opryland. They wanted to somehow be a part of what was promoted as Music City, U.S.A., the self-proclaimed and undisputed home of country music.

It was not always that way, however. Only a few decades ago, country music had no international capital. Most records were produced in New York City or wherever talented musicians could gather around a microphone. Radio stations across the nation often doubled as studios.

People lived in the houses on The Row as recently as the late 1940s and early '50s, when the roots of modern country music popped through the cracks in the sidewalks of 16th Avenue. At that time, Nashville probably wasn't blessed with any more good session players than any other medium-sized city. So Nashville imported them. This was no conspiracy; musicians just drifted in, slowly, to get work in radio and the Opry. Old Nashville had no guitar-shaped swimming pools, no disc jockey and fan conventions, no Hall of Fame. In fact, Cincinnati, Memphis, and perhaps a dozen other cities of their size boasted a strong local country music base.

But Cincinnati and Memphis were particularly strong. Even today, they share common traits with Nashville: all were basically the same size, all were cultural centers of their regions. all were located on rivers, all were industrial centers and transportation hubs, and all were hot music cities. I say this in the past tense because the competition is over today. Nashville is one of the three leading recording centers behind New York and Los Angeles. Nashville is a town spinning on a rhinestone, turning over millions of dollars a year on its musical reputation.

The record industry is the main cog in the wheel of the Nashville music economy. The record business and its satellite industries employ thousands of people. In the late '60s, the city estimated that its studios generated $180,000 of business a day, and that figure must be much larger now. Nashville's studio scene has grown tremendously.

Country music as we know it began as "hillbilly" music in the 1920s, when Vernon Dalhart recorded numerous folk songs for several record companies. Victor Records recorded Jimmie Rodgers and the Carter Family in the late '20s, but it was Rodgers who was to influence many other artists of his time. Many of "The Singing Brakeman's" songs — they included "Muleskinner Blues" and "In The Jailhouse Now" — are still recorded to this day.

During the Great Depression, records, like most other things, sold slowly. Yet country music became even more popular with the rise of country barn dance programs on local radio stations all over the nation. Chicago's "National Barn Dance" started the careers of such artists as Red Foley and Gene Autrey.

But it was a Nashville radio show, "The Grand Ole Opry," that was to become the most famous in the coming decades. The show was broadcast on WSM Radio, and its signal cut deeply into the heart of America. As the years passed, barn dance programs in other parts of the country faded, but the Opry did not. Soon publishers started working in Nashville and the better musicians moved to Nashville to get work in the shrinking radio barn dance market. By the mid-'40s, RCA Records was recording country artists at the WSM studio in Nashville, and other labels decided to record there, too.

By the late-'50s, Nashville had recording studios and its own "sound" — The Nashville Sound, a concoction of pop and country sounds featuring violins, a fat background chorus, and tinkling piano. The "sound" was pioneered by such people as Chet Atkins, a RCA executive and producer; Anita Kerr, of the Anita Kerr Singers, background vocalists; Owen Bradley, a Decca Records producer; and Don Law, a Columbia producer. The Nashville Sound eventually became a finely tuned machine. Session musicians provided the rhythm and orchestral tracks for the artist, whose only job was to show up for the recording session and sing. Nashville still operates that way, although room is being made for more diversity.

In Cincinnati, meanwhile, the local record industry is about dead. Several studios continue to operate, but gone are the days when many country singers headed to Cincinnati, Ohio, to start their music careers. Things were different in the early '50s, when King Records sought to sign every major country artist. And only fifteen or twenty years earlier, those artists had wanted to come to town to perform on WLW Radio's country barn dance shows. The station once broadcast with *500,000* watts.

"Most of the big-name musicians worked in Cincinnati at one time," the late E.T. "Bucky" Herzog Sr. said in 1984. "I worked at WLW Radio and knew all of the fellows. Then I opened my own recording studio in the early '40s. Cincinnati was way ahead of Nashville then in recording facilities. I remember when Fred Rose begged me to come down to Nashville to open a studio. He used to record in Cincinnati. I didn't go, though. Why should I think of doing that at the time? Record people from all over the country stopped in Cincinnati then to record because of the great sidemen we had in town. They worked for the station part of the time. We recorded so many singers: Hank Williams, Patti Page, Ernest Tubb, Red Foley, and more."

By the late '40s, however, the station reduced its live music programming and the musicians went South. Such shows as "Renfro Valley Jamboree" and "The Midwestern Hayride" were either stopped or, as with the "Hayride," put on television. The staff musicians found work at the Opry in Nashville. Chet Atkins was one who used his talent and intelligence to jump from one-time radio sideman to the head of RCA's Nashville operations. And, along the way, he became one of country music's most influential session guitarists.

As Cincinnati declined and Nashville set up its musical dynasty, Memphis continued on its fiercely independent way. That's the Memphis way.

They say Memphis is the home of the blues, and they're right, for Memphis has lured black and white, blues and country, from the cotton fields of the Mississippi Delta for a century. Poor blacks came in plantation boats, arriving at the doorstep of the blues on Beale Street in Memphis, between Hernando and Fourth, an area called "the underworld."

Memphis has long been known as a producer of cotton, lumber, tobacco, and the blues. Over the years, it has become known for attracting country and blues musicians, and for somehow blending the two styles into rockabilly.

The city's musical direction got started on the pathway to the blues in the first decade of the 1900s, when blues man William Christopher "W.C." Handy arrived in the area. Handy, a native of Florence, Alabama, is supposed to have starting playing music on the jaw bone of a dead horse before he took up the trumpet. (Another Florence native, Sam Phillips, would also come to Memphis and change the world's music. But that's another story.)

Handy became a top blues musician and composer, writing such blues hits as "Saint Louis Blues," "Memphis Blues," and "Beale Street Blues." Although he eventually moved to New York City, his memory still lives in Memphis.

Considering the city's tradition in blues and the area's devotion to country music, nobody should be surprised that rockabilly first erupted here.

Memphis has remained a strong American music center, but its recording industry has weakened since the days of the late '60s and early '70s. Then, the soul music of Stax Records and the white rock of such producers as Chips Moman and Dan Penn climbed the national charts with regularity.

But even if the recording scene diminishes in Memphis and Cincinnati and a host of other cities, the music will never die. It is a part of us.

This building on McGavock Street in Nashville, Tennessee, was the home of RCA's Studio A in the mid-1950s. Elvis Presley recorded "Heartbreak Hotel" there. Photo by Randy McNutt

The staff of WLWT's *Midwestern Hayride*, a program broadcast on Saturday nights in Cincinnati, Ohio. Many country and rockabilly performers were the featured guests. Kenny Price was a regular vocalist.

The Rise Of Sun

WHEN SAM C. PHILLIPS started getting his rockabilly records played on country music radio stations across the South in the mid-1950s, Nashville music executives paid little attention. They were a part of a close-knit group of singers, musicians, and producers who had made up that loose confederation of "folk" or "hillbilly" music — better known as country music in modern times. They lived in an insular world, one left alone most of the time by the general music industry. If they wanted something in country music, they got it. No questions asked. Their power was enormous. The overall country music establishment — that clique of producers, promoters, artists, and whatever — was The Power in 1954.

So who cares about Sam Phillips? That was their attitude. Who cares about his crazy music. These country music executives could not understand it. Not *all* of them were so close-minded, but many were and many remain so today. The Nashville elite simply underestimated the upheaval that was about to occur in music.

The rockabilly sound of Sun Records of Memphis was *not* country music. It also was not modern black music of the day. No, it was somehow a smooth combination of the two, and nobody really knew how to react to it. Least of all Sam Phillips. All he knew is that he liked what he heard in his little studio. He did not set out to find a white man who could sing like a black man. With racial tensions as they were in the South in the mid-'50s, that search would have been ridiculous. What Phillips wanted, however, was a white singer who could sing with the same feeling that many of the black artists projected in their music. A blues feeling. A certain rhythm. That is what Phillips needed.

When he put it all together, Nashville in general did not know how to react. Nor did it care to react. But despite Nashville's ambivalence, Sun simply would not go away.

Country hits followed by that upstart artist Elvis Presley, then by other Sun artists. By this time, 1954 and '54, Nashville had established itself as the top country music center of America, a position the city would further solidify by the end of the decade. This bastion of twang was not about to feel comfortable with Sun's new rocking rhythm.

Rockabilly was raw — pure energy unleased in about two minutes on scratchy vinyl. The music was like a tornado that touched down briefly, then pulled away to leave everything changed. The kids were moved by this sound long after the record ended. This was *their* music, not some schlock produced by Mitch Miller and the guys with pipes and tweed suits in New York and California. No, this music was explosive, a superconductor of energy. Nashville, as a collective consciousness, did not get that idea until after the young people had broken into a mild hysteria in the South.

Over the coming months and years, some Nashville-based labels did sign rockabilly artists. Some, like Ronnie Self, were good; others were not. And most were hampered by Nashville's insistence on stamping the Nashville Sound on its rockabilly records. Many labels used session players and arrangers who were talented studio creators but not enthusiasts of the new music. They were either pop or country players who were used to a formula. There were no preconceived notions in rockabilly. It was free-form music. Although someone like Chet Atkins could play about any kind of music on the guitar, the Anita Kerr Singers could sing only one way — the pop way, even though they were recording country music. The vocal arranger's group was used all too often on rockabilly sessions. Can you imagine a more incongruous sound?

Sam Phillips did not have to be told what players to use on his sessions, however. He *knew*. He matched singers with the proper songs, too. He knew, for example, that a rhythmic country singer named Warren Smith could handle a Johnny Cash song called "Rock 'n' Roll Ruby." Phillips also knew that a gritty bar singer named Billy Lee Riley would sound great on Ray Scott's "Flyin' Saucers Rock 'n' Roll." And so it continued.

In the beginning, too, he knew that a singing truck driver named Elvis Presley was rough but talented, lacking only in vocal coaching and direction.

But we will not tell the Presley story or the Sun story over again. Those stories have been told elsewhere and often. The Sun story has been the subject of entire books. Even many of its more famous artists have had books devoted to them. Instead, we will concentrate on a brief history of Sun so that we can have a perspective on the new music.

To say that Sun's roster was impressive is to understate the situation. Edwin

Bruce, Charlie Rich, Johnny Cash, Jerry Lee Lewis, Carl Perkins, Roy Orbison, Conway Twitty, Presley, and others all got their starts at Sun.

Phillips, the founder, became a father figure to many of them. Phillips was born in Florence, Alabama, in 1925. The family had eight children and Sam's father died when Sam was young, so life was tough when the Depression hit at full force in the early '30s. As a young man, Sam wanted to be a professional in some occupation, and he decided upon radio because the opportunity presented itself quickly. Eventually, he settled in Memphis. He had a family of his own. But somehow, it was not enough. He was not happy. With his radio station job going well and a part-time job lined up on the side, Sam should have been very happy. But like many Americans, he longed to work for himself in a field where he could see results. That's when he decided to open a little recording studio. He called it the Memphis Recording Service, and he opened it at 706 Union Avenue in early 1950.

By 1951, he had quit his other jobs and attempted to make a living from the studio. He recorded weddings and just about anything that people wanted. Folks could even come in, step before the microphone, and cut an acetate record for a friend or relative.

Phillips decided to record the many blues artists who lived around Memphis, and to lease the master tapes to record companies in other cities. He recorded such artists as Howlin' Wolf, B.B. King, Ike Turner, Bobby Bland, and many others. He cut "Rocket 88" by Jackie Brenston and other important records of the early '50s, many of which were leased to the Chess brothers' label in Chicago. Their Chess Records company was a major independent.

But the brothers and Phillips disagreed over a business deal, and other labels were cutting back on the number of blues masters they were accepting, so Phillips started his own label, Sun Records. That was 1952. After a slow and cautious start, he released a few blues records and then some country ones. Gradually, Sun got a little more successful in certain regions, and became Phillips' main passion. Young, white Southerners were pulled to Memphis to find Sun and success for themselves.

Johnny Cash was one of them. So was Carl Perkins. And Charlie Rich. Cash was always more country than rock. Perkins was true rockabilly. Rich was blessed with a feel for the blues. Phillips made them all stars. His label was filled with all kinds of different singers, and he got the most out of their abilities.

Sun's success encouraged other labels, such as Fernwood, which recorded a

Top, left: Sam Phillips with one of his few female artists, Barbara Pittman, in Nashville in 1958. Right: Sun artist Warren Smith, singer of "Ubangi Stomp" and "Rock 'n' Roll Ruby," from a Liberty Records publicity photograph from about 1960.

moody rockabilly ballad called "Tragedy" in 1959 by Thomas Wayne.

At Sun's peak, from 1956 to 1959, it was a basic operation, however, employing mainly four production-promotion people: Sam's brother, Judd, the national promotion director; Jack Clement, the producer-engineer; Bill Justis, the musical director who recorded the hit "Raunchy," and, of course, Phillips. He *was* Sun.

By the late '50s, it was slipping away from him. He had sold Presley's contract to RCA-Victor midway through the decade to get cash to finance the recordings of other artists. Then Presley finally achieved success nationally with "Heartbreak Hotel" and other records. Such sales had eluded Presley on Sun.

Cash and Perkins had left, too, for a lucrative Columbia opportunity. Lewis was pursued by scandal. Sun would never be the same.

Phillips himself was indeed a man peculiarly suited to times. Like rockabilly, he burned through the '50s like a comet, but never again achieving the success he had found earlier in the record business.

Jack Clement left in 1959. Brother Judd left the year before to start his own label, Judd Records, which gave the world Ray Smith's "Rockin' Little Angel."

Phillips decided to open a new studio on 17th Avenue in Memphis in 1961, but it has been more successful as a business than as a factory for hit records.

The old studio was closed. Only recently was it reopened for tourists to visit.

By 1966, Phillips closed his Phillips International Records subsidiary label, and in 1968 Sun was gone too. In 1969, he sold a major part of the label to Nashville producer-entrepreneur Shelby S. Singleton Jr., who helped establish Sun International Corporation. A new life was created for Sun, which had several chart records by The Gentrys. Singleton also started issuing old Sun recordings in economy albums.

Sun has now become known for reissues and compilations. But the label with the familiar brown and yellow logo will always be remembered as one man's vision of the future. As the incubator of rock 'n' roll.

This picture was taken in the mid- to -late 1950s, showing Marcus Van Story (left) and Warren Smith, Sun Records artist. "We were singing 'I'm Movin' On' when somebody snapped the picture," Van Story said. "I always threw up my hand and made a sound of a train whistle. Warren was such a great singer, but he never got the break he should have. Man, we used to do 'Ubangi Stomp' three times a night to satisfy the crowds. I'd hang a little rubber shrunken head on my bass keys. That went over well. A boy named Charlie Underwood wrote that song, and Sam Phillips liked it, so we cut it the same day we heard the demo. Only took about three hours, too. Warren and me put in a lot of hours together in the studio and on the road. I can't get over him being gone now. . . ."

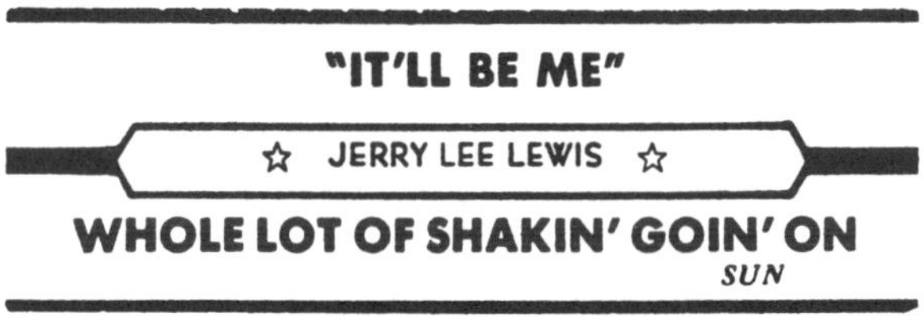

"IT'LL BE ME"

☆ JERRY LEE LEWIS ☆

WHOLE LOT OF SHAKIN' GOIN' ON
SUN

The Killer rocks on...
He also recorded for Phillips International as The Hawk.

Right: Chapel performs at the Brooklyn Paramount, 1956.

Sam Phillips was a dear man. He recorded a record for me called "Welcome To The Club" and "I Won't Be Rockin' Tonight." But Sun was pressed for cash at that time, about 1956, so Sam took my contract to RCA-Victor and sold it. He told me he thought I could do better on a bigger label. "I sold Elvis' contract to Victor and look what he's doing now," Sam said to me. Of course, Elvis was hitting about then with "Heartbreak Hotel" on RCA. So I became an RCA artist and got the tag "The Female Elvis Presley." I never could get over that title, though.

— JEAN CHAPEL, 1987.

Jean Chapel
WELCOME TO THE CLUB
and
WON'T BE ROCKIN' TONIGHT
SUN Record ——— No. 244

Harold Jenkins, left, walked into the Sun studios with a strong voice and a lot of old-fashioned confidence. He needed a few years, however, to develop into a hit-maker named Conway Twitty.

He played with a band called the Rock Housers in the early days, and for Sun cut such songs as "Give Me Some Love."

EDWIN BRUCE

Ed Bruce became a top country singer in the late 1970s and the 1980s. He even succeeded in an acting career. Before all that, he was a young rockabilly singer on Sun Records in Memphis in the 1950s. One of his records was "Rock Boppin' Baby."

Jimmy Williams of Memphis gravitated toward Sun in the mid-1950s, along with dozens of other would-be rockabilly stars. He recorded several sides, including "Rock-A-Bye Baby," "Rockin' History," and "Fire Engine Red." But Sun did not seem infatuated with Williams, so he left for other labels. He cut several Elvis-style sides, but got no big national hits.

"One guy just can't do it all at a record label," Sonny Burgess said of Sam Phillips. "That is simply too much to ask of any one person."

Bill Justis, musical director for the Sun labels, rode "Raunchy," an instrumental, to number 2 on the Hot 100 in November, 1957. He also charted with "College Man." Justis died in 1982 at the age of 55.

Bill Black, that bass-slapping backbone of the trio of Elvis, Scotty and Bill, started The Bill Black Combo when he left Presley's band. The combo had nineteen songs on the Hot 100 from 1959 to 1968. Black died in 1965 at the age of 39.

Sun's rich heritage included recordings by Charlie Rich, the Silver Fox. He turned "Lonely Weekends" into a hit (number 22 on the Hot 100) for Phillips International in early 1960. Later, he scored with "Mohair Sam" on Smash Records in 1965. By 1973 he was firmly in the country fold, with "Behind Closed Doors" and "The Most Beautiful Girl" on Epic Records.

Photo by Randy McNutt

In Nashville, the Sun International Corporation and Shelby Singleton operate a recording studio and office complex. A large brown and yellow rug with the Sun logo hangs on a wall of the studio, and a rack with albums for sale sits near the entrance. Sun staff producer and engineer Billy Self said, "I was listening to some of the old Jerry Lee Lewis stuff the other night, and I couldn't believe it. Bad notes, everything. But it's the feel that was important. A lot of that old-time rockabilly was so bad it's good...."

Although Johnny Cash was more of a country folk singer than a rockabilly, he found success at the eclectic Sun Records of Memphis, Tennessee. His records were hits in both country and pop markets in Sun's early days.

(Photo by Randy McNutt)

Top, exterior of the old Sun studio at 706 Union Avenue. Below, historical marker.

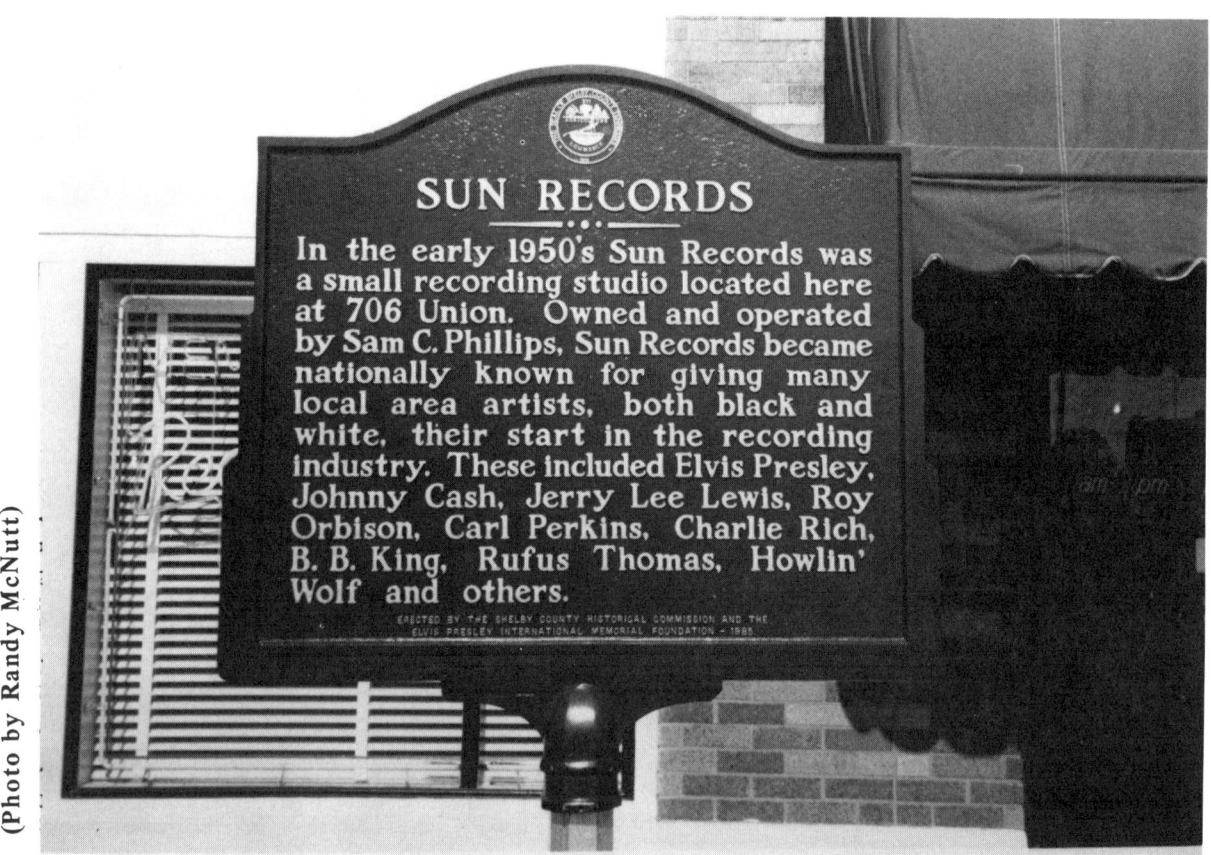
(Photo by Randy McNutt)

Roy Orbison recorded for Sun. He performed with a band called The Teen Kings. Orbison's Sun chart record was "Ooby Dooby," a top 50 hit in 1956.

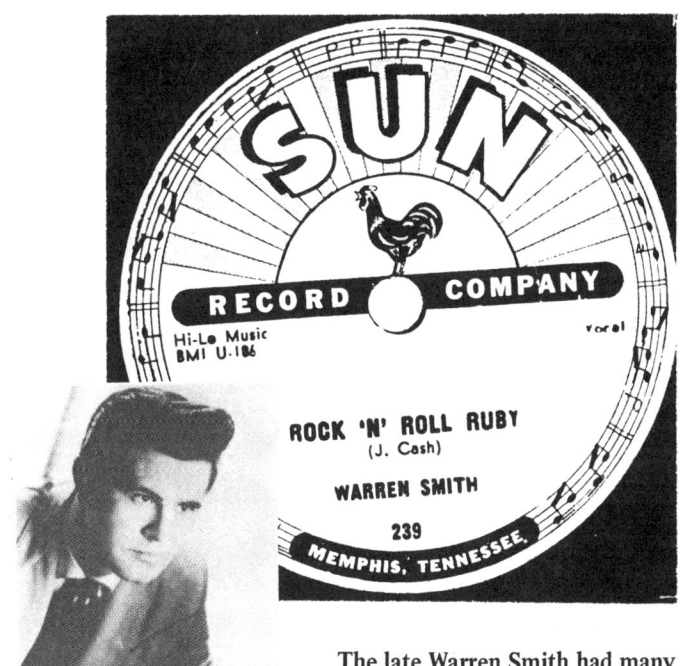

The late Warren Smith had many releases on Sun, but only one, "So Long I'm Gone," hit the pop charts. That was in 1957. His earlier effort, "Rock 'n' Roll Ruby," was supposedly composed by George Jones and sold to Johnny Cash for a small sum, according to a story that Warren Smith used to tell.

RAY SMITH

Ray Smith was good, no doubt about it. He sang with a strong and soulful voice and he pounded rock 'n' roll on his piano as well as any rockabilly performer. He was born in Melber, Kentucky, and grew up singing country music. In 1956, he left the U.S. Air Force and formed a band called The Rock And Roll Boys. Sam Phillips of Sun Records signed Ray to a contract, and about six singles were eventually released, including "Rockin' Bandit" and "Candy Doll." The Sun singles were not big sellers nationally, however, and Ray started recording for Judd Records – owned by Sam's brother, Judd Phillips – in the late '50s. A single, "Rockin' Little Angel," jumped to number twenty-two on Billboard's charts in early 1960. Ray Smith died in 1979 at the age of 41.

When King Was King

WHEN THE ROCK phenomenon refused to die, about 1955, Sydney Nathan took notice. He was, after all, the independent's independent, a record man who would try about anything to get a hit record. His King Records of Cincinnati had already grabbed a large portion of the rhythm and blues and country markets, signing many of the era's top artists to long-term contracts. So why not do the same thing with rock 'n' roll? Indeed, why *not*?

King was already recording some of the pre-rockabillies and boogie acts, including big Moon Mullican. They were doing a country boogie thing that often bordered on rockabilly. So Nathan reasoned that King could easily record the new rockers in its studio in Cincinnati, press a few thousand promotional copies of their records in the company's pressing plant, slip them to its company-owned distributors, and promote the records through an in-house promotion and sales staff. With the system that King had, rockers could be signed and ready for a few releases within a month. That doesn't even take into account the numerous artists whose records could be leased from smaller labels. Nathan was fond of that approach.

Before long, King Records boasted of one of rockabilly's most impressive rosters outside of Memphis. Sun may have started the genre, Nathan told his employees, but *he* would make more money that Sam Phillips could imagine.. Soon, King was releasing rockabilly records by such artists as Bill Beach, Charlie Feathers (Sun refugee), Bruce Channel, Hank Mizell, Joe Penny, Ronnie Molleen, Rusty York, Bonnie Lou, Boyd Bennett, Mac Curtis, Fuller Todd, Bob and Lucille, Teddy Humphries, and Louie Innes. Not a roster that will make any halls of fame, perhaps, but one that will undoubtedly be one of the largest rockabilly rosters of the 1950s. The number of rockabillies was so large then, in fact, that even former King executives can't recall who all recorded for the label. King was, in its glory days, the most impressive independent record company in America because it did *everything*. Distribution, promotion, sales, recording, pressing, art work — King did them all and did them right (well, let's don't talk about those hideous advertisements and album jackets!).

There were better independents, of course. Sun's product was to become a part of history, but Sun was a tiny operation when one considers the scope of King's operation. Yet King is unfairly ignored by many record historians today, just as it is forgotten in Cincinnati by many people. The label's rockabilly efforts were largely unsuccessful, despite Bonnie Lou's "Daddy-O" and Boyd Bennett & The Rockets' "Seventeen." But King was a seminal label that produced many talented producers, musicians, vocalists, promoters, and engineers.

King — and the independent label movement in the 1950s — deserves a closer look because those independents helped mold the early rockabilly sound. The independent owners, those entrepreneurs who gambled their own money and produced records on a ridiculously low budget, saw a need for a product and filled that need. Rockabilly acts could record without the interference of a big-label bureaucrat who neither understood nor cared about what they were trying to do in those early days. Not that all big labels were anti-rock music. They weren't. Such companies as Columbia recorded many fine rock records in the mid- to late-'50s. But the independents did it without as much restraint.

That was Nathan's way — and Sam Phillips'. They just let the artists come into the studio and perform. As early as the 1930s, Nathan had realized that black and Appalachian music would sell, and he went on to build a musical empire on that idea. At one time, the company's roster read like a Who's Who of American music. James Brown and the Famous Flames, Hank Ballard and the Midnighters, Otis Williams and the Charms, the Platters, Wynonie "Good Rockin' Tonight" Harris, Joe Tex, and Billy Ward and the Dominoes were but a few of the R&B artists under contract. Country — hillbilly music then — and bluegrass performers were not left out, either. Hawkshaw Hawkins, Cowboy Copas, the Delmore Brothers, Grandpa Jones, the Carlisles, the Stanley Brothers, and the Wilburn Brothers all recorded for King at one time or another.

But how could such a musical anomaly as King pop up in, of all places, Cincinnati, Ohio? The city on the Ohio River was heavily influenced by its European heritage, mainly German. The Cincinnati Symphony Orchestra was an important part of the local musical scene, not the players from the ghetto or the hollow. But Nathan was a man of great determination. And he determined that King was going to succeed.

About 1945, when King was founded, the Appalachian immigrants started moving into the area in large numbers. They worked in the factories and on the farms. They brought with them a strong desire to hear and play music. Country music had no international capital then, as Nashville is today. Country music was not even widely accepted in the city or the nation. The music existed in a rural vacuum most of the time, not crowded by the demands and competition of the pop music market.

Unlike today, country music was recorded and marketed in many cities, including Cincinnati. Today, most successful country records originate in Nashville, but in the 1930s and '40s many records came from other places. Nashville had not yet developed its massive "Music Row" of studios and record company offices. Only the Orpy lured musicians to town.

In the late '40s, Nathan used many local musicians who performed on Cincinnati country music radio shows. He opened a recording studio, a mastering lab and other facilities, and started making records. His twenty-six sales and promotion people traveled across the country to seek airplay for King's recordings.

Country pianist Moon Mullican, who had signed in King's first year, scored with four top ten hits in the early '50s, including "I'll Sail My Ship Alone" and "Mona Lisa." The hits continued to come.

In those days, King's maroon 78 rpm records carried this message under the logo: "The King Of Them All." And for good reason. King meant hits. Record executives came to Nathan to make deals, records and stars.

Each King release was personally approved by Nathan. The founder allowed his staff to debate the merits of each record, but, in the end, only Nathan's opinion mattered.

"The man was a pioneer," recalled Ray Pennington, a former King staff producer and rockabilly and country artist. "He was smart, too. Some people said he was gruff and mean. He mostly smoked big, foul-smelling cigars. But I tell you this: if Syd Nathan were alive today, I'd probably still be working for him. He had insight — a special way of seeing talent in people. It's sad that such a recording dynasty is gone today. But when Syd died, I don't think anybody could keep that operation going."

When Nathan died of heart disease in 1969 at the age of 63, the company had just finished one of its better sales periods, mainly because of James Brown's records. Most of the big-name country performers had already left for the safer confines of Nashville and its major labels. In 1967, Nathan and his family members — also his business partners — merged with Starday Records of Nashville, giving the Starday-King company a formidable catalogue of country music and a better position in the chart standings. The merger also created an impressive number of rockabilly master tapes from which to choose in later years. But Nathan never lived to see the rise of the collector market in reissues and compilation albums.

The marriage of King and Starday was an interesting one. Starday's roots ran deep into the country and rockabilly fields in the mid-'50s. Starday Records was founded in Houston about 1952 by Pappy Daily and Jack Starnes. Daily purchased the company from his partner a short time later and added Don Pierce as a partner. They operated the label until 1958, when they split the catalogue. Pierce stayed as chief of Starday; Daily left to form "D" Records and to work for the bigger labels. Daily discovered such artists as George Jones, Melba Montgomery, Judy Lynn, Webb Pierce, and Hank Locklin during the heyday of the Starday label.

"Pappy was like a father to George Jones," Sleepy LaBeef said. "He was good to all of us artists at Starday. At times he would have his people go into the Goldstar Studios in Houston and record a lot of sound-alike stuff — records that sounded like they were cut by Elvis, Hank Williams, Hank Snow, Johnny Cash. We'd get ten dollars a day for doing it. A radio station called XERF in Del Rio sold the records over the air, but the station people didn't mention that the records were sound-alikes. . . ."

Jones, LaBeef and other artists recorded rockabilly and country numbers under their own names and pseudonyms in the mid- to late-'50s. Starday also operated custom labels to record other artists.

Gusto Records of Nashville now owns many of the early King and Starday master tapes. The company has released many of them on single and compilation albums.

King's vaults were filled with various kinds of music, unlike many of the other independents. The bigger ones — Imperial, Dot, Sun and others — recorded different kinds of artists, but King, with its own studio and pressing facilities, recorded so *much*. And the company had the uncanny ability to market records in the strangest places.

"In the little hollows down in Kentucky, and in the coal-mining towns of Appalachia, you could always buy a King record," said Rusty York, a former King artist. "You couldn't buy too many Columbia or RCA Victor records down there in those days, but you sure could find the Kings. That's why Nathan was so successful."

King's sales were deceiving, at least by today's standards. In the late '40s and early '50s. King and other independents sold hundreds of thousands of records without much notice. The publications usually didn't bother writing much about the so-called hillbilly music, unless, of course, it was by somebody like Hank Williams and Hank Snow. King's roster was also deceiving, for Nathan often leased masters from smaller independent labels. The artists were not necessarily under contract to King, or recording directly for King, yet their records were released on the label. Ferlin Husky said King bought some of his old masters in the '50s, although he didn't record for King.

Another interesting point about King was its promotional copies. Some were covered with a mini-biography of the artist. These are sought by collectors today.

But perhaps the most discussed aspect of King was its "sound" — that undefinable combination of proper acoustics and musicianship that developed into the King sound, as many people call it. At first, King shared its headquarters with a combination ice house and carryout. The offices were rudimentary. So was the studio. But somehow, that little two-track studio was becoming magical. The studio quickly gained the reputation of a hit-maker, with a dynamic, clear, funky sound.

"Virtually every major country artist on King cut in that little studio in the 1950s," noted Gene Lawson, a former King session player and owner of a Nashville studio today. "Although the sound was funky and unusual, I believe the real difference was created by the talented musicians who recorded there."

"One week I'd be doing country, then bluegrass, then R&B," Pennington added. "I got a college education in the record business. King had just about every top country act of the time — Cowboy Copas, Patsy Cline, Hawkshaw Hawkins, Merle Travis, Red Foley, Grandpa Jones. And then, there were the R&B artists. And the rockabillies. If Nathan didn't have them under contract, he'd buy up their old masters and release them. That's what he did with Patsy Cline."

The musicians on the King sessions were a variety of white, black, country, R&B, big band — anybody who was good and available that day.

Somehow, Nathan built a hit machine in a city that didn't seem to care about the music of the "little people," poor blacks and Appalachians, as Nathan said. "The newspapers weren't interested in those people," the late Dorothy Halper, Nathan's sister and business partner said in 1981. "Nobody cared about King Records of Brewster Avenue. The city wasn't proud of its association with King. I think people in other cities were more interested and proud of King's accomplishments than the people of Cincinnati."

Although Nathan had partners, King was essentially a one-man operation. Nathan had taken King from a record store to an idea to a record company, and made it work. He chose his label names carefully: King, Queen, DeLuxe, Federal. "He always had regal ideas," Mrs. Halper recalled.

Today, however, the only sound on Brewster Avenue is the sound of tires whining from nearby Interstate 71. The old building is ugly, unbefittingly ugly. And King Records, that seminal voice of Sydney Nathan's "little people," is so unfairly forgotten.

We even made up our own vinyl mix. Nathan even ground up his returns and made new records. We all had meetings on what to release, but Sydney Nathan had the final say. He didn't care whether we agreed or not. If he liked a record, it would go out. King Records was a dynasty. We did everything, from mastering to pressing to art work to distribution. It's sad to see a label like that go out of existence.
—*Ray Pennington, former King producer and successful Nashville writer and record executive.*

I signed with King about '56. A talent scout found me. I had mentioned to a fella that I had done this thing called "Tongue-Tied Jill," a demo cut by Wink Martindale at WHBQ in Memphis. I sent a tape to that talent scout, and we went up to Cincinnati. We cut four tunes in that King studio. I was disappointed in them, though, 'cause I was used to slap-back — not that echo that King used. Later, King sent me to Nashville to cut four more sides. Then that was that. I lost contact with them at King. I remember that the people there were into black and country things. Now, Sun down in Memphis didn't have the studio suited to country. They couldn't do it well. King tried to copy the rockabilly thing that Sun did so well, but there was a problem because King had too many Northerners as artists. The accents were different. I think we got it all goin' down here, man, 'cause we had the accents. . . .
—*Charlie Feathers, former Sun and King recording artist.*

I remember that the studio had a live echo chamber upstairs with an ultraviolet light in the ceiling. Don't ask me why.
—*Gene Lawson, former studio drummer and a Nashville studio owner.*

●●●●●●●●●●●●●●●●●●●●●●●●●●●●●●●●

Anything could happen at King. One day they took me into the studio to cut Hank Ballard's "Tore Up Over You." But we used the black guys in Hank's band. So here was this rockabilly cutting with R&B guys, and were they ever drinkin'. What a session. But then, that's the kind of thing that happened over on Brewster.
—*Rusty York, former King artist.*

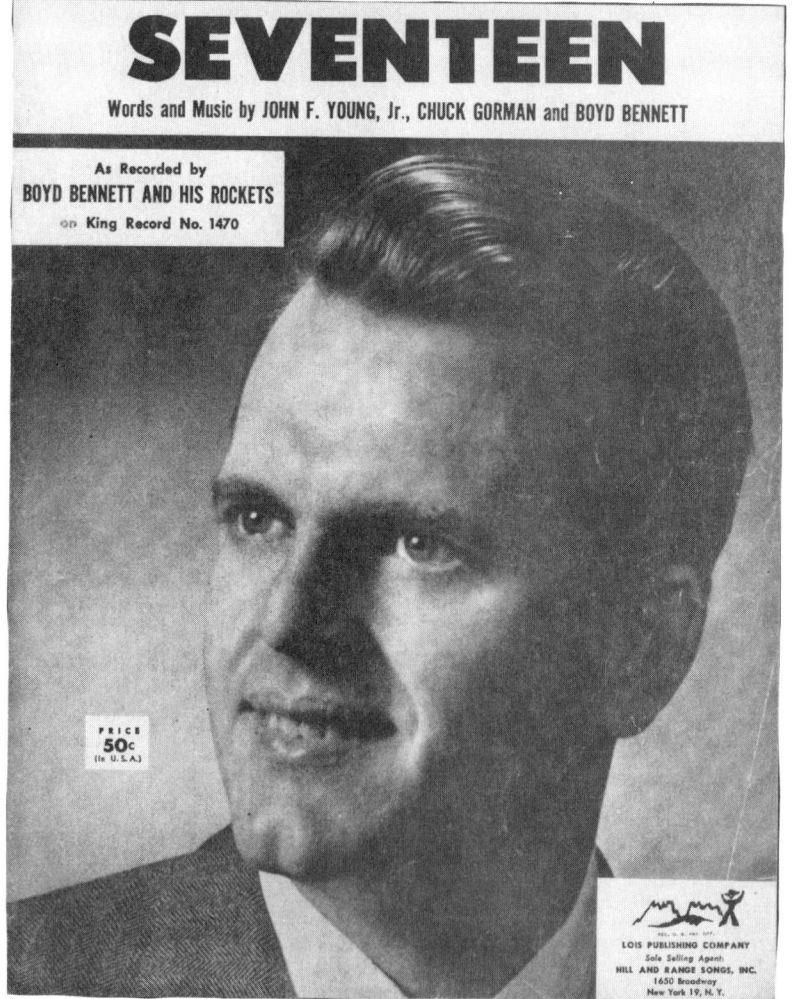

Sydney Nathan

LAH-DEE-DAH
b/w
LET THE SCHOOL BELL RING DING-A-LING

BONNIE and RUSTY
KING 5110

Promotional piece for a cover record
by Rusty York and Bonnie
Lou in 1958.

Boyd Bennett and His Rockets rocked to number five on the pop charts in 1955 with "Seventeen," one of King Records' first rockabilly hits. The band followed that hit with "My Boy — Flat Top," which reached only the thirties on the national charts. Both records were sung by vocalist Big Moe.

STARTING 1958 WITH THE HOT RECORDS
TOP TWENTY

45 78	**1**	SWINGING SHEPHERD BLUES THE ELDER JOHNNIE PATE QUINTET—King 12312	**11**	DON'T BE ASHAMED DEDICATED TO THE ONE I LOVE THE "5" ROYALES—King 5098	45 78
	2	LEAPS & BOUNDS PARTS 1 & 2 BILL DOGGETT—King 5101	**12**	HAVE I SINNED LEONA DONNIE ELBERT—King 6148	
	3	OH JULIE COULD THIS BE MAGIC OTIS WILLIAMS AND HIS CHARMS	**13**	YOU KNOW MY LOVE IS TRUE WHAT A FOOL WAS I ROY & GLORIA—King 5053	
	4	SOFT HOT GINGER BILL DOGGETT—King 5080	**14**	WHAT SIN WHEN DAY IS DONE JIMMY SCOTT—King 5086	
	5	SHAKE SHAKE OH YEAH! THE BLUE NOTES—King 5088	**15**	MUDDY WATER THE WHISPERERS BUBBER JOHNSON—King 5089	
	6	PEGGY SUE SHAKE 'EM UP BABY RUSTY YORK—King 5103	**16**	WISHBONE DOWN BOY BILL JENNINGS-WILLIS JACKSON—King 5087	
	7	WALKIN' WITH MR. LEE PATTIN' WITH PATE JOHNNIE PATE AND HIS ORCHESTRA	**17**	MISS YOU SO AW! SHUCKS BABY TINY TOPSY—King 12302	
	8	I'M AVAILABLE WAITING IN VAIN BONNIE LOU—King 5094	**18**	THE SEASONS ROLLING HOME LARRY HARVEY—King 5093	
	9	PERSON TO PERSON UNTIL YOU DO LITTLE WILLIE JOHN—King 5091	**19**	I KNOW YOU'RE MARRIED BEER BARREL POLKA DON RENO-RED SMILEY—King 5016	
	10	JOSEPHINE JEANNINE I DREAM OF LILAC TIME EARL BOSTIC—King 5092	**20**	NO LONGER A SWEETHEART OF MINE RICHMOND RUCKUS DON RENO-RED SMILEY—King 5079	

In 1958, King Records released its own charts. This one featured many rhythm and blues records as well as a little rockabilly. Below, Boyd Bennett and His Rockets. They recorded an early rockabilly hit for King called "Seventeen."

"GO, CATS, GO!"

BUT PLEASE DON'T COVER MY COVER

WHEN VIEWED FROM today's perspective, rock 'n' roll is history repeating itself and enjoying the process. In 1956, however, things were different. There was little history to repeat, so rock records were "covered," meaning in part that they were cut to compete with originals.

Carl Perkins found this out for certain. After hearing a fellow tell his date not to step on his blue suedes, Carl rushed back to the housing project in Tennessee and wrote the lyrics on a brown potato sack. Sun Records released the single and it leaped onto the pop, country and rhythm and blues charts. By March, 1956, the record had reached number two on Billboard's top 100 chart.

That's when the competition jumped in to fight. King Records of Cincinnati, that ever watchful label of covers and crazies, returned Boyd Bennett and his group the Rockets to the chart with his interpretation of "Blue Suede Shoes." He had been in the top ten in 1955 with "Seventeen," and this time his cover record of "Blue Suede Shoes" went to number 63 on Billboard's chart. That was April 14, 1956.

The week before, however, Elvis Presley — yes, the phenomenon of the era — had reached number 20 with *his* version of the song on an extended play record.

We cannot understand such a thing as the cover version in this day. Few companies release records that way anymore because of the extremely high costs of production, manufacturing, and promotion. Besides, getting airplay is difficult enough. Only odd cases, usually when the original is not yet hitting, spawn covers today.

But in 1956, the larger labels could always out-promote the smaller ones, so the majors didn't mind covering anything. And often the smaller ones thought they could succeed with a cover if it managed to sell only a few thousand copies. (King reveled in covering rock records; the majors didn't mind covering King's R&B records with white acts. In fact, King even covered Buddy Holly's "Peggy Sue" with Rusty York's version.)

Such warfare left the listener befuddled, no doubt. Some probably heard all three versions of "Blue Suede Shoes," the rockabilly anthem. Some probably heard only one. So which record was the best?

Perkins' record reflected the blues and country inclinations of the singer and his Memphis players of that period, but somehow both styles can be distinctly heard. Although the singer sounds like a country vocalist and the record *feels* country, the record also has that choppy rhythm — a blues feel. And the singer delivers his message with a rural flair and detachment that makes the record so effective. In short, everything worked.

Presley, on the other turntable, was recording in Nashville by early '56, but with his Memphis accomplices Scotty Moore, the guitarist, and Bill Black, the upright bass man. They supplied that old rockabilly feel that had started Elvis upward. This time, they were augmented by D.J. Fontana on drums and supplemental players. At the time, Presley's music was progressing from rockabilly to a middle state, between what he was and what he would become. It was still rockabilly, but the edge had hardened a bit. So his version of "Blue Suede Shoes" was more energetic, punched up by a hipper beat and vocals that rocked. The country feeling was not so distinct. Presley's version was indeed a master interpretation.

Bennett's record was the least significant of the 1956 hits of the song because it was a routine, uninspired clunker. It was, well, square. King or Bennett even changed the lyrics to be more cleancut. Gone were the references to drinking liquor and stealing. In their place were: ". . .burn my house, wreck my car, spend my dough at the soda bar. . ."

"Blue Suede Shoes" was not finished, however. Dozens of versions were recorded over the next few years, and it continues to be recorded. Jim Lowe, Syd King, Pee Wee King, Johnny Mercer, and Roy Hall were but a few artists who tried to cover the song at the time.

But Carl Perkins' version remains the definitive rockabilly record. He defined the new music with one song, while Elvis interpreted the message. Nobody is complaining.

3

ELVIS PRESLEY: 'I HAVE TO MOVE'

Elvis Aaron Presley grew up poor in Tupelo, Mississippi. No doubt he listened to black music when he was playing in the yards of that city in the 1940s. Although his biographers have stressed the influence of Beale Street on Presley, Tupelo is the place where his earliest musical memories were made. He did not move to the city of Memphis until the late '40s, when he was about thirteen years old. In Tupelo, the Presley family lived in an integrated neighborhood, where many front-porch bluesmen strummed their lives away. Later in his life, Presley said all he knew as a boy was church music, or gospel. But a combination of that rhythmic white church music and black blues surely molded to contribute to his early musical leanings. After all, he once said he enjoyed listening to black Mississippi singers, including Arthur Crudup, whose song "That's All Right (Mama)," was recorded by Presley at the Sun Records studio in Memphis in 1954.

Presley's musical history – and the affect he had on the history of music – is chronicled throughout this book. There is no point in retracing his personal journey. What we will discuss is what happened when the whirlwind named Elvis Presley unleashed himself on an unsuspecting world.

"The poor man's Liberace" is what disc jockey Dewey Phillips once called Presley during an intermission at the Eagle's Nest nightclub, but Presley quickly went on to become popular with all social classes, races, and nationalities.

Presley affected country music in the mid-'50s by cutting into its sales. This came at a time when country records were not nearly as popular as they were later, in the 1970s and '80s. A drastic reduction in sales and overall popularity hit most of the country artists hard. Young people started buying rockabilly records. Interest in the new music ran high.

Elvis was treated as a king by his new following, but as an outcast by most of the adult world. He was looked upon as a rebel, as a sexual menace to the youth of America. "People say I'm vulgar," he once said. "They say I use my hips disgustingly. But that's my way of putting over a song. I have to move. When I have a lot of energy, I move more. I lose three or four pounds a performance. I've always done it this way...."

Then he explained exactly why he *had* to move: "When I stand still, I'm dead."

Elvismania exploded among the nation's youth with Presley's signing with RCA-Victor Records. The country music establishment would not forget. Sun artists — even the benign Johnny Cash — were considered outcasts and treated accordingly. Only time would correct this prejudice against the little Memphis label's artists. Ironically, the country music elitists would one day claim Elvis as one of their own.

Yet Presley remained above such petty activity simply because he was bigger than life — a musical institution unto himself. He remained the embodiment of rock, pop, and country music at the time of his death in 1977. What he once took away in sales to country music he returned a million times and more.

His old songs continued to be recorded over the years, and his old records repackaged and rereleased. Hundreds of thousands of tourists have made the trip to Memphis just to be near his mansion, Graceland, and to see the artifacts of The Hillbilly Cat himself.

Perhaps this is good for country music, an industry based on love and tourism. Country music needs an artist bigger than anybody else. It needs Elvis Presley.

Elvis Presley returned home to Tupelo for the Mississippi-Alabama Fair & Dairy Show on September 26, 1956.

THE WILD DAYS: Elvis Presley, mid-1950s.

Top, left: Elvis Presley sings in 1958.
Top, right: Elvis in high school.
Botton, right: Elvis in the movie "Jailhouse Rock," 1957. D.J. Fontana on drums and Scotty Moore on guitar.

The Hillbilly Cat Lives...

Elvis Presley in the mid-1950s.

B U D D Y H O L L Y

Charles Hardin Holley was born in Lubbock, Texas, in 1936, the son of Ella and Lawrence Holley. The parents named the boy after his grandfathers, but Charles seemed too formal for the family's tastes, so they simply called the youngster Buddy.

He grew up in a home filled with music. Buddy first appeared with his brothers in a talent contest, and in time everybody realized that music was the focus of Buddy's life. Buddy was rather quiet. He wore glasses to correct his nearsightedness. By the age of eleven, he was taking piano lessons from a local music teacher. Then he started playing the guitar.

Buddy met Bob Montgomery at Hutchinson Junior High School about 1949, and Montgomery helped Buddy develop his guitar playing. The boys were good friends. By this time, Buddy was intrigued with the music of Hank Williams and other country stars. One of Buddy's favorites was Williams' "Lovesick Blues."

Soon, the two boys were performing locally as Buddy and Bob. Their business card read: "Buddy and Bob...Western and Bop."

Eventually, the boys were featured on KDAV Radio in Lubbock. They added bassist Larry Welborn, and they pushed their bluegrass sound to one that featured more rhythm and blues. In high school, Buddy met a guitar player named Sonny Curtis, and he was invited to join their group.

"Buddy and I met when I was a sophomore in high school," Curtis recalled. "In no more than a minute and a half after being introduced, we had our guitars out and were playing. In those days it was this way: 'Hi, ya, Buddy, glad to meet you. Now let's pick!' Buddy was like that. We used to hang out a lot and sit in his car. We'd fall asleep listening to the blues on the radio. Buddy was on fire in his enthusiasm for rock 'n' roll. We'd get excited over lunch. We didn't think much about anything but music in those days. We *loved* it. That's all we used to think about in high school."

Curtis was a fine guitarist for his age, and he would develop into one of the top ones in west Texas. The group was also excellent. By 1954, Buddy was determined to make music a career. He was single-minded in his determination to succeed.

Then the band played on the same bill in Lubbock with Bill Haley and the Comets in 1955. Buddy became infatuated with rock 'n' roll.

The group made some country-oriented recordings for Decca in Nashville in 1956, but they were not successful and Buddy returned to Lubbock to play music. The group – called The Three Tunes by now – returned to Nashville and cut some interesting songs, however, including a Curtis song called "Rock Around With Ollie Vee." By this time, Buddy was learning to write his own material. His name was misspelled on a record label – the label called him Holly – and he decided to keep it that way.

One of his songs, written with drummer Jerry Allison, was inspired by a John Wayne movie called *The Searchers*, in which this line was uttered: "That'll be the day...." The young musicians picked it up as a song title.

The group's personnel changed. Curtis left to play with Slim Whitman. Others came and went. But Buddy became the leader through sheer willpower. By late 1956, Holly went to Clovis, New Mexico, to record in Norman Petty's little studio. Petty had gained notoriety locally for producing a number of acts and leasing their tapes to big record labels in New York City. Holly was interested in such connections.

In early 1957, Petty recorded the band in a historic session. "That'll Be The Day" was cut, backed with "I'm Looking For Someone To Love." Holly decided to use a new group name, The Crickets, to avoid any possible legal trouble with his former label, Decca, which had dropped him but still had contractual options. Petty arranged a deal with Coral Records, an independent subsidiary of Decca, and the label released the two tracks as a single. Holly was surprised. He had intended the tapes to be used as demos.

Nobody knew the difference. By September, 1957, "That'll Be The Day" by The Crickets had jumped into the top five nationally.

Petty also arranged for Holly to release records as a solo artist, and, in 1957, "Words Of Love," another Holly original, was released. It was not a big seller but it was successful in vocal execution and production technique. Buddy sang unison with himself.

His first big hit by himself was "Peggy Sue," which peaked at number three in November, 1957. He followed with "Rave On," (37), "Early In The Morning," (32), "Heartbeat" (82), and a double-sided hit, "It Doesn't Matter Anymore" (13) and "Raining In My Heart," (88). The records spanned late 1957 to early 1959. None were big hits, except for "Peggy Sue" and "It Doesn't Matter Anymore." Holly's style also changed during this period. He went from rock to middle-of-the-road. He became interested in the big pop ballad, complete with string sections, and he felt that such an approach would help his career.

The Crickets, meanwhile, produced chart records from the summer of 1957 to the summer of 1958 on the Brunswick label in America. "Oh, Boy!" (10) and "Maybe Baby" (17) were their biggest hits. Today, these rock recordings of The Crickets and Buddy Holly as a single artist are perhaps the performers' most well-known works. Who has not heard "Peggy Sue"? It is the quintessential Holly recording.

The records of Buddy Holly and The Crickets — particularly their *rock* records — were rockabilly in that they were basic and an obvious combination of country and beat-blues. But these early recordings, including "That'll Be The Day" and "Maybe Baby," were of a different nature than, say, the early Sun recordings. The Crickets' style was heavier on the rock.

Unfortunately, Holly never got the opportunity to evolve. He was killed in an airplane crash on February 3, 1959, in Clear Lake, Iowa. He was only twenty-two years old.

His music has continued to live, however, in reissues and new releases. The years have come and gone, but Buddy Holly is still rockabilly's gentleman.

Buddy Holly

Charles Hardin Holley — Buddy Holly to his fans — was born in Lubbock, Texas, in 1936. He grew up to become the rockabilly gentleman of the late 1950s. His rich music was popular and diverse enough to include such rockers as "Peggy Sue," "Rave On" and "That'll Be The Day," and such middle-of-the-road ballads as "Raining In My Heart" and "True Love Ways." Holly was one of the most talented of the early singer-songwriters of the rock era. He left the basic rockabilly sound behind — actually, it was never primitive rockabilly — for what he considered to be more commercial: softer sounds. Holly was killed in a plane crash in early 1959.

Photographs: Top, left—(l-r) Joe B. Maudlin, Jerry Allison, Niki Sullivan (The Crickets). Bottom, left—Holly with his familiar black glasses.

Rocking Guitar Man

CARL PERKINS REMAINS A rockabilly original. Elvis is gone. So are the Dorsey brothers, Eddie Cochran, and Gene Vincent. But the Rockin' Guitar man from Jackson, Tennessee, is still performing for enthusiastic audiences all over the world.

When Presley abandoned his rockabilly roots in favor of contrived pop formulas, Perkins fought back from the effects of personal tragedy, injuries, and changing tastes in music to become the number one rockabilly in America. He has remained faithful to his peculiar blend of hillbilly and blues, going through lean times and times of plenty. Whatever fad happens to come along is of no matter to Perkins. He will not alter his style to fit a passing infatuation.

Carl Lee Perkins, the Pied Piper of Rockabilly, was born April 9, 1932, in Tiptonville, Tennessee, the son of a tenant farmer. In 1945, the family moved to Bemis, and Carl got a job in a factory. He later went to work in a bakery near

Jackson.

But Perkins was destined to cook hot licks, not donuts, so he entered a talent contest in Bemis with his brothers, Jay and Clayton. The three performed locally as the Perkins Brothers Band. The group become popular in the area, but Carl decided to move to Jackson in 1953 with his wife, Valda. They lived in Parkview Courts, a government housing project.

Carl recorded demos of his music and tried to get a contract with one of the major labels in New York City, but none were interested in his country music with a flavoring of blues. Then Carl approached Sam Phillips of Sun Records in Memphis in late 1954, and Phillips eventually released "Movie Magg" and "Turn Around" on his Flip label. In early 1955, the record got some attention in Memphis and other areas, and Phillips brought the new singer into the Sun stable.

Perkins seemed to develop his blend of country and blues independently, about the time that Elvis and a few others were putting the same ingredients together. But Elvis hit first. He had that contagious energy and dark, young looks. Perkins had talent but not the sexuality that Elvis promoted so effectively. And, Perkins was a married man.

Although he had big hits on Sun — "Blue Suede Shoes" was the biggest — he had relatively few releases over the years. In the late '50s he signed with Columbia and recorded some good records in Nashville, but they lacked the intensity of his earlier releases. Nevertheless, he stands out as a favorite because of his originality. He was the

prototypical rockabilly artist-composer, a smooth vocalist, and a quality guitarist. Elvis was usually an interpreter of other people's songs; Perkins was usually the rockabilly social commentator who wrote his own songs. Who can forget such lyrics as "Dixie Fried" and "Put Your Cat Clothes On"? They were the anthems of the poor, young, white Southerners in the mid-1950s.

Perhaps Perkins is so fondly remembered today for his style, however. That undefinable quality, that special charm, set him apart from his peers. He was always under control. Elvis was explosive and suggestive to a point, giving the impression that he was somehow managing to hold the line against full-blown expression of sexual energy and rebellion. But Perkins was different. He was restrained, preferring to

Perkins, center, in a publicity photograph from the Cinemax program "A Rockabilly Session: Carl Perkins And Friends," from 1986. Left to right: Lee Rocker, Eric Clapton, George Harrison, Perkins, Earl Slick, Ringo Starr, Dave Edmunds, and Slim Jim Phantom.

concentrate on his guitar playing and his message.

"I think we all knew we had ahold of something," he told the Associated Press in 1985. "We were just taking country music and putting that black rhythm in it. It was a marriage of the white man's lyrics and the black man's soul. I played on country shows and they were reserved, good audiences, but these kids were coming up out of the seats. You saw dust coming from the old high school gyms that had been settled for years. I think we all knew that something was happening. . . ."

So Carl Perkins became a rock 'n' roll institution. He was revered by rockers then and he is revered by them now. People of all ages enjoy his music because it is unpretentious. Because it is real.

He is proud that his music has influenced so many younger people, including the Beatles, Eric Clapton, and the Rolling Stones. In fact, Perkins alone was nearly responsible for reuniting the three remaining Beatles — or former Beatles, but we never think of them in that context, do we? — for his 1985 Cinemax television show, "Carl Perkins and Friends: A Rockabilly Session." Ringo Starr and George Harrison appeared on the program, but Paul McCartney was recording then and couldn't participate.

The Beatles recorded Perkins' "Honey Don't" and "Matchbox" in the early part of their careers. All members have acknowledged that Perkins influenced them. He first met the Beatles in 1964, when he was a 32-year-old rockabilly trying to find his niche in a world gone mad over long-haired, young English rock bands. What finer tribute could such a group pay than to record Perkins' songs?

"I don't hear myself in their playing," he once said of the Beatles. "I do in some early Beatles songs, but they advanced so much. That rockabilly sound wasn't as simple as I thought it was."

The high-powered rockers have continued their friendships with Perkins. One year, McCartney sent him a full-sized guitar birthday cake, complete with frets. Perkins even wrote a song for McCartney called "My Old Friend."

Considering Perkins' adversities over the years, his biggest asset was not influencing other musicians but staying alive. He was seriously injured in an automobile accident at the height of his early career in the '50s, and he spent a year recovering. His brother Jay eventually died as a result of injuries from the crash.

Perkins then spent fifteen years trying to stop drinking. He overcame the problem in 1967, when he threw his last whiskey bottle into the Pacific Ocean. About this time, he turned to country music to revitalize his sagging career. Country songs had always been a big part of his presentation, and now he concentrated on the country charts. He had success, too. His Columbia singles dotted the country charts in the late '60s.

Most of the time, however, Perkins played and sang for Johnny Cash, and even wrote Cash's hit, "Daddy Sang Bass."

Lately, Perkins has settled into a busy schedule of touring and recording. He plays himself – revered rockabilly. And he enjoys himself. The Rockin' Guitar Man is still rockin'. Isn't that the way it should be?

Carl Perkins' recordings have continued to be popular over the last several decades. They have been released, re-released, re-packaged, and bootlegged. This interesting disc is a compilation of Perkins' Sun recordings, complete with his photograph.

Above, Carl Perkins in a Mercury Records publicity photo, 1973. Below, Perkins performs with Johnny Cash on the ABC-TV special "Johnny Cash Presents The Country Music Story," in 1971.

At the Carl Perkins Musuem off of Interstate 40 at Jackson, Tennessee, you can visit a railroad car filled with the singer's memorabilia, including guitars, stage clothes, and this original lyric sheet for "Blue Suede Shoes" from 1955. It was written on a paper sack.
(Photo by Randy McNutt)

Below, Carl Perkins inspects the Carl Perkins Musuem at Jackson. (Photo courtesy Tennessee Tourist Development)

Be-Bop-A-Vincent

In the spring of 1956, radio stations across the nation treated listeners to a strange and provocative new sound — "Be-Bop-A-Lula." The record soared to number seven in June and opened a new dimension in rockabilly music.

The artist was Gene Vincent, who had a band called The Blue Caps. Vincent was not another Sun Records artist, although he was as talented as anybody on that label. He was a rockabilly from the Norfolk, Virginia, area, and his music was different from most of the other rockabilly music of the day. Vincent's style was not so dominated by country music, nor was it dominated by rhythm and blues. It was a perfect synthesis of both styles. He was no hyperactive hillbilly crooner. He was a part of the developing rock 'n' roll phenomenon.

He was also a rather pathetic figure, with his severe limp — a result of an accident — and his never-ending quest for another big hit. Capitol Records signed Vincent as its answer to Elvis Presley, but such universal success was not to be. His few chart records included big hits, of course, and represented an emerging rock 'n' roll, but Vincent never did equal the pure energy and sales power of his "Lula." Although he wrote it, he never really wrote or sang anything else that could duplicate its rare qualities of originality and excitement. His other hits, including "Bluejean Bop" and "Lotta Lovin'" continued through 1957. But a singer cannot follow a legend, and that is what "Be-Bop-A-Lula" has now become.

By the late '50s, the slick city boys had rattled the charts, and Vincent and many other rockabillies were fading. Vincent, in constant pain with his leg injury, embarked on a tour of Great Britain with Eddie Cochran in 1960. They were successful there, but a car crash killed Eddie and hurt Vincent.

Vincent turned to alcohol, making his life a blur. He died in 1971, at the age of 36.

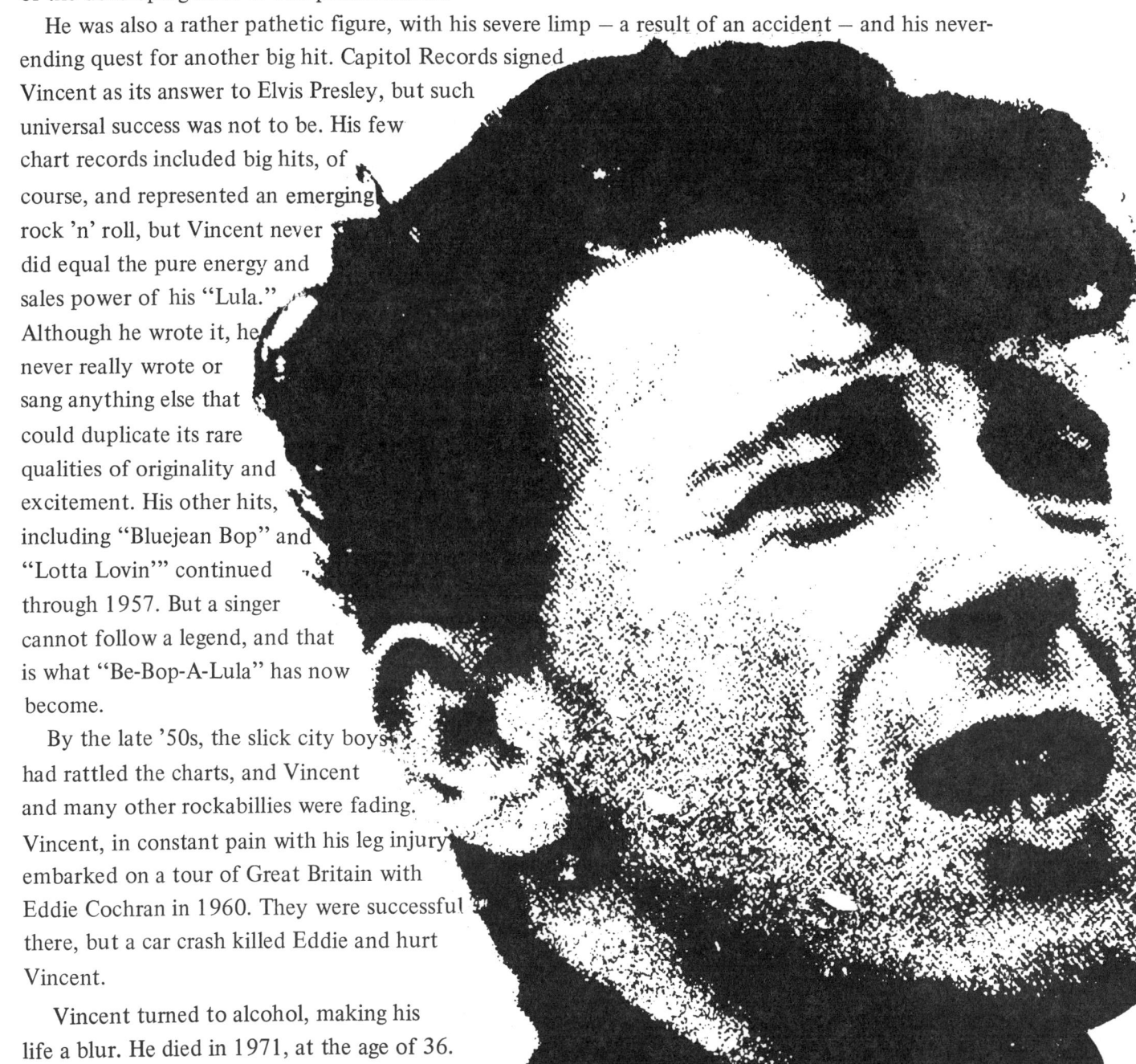

Gene Vincent, right and left, from the 1950s. The record is one of the last made by the "Bop-A-Lula" man.

Lonely Blues Boy

THE FIRST THING YOU notice about Conway Twitty is the hair. In those photographs from the late 1950s, he stands defiantly, dark hair firmly set in grease. Through the years that bushy hair has been held tightly in place with cream and spray, but, to this day, Twitty's hair is still distinctive for a man in his fifties.

He was one of the top rockabilly performers of the late 1950s, even though the genre was already on the decline. "It's Only Make Believe," his anthem of the lonely lover, jumped to number one on the charts on September 15, 1958, on MGM Records. The disc — two minutes and ten seconds of unrestrained emotion — seemed to increase in intensity as it pushed to a climax. It was one of the few rockabilly records that successfully mixed a good melody with a strong vocalist and a lush string arrangement. No gimmicks, no shouting. Just *soul*. Twitty's ballad, which he cowrote, was simply a great song. Thirteen chart records followed it, including "Danny Boy," (number ten) "Lonely Blue Boy," (number six) and "What Am I Living For," (number twenty-six), but none equaled the concert popularity of "It's Only Make Believe."

Twitty was destined to perform in some capacity, it seems. He was born Harold Jenkins on September 1, 1933, in Friar's Point, Mississippi, where he learned to the play the guitar from his father, a river pilot. Captain Jenkins later moved the family to Helena, Arkansas, when Twitty was a boy. On Saturday nights, they sat around a radio and listened to the Grand Ole Opry show from Nashville. Young Harold was entranced. He started singing at family gatherings.

Yet he was apprehensive about entering the field of country music as he grew older because its stars seemed bigger than life. He wondered how he could ever compete with such singers as Ernest Tubb and Hank Snow. So, he signed a contract with the Philadephia Phillies after high school (he had stroked

a cool .469 in school ball). Before he could slip on a minor league baseball uniform, however, he was drafted into the U.S. Army and sent to Korea. Upon his discharge in the mid-'50s, he heard a record by Elvis Presley and figured he'd better head for Memphis as fast as possible. Sun Records liked his soulful voice, and the label recorded a few sides with Harold Jenkins. But they were not released at the time, and the singer set out on the road to perform. One day he decided to change his luck by changing his name to Conway Twitty — after Conway, Arkansas, and Twitty, Texas. A classic rockabilly name was born.

"It's Only Make Believe" brought success, but, like everything in the temporary world of rock 'n' roll, he eventually slipped. He could not sustain the big hits needed to keep him in the public's eye, despite a hectic touring schedule. Yet he continued to sing. In the early 1960s he toured extensively in the Midwest and Southwest, giving what some observers say were the most powerful shows they

have ever seen. But his recording decline continued; rockabilly drifted from its roots. Twitty had to compete on the charts with too many manufactured stars of dubious vocal ability and with songs of little merit.

As the decade of the '60s pushed toward its halfway point, Twitty decided to move to Oklahoma City. He was determined to become a country music star. While other old rockabilly artists continued to fight a losing battle with the new groups and artists (Gene Vincent is one prominent example), Twitty set out to establish himself in country. The change was not that radical — he was already country in style and thought. As he told a writer once, "One night I sang rock, the next night country. . . ."

So Conway Twitty and his House Rockers went on to move the honky-tonk crowds. The way they played was essentially the same, only softer. By 1985, about twenty years after he had went into country music, Twitty had amassed fifty number one records on the country charts, and had gained the respect of the Nashville music establishment. He is now an industry unto himself, owning a part of the Nashville Sounds minor league baseball team, a production company and other businesses. He is also the namesake of Twitty City, an entertainment complex in Music City.

He built that "city" on hit records — big hits. "Next In Line," his first number one record for Decca in August, 1968, was followed by others, including "I Love You More Today," "To See My Angel Cry," "Hello Darlin'" and "How Much More Can She Stand." His style has not wavered, either. He still sings with soul and power, and he is still working almost nonstop. The focus of his songs have since shifted to the more macho country ballads, but he still closes his concerts with "It's Only Make Believe."

And his hair still makes its own statements.

Mr. Pumping Piano

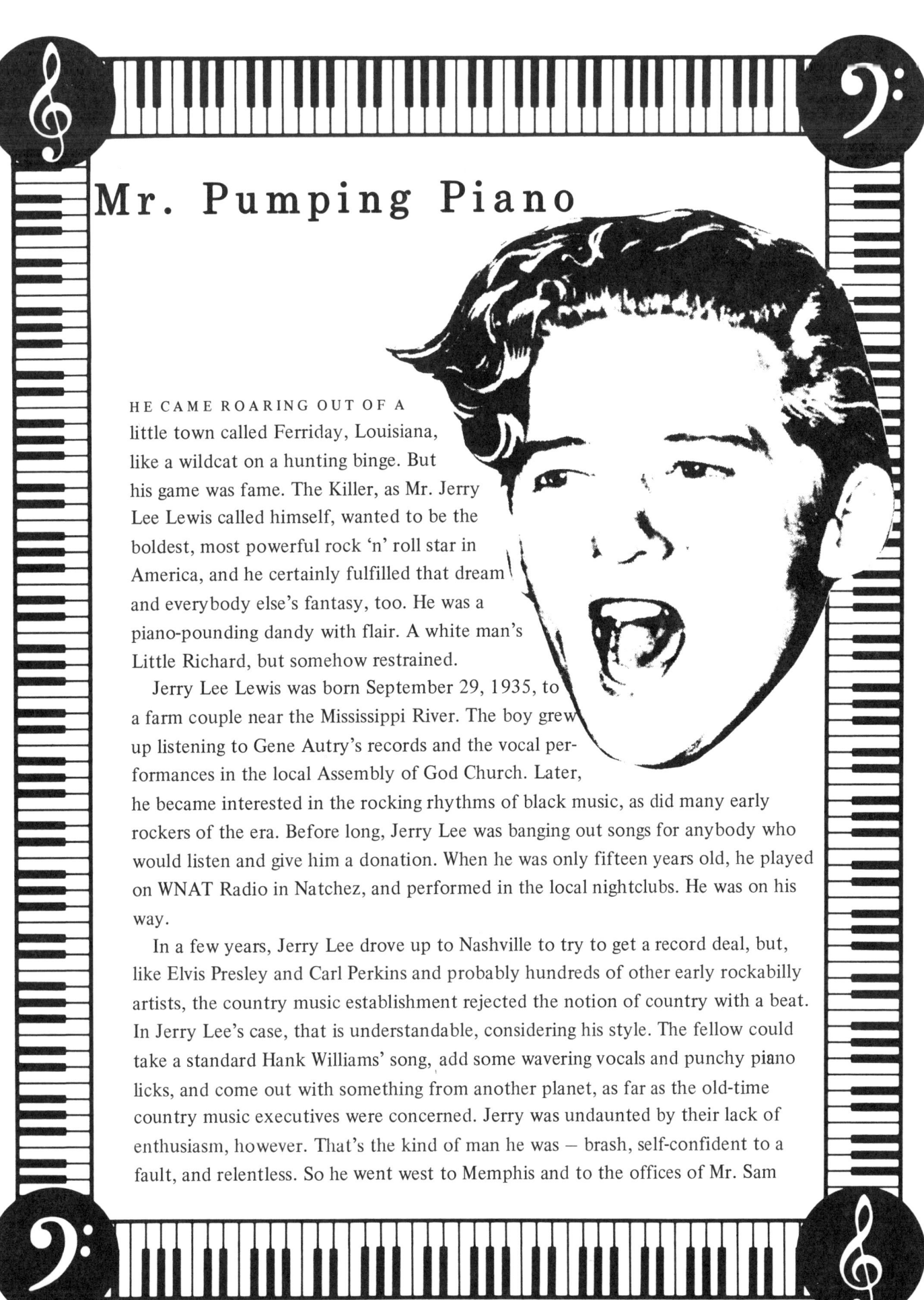

HE CAME ROARING OUT OF A little town called Ferriday, Louisiana, like a wildcat on a hunting binge. But his game was fame. The Killer, as Mr. Jerry Lee Lewis called himself, wanted to be the boldest, most powerful rock 'n' roll star in America, and he certainly fulfilled that dream and everybody else's fantasy, too. He was a piano-pounding dandy with flair. A white man's Little Richard, but somehow restrained.

Jerry Lee Lewis was born September 29, 1935, to a farm couple near the Mississippi River. The boy grew up listening to Gene Autry's records and the vocal performances in the local Assembly of God Church. Later, he became interested in the rocking rhythms of black music, as did many early rockers of the era. Before long, Jerry Lee was banging out songs for anybody who would listen and give him a donation. When he was only fifteen years old, he played on WNAT Radio in Natchez, and performed in the local nightclubs. He was on his way.

In a few years, Jerry Lee drove up to Nashville to try to get a record deal, but, like Elvis Presley and Carl Perkins and probably hundreds of other early rockabilly artists, the country music establishment rejected the notion of country with a beat. In Jerry Lee's case, that is understandable, considering his style. The fellow could take a standard Hank Williams' song, add some wavering vocals and punchy piano licks, and come out with something from another planet, as far as the old-time country music executives were concerned. Jerry was undaunted by their lack of enthusiasm, however. That's the kind of man he was — brash, self-confident to a fault, and relentless. So he went west to Memphis and to the offices of Mr. Sam

Phillips at Sun Records. Phillips had discovered Perkins and Presley, Jerry Lee reasoned, so he ought to *welcome* The Killer. Phillips' assistant, Jack Clement, heard Jerry Lee play, and he knew that music would somehow never be the same. So Sun Records cut Jerry Lee Lewis over the next few months, and used him as a sideman on other Sun sessions. Jerry Lee didn't like that job, however, and didn't mind telling anybody who asked about it. After all, Jerry Lee thought, a star should play on his own records, not other people's. Period.

In the spring of 1957, Lewis recorded a new single, "Whole Lotta Shakin' Goin' On," a song originally recorded by a black group called the Commodores, and "It'll Be Me," an original Jack Clement song. Judd Phillips, the Sun promotion man and Sam's brother, charmed his way into the offices of *The Steve Allen Show* in New York City and let Jerry Lee pound a piano. The producers agreed to let The Killer on the air, and as a result the new rocker had a national hit record. Before long, every kid in every dance hall across America was doing his imitation of the blonde singer who stood up and kicked his piano bench away on stage. "Jerry Lee," said session player Bobby Wood, "was the one who started it all for the piano boys."

Next came "Great Balls Of Fire," written by Otis Blackwell, a black writer who composed "All Shook Up," and Jack Hammer. The record was pure spartan rockabilly – vocal, piano, drums. But, oh, those vocals! They seemingly brought out every suggestion of sex and wildness. Suddenly, Jerry Lee had a *reputation*. He was the singer who dared to croon what teenagers were really thinking, the adults wrote in magazines and newspapers. Jerry Lee was hot. He followed with such hits as "Breathless" and "High School Confidential," the latter song from a movie of the same name. With "Confidential" riding the charts in the spring of 1958, Jerry Lee went to England on tour. There the tabloids revealed that the 22-year-old singer had married his 13-year-old cousin, Myra Brown, his third wife. No big thing, Jerry Lee thought; the English stood aghast. Crowds heckled him, and soon he returned to the United States, although he never did recapture the momentum he had achieved earlier in rock music.

Not until the late 1960s, in fact, did the hits start coming again, and this time they were in country music. Lewis was not really doing much different, except calming himself a bit. He still played the boogie-woogie piano. He still leered at the crowds. Only this time, he attacked ballads. And people loved it.

Jerry Lee Lewis is still pounding that old piano, too. The Killer is still rocking his life away.

In 1958, after three top ten hits on Sun Records, Jerry Lee Lewis took a song called "High School Confidential" into the low twenties on the national charts. The song was from the movie of the same name, starring (left to right) Diane Jergens, Russ Tamblyn, Jan Sterling, John Drew Barrymore, and Mamie Van Doren. (She's the one with the torpedo bra!) This photograph is from a Sun record sleeve.

4

Dumpy

LATE, SOMEWHERE BETWEEN MILLVILLE and McGonigle, Dumpy Rice slow-danced in his mind with a melody. Past the fields and the farm bureau he held it, because all he wanted was to play it before somebody said hello and it was gone.

The melody lingered as he drove into the parking lot of the Rusty Nail. Through whiskey-soaked air, he glided toward the red-carpeted bandstand and the piano, forgetting to take off his coat and the old brown fedora pulled snugly over his bushy hair. With each step, a cigarette bobbed in his lips. A wide-bellied man followed closely.

"What's goin' *on?*" the man asked breathlessly, patting the bulge in his tight-fitting nylon shirt.

Dumpy smiled absently and plugged in the electric piano.

"Haven't played no music for a long time," the man said. "Busy with the kids. Busy at the plant. . . ."

Dumpy's smile was the vacant smile of a man looking over his desk and seeing a trout stream where his filing cabinet used to be. It was a Wednesday morning smile thinking Saturday night.

The old friend, sensing a familiar preoccupation, stepped back. "Well, Dump," he said, almost apologetically, "I'd better go. You got bigger things to do right now."

Dumpy pecked at the keyboard. It wasn't there anymore. The melody was gone. He looked up, then he laughed. "Brother," he said, "the biggest thing I gotta do right now is *find my Miller.*" Together, they walked toward the bar.

Once they had shared more. They had played together. There had been five of them, boys with shot-glass wisdom and an ear for rockabilly music. But, gradually, the more sober notes of factory jobs and mortgages took over, and only Dumpy was left.

For twenty years, he blended quietly into roadside honky-tonks, pounding out lonely songs for lonely people. From gritty dance floors and teetering bar stools they watched each other. Only Dumpy was the closer observer. He took them — and himself — and wrapped them up in melody. They became the characters in his songs, in "Missing You, Missing Home," "You And Me," "Beware Of The Night."

Dumpy said he was forty-three years old but that he had the experience of a sixty-five-year-old. His friends agreed. They said if facial lines meant character, then Dumpy was a *statesman*. There was a photograph of Willie Nelson at a Cincinnati recording studio, and on it were these words: "This man is *not* Dumpy Rice." Dumpy was repentant of yesterday, somewhat jaded about today, but still hopeful about tomorrow. He said his heart had been broken like a full Mason jar on a hardwood floor, but no mind, because it helped his music.

His real name was Denzil, but nobody — not even close friends — ever called him that. His name had been Dumpy ever since an aunt peered at the hefty infant Denzil and said he looked "dumpy." When somebody in a bar happened to see clearly enough to notice the name Denzil on an Elvis Presley or Conway Twitty or Dobie Gray record, Dumpy just grinned shyly and mumbled something or another into his beer.

In 1974, Twitty recorded "There's A Honky-Tonk Angel (Who'll Take Me Back In)." The record went to number one on the national country music charts. When folks asked about that, Dumpy said, "Good, ole Conway." A few years later, RCA released Presley's version and it jumped into the top ten. "I'll be dang," Dumpy said. "*Elvis.*"

With one song, it seemed that the scratchy-voiced singer and piano player from Hamilton, Ohio, had written something permanent, without trying. Royalty checks came in the mail and, for once, he could afford a few luxuries. But only a few. A man can't support himself on one country hit, and that's one reason why Dumpy played at the Rusty Nail.

The night was like the others: darkness covering darkness; faceless people laughing to themselves and moving in slow-motion through blue haze on a dimly lit dance floor. The place was so dark a man needed infrared eyes if he cared any about seeing whom he was dancing with. And when the dancing was over around two the next morning and the doors opened, an ominous ball of gray smoke rolled out into the parking lot.

Through the night Dumpy played, sitting hunched over his small electric piano as if he'd been punched in the stomach. His singing wasn't beautiful, but it was real, and his mustache bristled against the microphone as he sang his song:

"So tell me if you think it's over, And I'll leave it up to you how it ends. 'Cause if you don't want a love I can give you, There's a honky-tonk angel who'll take me back in." (℗1973 Danor Music, BMI).

Then the band leader, Lonnie Mack, signaled for a tempo change, and the group rollicked with "We Still Play Rock 'n' Roll Like We Used To." Mack, a bear of a man, tenaciously grabbed his old Flying V guitar as if it were a fire hose. The sound ricocheted across the tables and off the mirrors.

Mack and Rice performed together before 1963, when Mack succeeded with his record, "Memphis." After that, Mack went on to have two Cadillacs a year, press parties and an endless night of one-nighters. Dumpy had a beer and went back to the small clubs. In the 1950s they had been rockabilly players. Mack developed, ultimately, into the link between blues-rock and hip guitarists of the '60s. Dumpy stayed rockabilly, however. Oh, he could play about anything, they said, but he was just a simple country player with a passion for boogie-woogie.

So the coliseums and large concert halls faded into such places as the Rusty Nail and the Golden Key, and Mack, for a time, was back in the country, playing the clubs where he started. He would eventually go on to have a second life on Chicago's Alligator Records in the mid-'80s, but, on this night, he was just another roadhouse player.

"Remember the night we met in McGonigle, Dumpy?" Lonnie asked.

"I don't remember," Dumpy replied, "but I know you fired me after the first month."

"Well, Dump, do you remember the night you set yourself on fire on stage? Musta been early '60s. We were backin' Jackie DeShannon. She had one of those short skirts on, and you leaned back so far to look up her dress that you. . . ."

"Aw, Lonnie," Dumpy said, looking embarrassed and turning his head. Lonnie went on anyway.

"Well, your hair was longer then and you always kept a cigarette in your mouth and two lighted ones behind your ears. You kept insistin' on leanin' back farther and farther at the piano, tryin' to get a good look, and pretty soon – BANG! Off your seat and set your hair on fire. Guess you had the *hots*."

"Aw, Lonnie," Dumpy said, staring at the table. Lonnie giggled.

"I gotta say something," Dumpy said suddenly.

"Well, tell it *right*," warned Lonnie.

"One night I went to the drive-in with some chick I never was with before."

"There was a lot of them," Lonnie said, laughing.

"No, Lonnie, we went and saw this movie with Bill Haley and the Comets and

Chuck Berry. I heard the song "Memphis," see and I *loved* it. So I ordered it from the record store in Hamilton. Lonnie, you liked that song so much that you started doin' it as an instrumental."

Lonnie looked at him increduously. "No, no, that ain't it, Dumpy. *You* started playin' it, and one night you didn't come to work, and *I* had to play guitar on it myself. You were my guitar player then. I usually played bass on it."

Dumpy shook his head knowingly and insisted, "No, you started playin' it."

"You learned it first," growled Lonnie, with a look that showed the discussion was finished.

Who played the song first wasn't important. Mack recorded it in the last minutes of a session for Fraternity Records of Cincinnati, and he had the hit record. It became his fusion of country and rock and established him as a premier guitarist.

"I had a record out on Fraternity once myself," Dumpy said.

"Oh, yeah, what was it?"

"A little rockabilly thing called 'Rinky Dink.'"

"Ha! Dumpy plays rinky dink," Lonnie said. "Rinky *dinky*."

Dumpy looked hurt, and Lonnie stopped laughing. "Really," Lonnie explained, "Dumpy Rice is one of the all-time great piano players, but he never got the credit for it. He just wouldn't leave Hamilton long enough."

"Those days, things were fun," Dumpy said.

"Yeah, you always used to be a clown, Dump, and do flip-flops and land on your feet. We'd march five or six hundred people out of here and down the road and back. You'd bust your tail every time you'd flip-flop through the window and hit the dance floor."

"Lonnie, remember the night I came to work in shorts?"

"*Remember*? One of your trademarks was always bein' late, and when the band dressed in matching suits, you'd show up in T-shirts and jeans."

"Well, Lonnie, you knew I just came to play."

"Yeah, and you'd come in a '49 Plymouth that'd been through World War Three. Your cars always looked that way and, come to think of it, they still do. And you still look like a hundred-year-old Mexican."

Dumpy grinned and lit another cigarette.

"And you always tried to steal my women," Lonnie said.

"How do *you* know, Lonnie?"

"Oh, I know."

"I never did take any of your women."

Lonnie looked unconvinced. "One thing about you, Dumpy, is that you are the same as you were twenty years ago."

"Thanks, Lonnie."

"I mean, you don't practice and you don't give a darn."

"Yeah, I guess everything I know is accidental," Dumpy said.

"That's a true statement," Lonnie chuckled. "That's a great statement."

Without interrupting, a young musician approached the table. "You play *my* kind of music," he said, although he was a baby twenty years ago.

"We're back and we're gonna do it because we're not getting any younger," Lonnie said. "We're going for the last run before we leave this life."

"Uh, Mr. Rice," the young man said. "The studio engineer said our record is hot. A smash. He said, 'Get Dumpy Rice to put some rockabilly piano licks on it.' I told him the band was out of money, and we couldn't pay. He said, 'You from Hamilton? Dumpy'll do it for nothing.'"

"For *nothin'*?" Dumpy said, feigning disbelief. He paused, then he said, "Yeah, kid, I'll do it for nothin'."

Dumpy estimated he has played on more than three hundred albums and even more singles in the last eighteen years. With sporadic session work and a few royalty checks, he tried to stay alive.

"I don't have much interest in material things in life," he said. "If I've got a little change for cigarettes and a place to stay, I'm happy. If everybody had my attitude, there would be no use for safes. Why do we have safes? What *for*? Because people are materialistic. I look at things almost fundamentally barbaric. I might as well be out there pullin' some chick's hair and draggin' her on the ground and carryin' a club. All you can enjoy are the senses. I guess there's a name for people like me, but I don't know *what* it is."

Dumpy has had his joys and sorrows, money notwithstanding. "One time," recalled his friend Rusty York, "Dumpy came to a session with a mattress strapped to the top of his car. I said, 'Dumpy, where you going?' He said, 'I've had my last argument with that girl. I took her mattress because I couldn't bear to think of her ever stayin' with another man.'"

But that was a girlfriend and a lifetime ago, and all that was the same was that Dumpy Rice was still a musician. Which was all he ever wanted to be, ever since he was eleven and found his father's cheap guitar. Then he discovered his sister's old upright piano, and decided to be a classical pianist. He fell short of classical anything, however, and quit school in the ninth grade. No interest.

"Then one day I was playin' guit-ar on the front porch and a guy came up to me and said, 'Would you be interest in playin' in a band?' Well, I was only seventeen, and I said, 'I never played *out*.' But he got me to play at a teen hop, and two weeks later he got me a job playin' in a beer joint for twelve dollars a night and all the beer

I could drink. I wasn't even eighteen yet. I played around the area for a while, and one night I met Troy Seals — he's a big Nashville songwriter now — just ridin' through the humps at Frisch's restaurant. We played with Lonnie Mack for a time, and then Conway Twitty took a likin' to my piana playin' and offered me a job. Conway was a big rock star then, having had a hit with 'It's Only Make Believe' and other songs. When he asked me to work for him, I gladly took the job. But I only got to come home about once every three months, and I took what you'd call a bad look at bein' a star. We played all over the United States — the hops, the nightclubs, the county fairs. Just about *everything*. Even did a telethon in Oklahoma City. After three and a half years, I wanted to be home. See, I'm a down-home fella and I don't mind bein' called that."

With Twitty, the musicians rode 125,000 miles a year and drove ninety miles an hour to get to the next town. "So I came *home*," Dumpy said. "I never got used to living out of a suitcase. What's kept me here is that I'm around people I know. I'm satisfied here; satisfied with bein' a sideman. I've always been a homebody. I don't like changes much. The pressure is less when you stay around your hometown and don't try to be somebody."

Dumpy never wanted to be *somebody*, only himself. Difficult enough for anyone to attain, even more difficult for a twenty-one-year-old piano player just coming off the road. He was used to doing what he wanted, but he thought perhaps he should conform. Be a little normal. And the way to do it, he thought then, was to marry and get a job. A few months later, Dumpy got a bride in Hamilton, a diploma from an electronics school and a job in a television repair shop.

"It's the only time I ever had a *real* gig," he said. "I quit music for six months, just to take the insides out of televisions and look for bad tubes. Hard to concentrate when you're not into it, though. You're cut out for something, you're cut out for it. Right? My hands like to froze to death every time I was up on a roof lookin' at an antenna. I'd stand there, freezin', sayin': 'Boy, you're gonna go home and *practice.*'"

So he quit his job. How could he reject a six-night job in a respectable nightclub in Cincinnati? After all, he somehow needed the performing life. But he believed his decision to return to the bars doomed his marriage. Music and marriage are often incompatible, he thought. Too many *distractions*. It was distraction, however, that later gave him enough experience to write his first lyric: "Honky-Tonk Angel." "I just felt about how lonely I was. I was feelin' like life was passin' me by. I didn't want to be where I was, so, well, I thought: There's an old gal here who this old boy's crazy about. And I wrote 'Angel.' Since then, though, I've had no major cuts out of Nashville. Oh, I *plan* on goin' to Nashville with my songs, but I never do go. A year from now I'll *still* be sayin' I'm goin'. I'm just too laid back. I never had an ambitious bone in my body. If everybody looked at life the way I do, things would go at a much slower pace and nothin' would ever get done. You see, everything to me is so temporary. I keep askin' myself: Am I doin' right by doin' wrong? Hey, that sounds like a song title, don't it. . . ?"

Song titles, it seemed, came easier than trips to Nashville. Dumpy had plenty of songs on just about every subject. One song was even named in honor of his former wife. "I named it after her only because she wanted me to," he said, grinning. "It wasn't an emotional outburst."

Early morning at the Rusty Nail. Dumpy looking over four empty cans of beer on top of the piano, toward an old cowboy. Somebody said play one more slow song, and by then the cowboy wobbled near the pinball machine, cajoling into the well-worn ear of a regular. He walked with her toward the dance floor, love at last sight, but the band was already saying goodnight.

Dumpy walked slowly through the darkness, laughing and talking with friends. "I got a new song called 'When The Fire Goes Out, She's Gone,'" he said. "Got sort of a blues feel. I've always been a blues man myself. Used to lay on my bed as a kid, just listening to that old blues radio show from Randy's Record Shop in Gallatin, Tennessee. It gave me a blues feel. I'm a blues and country man."

He slipped on his coat and old fedora and walked silently into the bone-cold morning air, alone. He'd take a country road, the long way home, and he'd be *listening.*

Hamilton, Ohio; January, 1985.

Dumpy Rice, second from right, with Jimmie Skinner, center, and Dumpy's sister, Marvain Calhoun. From mid-1960s.

Dumpy and his wife (unidentified), mid-'60s.

Dumpy Rice, 1986.

Photos courtesy Marvain Calhoun.

Dumpy Rice at Grand Forks Armory in North Dakota. January, 1964.

Lonnie Mack (right) and Dumpy Rice perform in Ohio in the late 1950s.

Photo by Randy McNutt

Looking For The Cool Spot

BY EIGHT O'CLOCK SATURDAY NIGHT, a long line had started to form already outside of Bobby Mackey's Country Music Ballroom near Wilder, Kentucky. A buxom woman of about forty years old pushed her way up to the door and thrust out her chest to reveal more clearly the black letters printed on her tight-fitting T-shirt: "Rick Saucedo – The Legend Lives On."

She and several hundred other admirers would pay six dollars this night to see an Elvis imitator from Chicago. They would also see D.J. Fontana, the man who kept the beat for The Hillbilly Cat, Elvis Presley.

Before the show, Fontana sat in a dimly lit storage room, eating fried chicken with Saucedo's security people, stage crew and band. Food was spread over several small tables, like a picnic, but with the enthusiasm of a wake. The room was hot and stuffy, not unlike the clubs Fontana performed in thirty years ago when Presley was beginning his incredible ascent. Tonight, things seemed the same somehow, from the fried chicken to the enthusiastic crowd to the unbearable 100-degree heat and high humidity. Even the limber singer in the gold jacket could temporarily suspend belief when he wailed, "Well, since my baby left me. . . ."

But D.J. Fontana did not pause to consider history. He was too busy meeting the people and signing autographs. He earns his living these days playing on recording sessions in Nashville, where he lives with his wife and children, and making personal appearances such as the one tonight. He has had a front-row seat in the long run of musical history, but he will tell you that he was only in the right place at the right time.

"In '54," he said, putting down his cole slaw, "I was playin' on the Louisiana Hayride as a staff drummer. I'm from Shreveport, you see, and I played in bands there from the time I was fifteen. After high school I played the strip shows, little clubs, anything I could find. On Saturday night, I played the Hayride, though. The funny thing is, I never listened to country music when I was growing up. I didn't listen to it until I joined the Hayride in '53 or '54, and the only reason I did it then was because I had to back the country performers. When I was in school, all of us kids listened to the big band records. I played light jazz or pop stuff. Then Elvis came along. His records were getting a lot of play in the area and he got to appear on the show. A fellow said to me, 'Will you back him?' I said, 'Well, sure, I'll back him. That's what I'm here for.' So I played with Elvis and his players, and I thought he had a unique sound, one that I shouldn't clutter up. I kept it simple."

Fontana backed the odd trio of Presley, electric guitarist Scotty Moore, and upright bassist Bill Black. Their Hayride performances went well, and Presley enjoyed working with the drummer. Whenever the trio returned to the Hayride, Fontana kept a heavy back beat, smooth and uncluttered, with a few tasteful licks thrown in. Fontana did not hesitate to accept Presley's offer to join the group.

Presley was rapidly becoming a teenage sensation in the South and in other areas. His energetic, gyrating stage appearances were attracting new audiences to the Hayride, ones with the young people. Fontana realized that something was happening.

"When Elvis first came on the Hayride," he recalled, "the country artists were really thrown. They said, 'What is this kid doin'?' Then they went home and told their kids about him, and they came to the Hayride to see what was going on. In those days, Bill Black was the mainstay of the band. He was a comedian who could warm up a crowd. That was necessary for us because we played for a lot of country crowds that weren't used to people jumping up and down on stage. Well, Bill was a big guy, as you'll remember, and he used to slide up and down on that big upright bass, slapping those strings on the wood. You get such a fat sound with an acoustic bass. You can't duplicate that sound. No way."

Fontana wiped his brow, tugged at the collar of his white shirt and shifted uncomfortably in his blue-gray suit. The heat was oppressive, even inside the air-conditioned nightclub, so he decided to move up to the bar.

"D.J.," a band member said, "are you keepin' cool, man?"

Fontana stared in disbelief. "*Cool?*" he replied.

He groaned and ordered a beer. He lit a cigarette and stared up toward the ceiling. "There's a cool spot around here somewhere. I know there is," he said. Finally he found the air-conditioning vent on the wall.

By 8:30 the crowd had wound its way fifty feet outside the door. The people inside had already sucked up any cool air. As smoke drifted all around, middle-aged women in polyester suits filed past a table lined with Rick Saucedo memorabila: key chains, fan club items, bumper stickers, buttons, glossy photographs. The women looked reverently at the table, as though it were a shrine.

Fontana sat at the bar, talking. A heavy woman walked up and touched him gently on the arm. "Hi, D.J.!" she bubbled. "Remember me?"

"Hi," he said, lowly.

"I'm Dottie's sister. From the convention...."

"Oh, yeah, hi," he said.

She walked away smiling. Fontana got up and inspected the corner of the bar. Suddenly he grabbed a stool and sat it down carefully. "*Here* it is," he announced to no one in particular. "The cool spot. It's right here."

A cool stream of air indeed. It flowed from the vent, right into his face.

"The tie's *gone*," he said, pulling it off. "Let's have another beer."

"I learned the value of simplicity at the Hayride," Fontana said later. "I heard Scotty and Bill and Elvis one night and knew that I couldn't mess up that sound. That's why I always play what I feel. If that won't work, I just won't do it again. I think the simple approach comes from my hearing so much big band music. I mixed it with rockabilly."

He does not remember the details: what tracks he played on, what studios he recorded in, why songs got cut and others didn't. Everything seems to run together now, more than thirty years later. Record historians tell him he first appeared on sessions in the mid-'50s on Presley's later Sun recordings. He shook his head at the thought. "There were so *many* songs over the years, so many performances. We recorded live in those days, on one-track equipment. But Elvis didn't care if we made a mistake if the track sounded right to him. He wanted quality, sure, but Elvis had an ear, too, and he wanted the records to have that certain feel to them. That's what it was all about — the feel."

Fontana has told the stories over and over, to fans and writers and collectors. It's a job that somebody must do. Elvis and Bill Black are dead; Scotty Moore is busy with his business interests in Nashville. That leaves D.J. Fontana to talk.

The band played an effective version of "My Girl." Just then a pretty woman of about twenty tapped Fontana on the arm.

"Dance with me," she pleaded.

"Well, uh," he said, trying to be polite, "I've been looking for the cool spot in here all night, see, and this is the coolest place in the building. I just can't move. But thank you, though."

He wiped his forehead again and sipped on a beer.

"The jacket's *gone*," he groaned.

"Who put the glue on my microphone?" the band leader asked.

D.J. Fontana laughed. "I'll do my five songs soon," he said. "When you do only five songs, you don't *sweat* so much. . . ."

August, 1985

Even Cowboys Get The Blues

LLOYD COPAS CALLED HIMSELF cowboy and the world believed him. He was, after all, a Grand Ole Opry star in a time of western swing. In the hollows near Blue Creek, Ohio, old friends just smiled knowingly and welcomed him home each Christmas. They never did get used to calling him the Oklahoma Singing Cowboy, for they remembered him as the quiet son of Elvin and Lola Copas, poor Adams County farmers who entertained at the Saturday night barn dances.

Cowboy Copas was never a cowboy. He was in fact a prototypical country singer of the 1940s who went to Nashville with a cheap guitar and a worn dream. He helped mold a disorganized country music into what it is today — an amalgamation of popular sounds — and he explored its softer side. Yet for all his fame, the name Cowboy Copas now evokes more curiosity than respect. The man who gave the world "The Tennessee Waltz" has become an anachronism in 4/4 time. He is perceived as the quintessential rhinestone troubadour, whose stage name is enough to cause a hearty chuckle in today's slick world of country music. The music historians don't even know that he was an Ohio Appalachian, not an Oklahoma cowboy. Copas himself spread the misinformation all his adult life, saying he grew up on a ranch near Muskogee, Oklahoma. He figured anybody with such a dusty past was born to be a singing cowboy.

Music was his beginning and end. As a boy of ten, he used to sit for hours on a wooden fence and strum an old guitar. His father gently reminded him of the merits of farm work, but the boy said he intended to work hard to become a famous hillbilly singer like Vernon Dalhart. Lloyd said he could never be happy working on a farm or in a mill, not even if he could play the barn dances every Saturday night. So, he strummed. He wanted recognition.

In 1927, when he was fourteen, he convinced a local musician named Fred Evans to let him join the popular Hencacklers String Band. Evans was wary of hiring a boy, but the kid possessed a sweet tenor voice and quick fingers. That was enough. By summer the group set out in a big automobile to perform at county fairs in the area and during intermissions at the old Palace Theater in the village of Peebles. In that theater in 1928, young Lloyd Copas lost his heart to the western movie.

By his sixteenth birthday, however, he realized he could never become famous by singing at the Palace. He needed a larger audience and phonograph records, so he left home to seek them. Instead, he found a fellow named Natchee, a champion fiddle player whose real name was Vernon Storer. They formed a team, and by 1935 Natchee was playing the fiddle and Lloyd the flat-top guitar all over the region. They performed in talent contests and on radio shows in hundreds of dusty towns. On day, at an amateur contest in Cincinnati, the organizer saw Lloyd waiting for his turn on stage. "All right, cowboy," the man said to Lloyd, "let's see what *you* can do." Lloyd liked that word, cowboy. He told Natchee that it seemed proper somehow: Cowboy Copas. "I'd rather be an Oklahoma cowboy than an Ohio ridge runner any day," Lloyd said with a laugh.

The name stuck but his association with Natchee did not. Lloyd went home to Blue Creek and formed a band called the Gold Star Rangers with his brother, Marion Andrew, and some other local men. They performed on WCHS in Charleston, West Virginia, and in the clubs in the hill country. Not even his band could hold Lloyd, however, for he had deeper needs.

He convinced his brother to go with him to Nashville to seek work on the Opry. Lloyd was confident. Broadcast every Saturday night, the Opry was the most popular barn dance show in America and the country performers' lifeline to the populace. Singing on that show, Lloyd said, was a man's ticket to success. Marion just smiled shyly and tried to explain that a man just can't walk into the Ryman Auditoriun and announce his availability, but Lloyd would not discuss reality.

Somewhere between Lexington, Kentucky, and Nashville, Marion turned to Lloyd and said, "I ain't cut out for this life. I'm goin' home."

Lloyd did not flinch. He kept his eyes on the road and his mind on his dream. "Do what you must do," he said, "but I'm going to Nashville."

In a few months the city turned cold and Lloyd returned to Ohio, rejected. If he could not sing on the radio in Nashville, he said, he would sing in Cincinnati. Soon, the "Boone County Jamboree," a popular program broadcast on WLW Radio, featured Cowboy Copas. He continued to sing on the show for several years — he even married Lucille Markins of Peebles on its stage with a borrowed ring in 1935 — but somehow he was not contented. What Lloyd needed was a band. One that made records.

A band found him in Knoxville in 1940. Lloyd had decided to go south to sing on the radio, and one day he met accordionist Pee Wee King and his Golden West Cowboys. King had introduced big band music to the Opry in 1937, the year another cowboy singer, Leonard Slye — who grew up about twenty miles east of Blue Creek — became Roy Rogers for Republic Pictures. King immediately liked Copas and his straightforward, emotional delivery, and he asked the singer to become vocalist for the band. Cowboy Copas slipped on the colorful western suit of the Golden West Cowboys and never looked back toward Ohio.

He did not disown his past, he just decided not to mention it to the publicity agents. He wanted them to think of him as a ranch hand who simply eased on out of the west and into the studio. "Some people change their names to get ahead in life," said his sister, Mildred Rothwell of Blue Creek. "Well, our Lloyd changed his name *and* his life."

By 1944, however, Copas knew he was going to need more than a cowboy name to become famous on his own. King informed him late that year that the Golden West Cowboys would soon move their base from Nashville to Louisville. Copas didn't want to leave the Opry, so in January, 1945, he became a solo performer with those same old dreams of fame.

In Cincinnati, meanwhile, Sydney Nathan was dreaming too. At least that's what his friends told him. With the war's troublesome restrictions on shellac eased, Nathan wanted to set up his own independent record company, King Records. He finally obtained help from partners to set up his label to record music for poor Appalachians and, later, blacks.

Nathan heard Copas sing on the radio, and offered the singer a contract. Copas walked into the ugly gray studio on Brewster Avenue in the Cincinnati neighborhood of Evanston and left with such country hits as "Filipino Baby," "The Tennessee Waltz," "The Kentucky Waltz," "Rose of Oklahoma" and "Signed, Sealed and Delivered." He then went to California to make a cowboy movie of his own, and returned to go on tour with Hank Williams.

In photographs, Copas appeared a smiling man with hazel eyes and dark hair. On stage, he wore a powder blue suit, green boots, and a white cowboy hat. He was one of America's most popular country singers of the late 1940s and early '50s. By 1951, however, the hits suddenly had stopped. Copas could not equal the sales of "Strange Little Girl," his top ten hit of that year. Not that he didn't try. For some reason, he descended on the charts as swiftly as he had risen. Nobody at King Records could understand the problem. Copas remained popular in concert, but his records were not selling well.

He attributed the problem to a general slump in country music, and he stopped performing for several years to regroup. Desperate for another hit, he turned to a new music, rock 'n' roll, and a new label, Dot Records, in 1956. Nothing happened with his rockabilly effort, "Circle Rock," however, and Copas was disillusioned. He was, after all, a 43-year-old country singer. A waltz man at heart. He could not bring himself to *wiggle*.

As the '50s wore on Copas nearly dropped from the horizon of country music. Then as the decade ended so did his bad luck. The transformation came quickly: Starday Records, a Texas label that had found success with country and rockabilly artists, promoted his new record, "Alabam," all the way to Number One. The record clung to the country charts for thirty-four weeks before it spilled over onto the pop charts. Cowboy Copas was now a star in three decades.

When he returned to Adams County, Ohio, just before Christmas in 1962, he must have been proud. He sang well for old friends at a benefit concert that day, and he had a new record, "Goodbye Kisses," ready for release.

On March 5, 1963, two days after the record was mailed to the radio stations, Copas appeared at a benefit for a disc jockey in Kansas City with Patsy Cline and Hawkshaw Hawkins. Later, they flew to Nashville on a small private plane flown by Randy Hughes, Copas' son-in-law and Cline's manager. As Hughes struggled to see in a thunderstorm, the plane crashed near Camden, Tennessee. All four passengers died.

Now Copas' music is being re-evaluated by music scholars who are finding his records exceeding good for the period. "Cowboy was a favorite here on the Opry for twenty-two years," said Ronnie Pugh, head reference librarian at the Country Music Hall of Fame in Nashville. "He did some marvelous songs, but he was never elected to the hall for some reason. But he was an important performer."

No finer tribute can be given to any man. Even an *Ohio* cowboy.

Requiem For A Bantamweight

JOHNNY PAYCHECK CAME HOME to Highland County, Ohio, for Christmas in 1985, and ended up in the Highland County Courthouse in Hillsboro on a shooting charge. The bullet hit a guy above the right eye, only grazing him, and he lived to joke about the incident to a nurse. "Like bein' in the Long Branch," he told her, shortly after he was shot in a tavern in town one night. With one squeeze of the trigger, Johnny's homecoming went awry, and his latest record, "Everything's Changin' (But Me)," became a requiem for a bantamweight.

Johnny always was more than just a country singer; he was a man seemingly destined to live out his own lyrics. He was one of the last of country music's self-proclaimed outlaws, who turned the conservative Nashville establishment on its head in the late 1970s. Times moved on, though; Waylon went straight, Willie headed out to Hollywood, and Johnny went to the courthouse. What luck.

Johnny Paycheck did not grow up bad, though, just feisty. He was, in his own words, a boy who never passed a puddle he didn't jump. He was born Donald Eugene Lytle in 1937 in Greenfield, Ohio, a tough little town carved from the rolling farmland of southwestern Ohio. In a community fed on corn and country music, Donnie grew up humming the songs of Hank Williams and Lefty Frizzell. At thirteen, he was already playing the guitar. Music was his one passion, taking him away from the strife of a poor family. Donnie didn't play all that well by his fifteenth birthday, but when he opened his mouth to sing, everybody around him stopped to listen. The kid could wail the country blues, even if he wasn't old enough to feel them yet. Give him time, folks said, for the boy was small in stature but big in voice.

Donnie decided early on that he wanted to be a country music star. Not just a local musician content to play on weekends, but a singer on the Grand Ole Opry in Nashville. And a likely start, he reasoned, was through the front door of the Club 28, a Greenfield nightclub on State Route 28 that featured some members of WLW-T's "Midwestern Hayride." One day he just strolled in with his guitar and asked the owner for a job. The owner heard the kid sing, and that was that.

The only trouble was, Donnie couldn't stay in one place for long. At seventeen, he realized he would have to leave Greenfield if he wanted a successful recording career. He promptly quit the Club 28 job and went to Columbus, where he got bored. He longed to explore the next highway, so he figured he'd join the Navy. The advertisements promised he would see the world, but he didn't know it would be done with mop in hand. He simply did not fit in, and in a year he was accused of having a little set-to with an officer. Donnie decided that as soon as he got out he would go to Nashville, where he wouldn't have to say "Yes, sir" to anybody.

Don Lytle arrived in Nashville in 1957 with nothing but a guitar, a lead and a dream. Somebody had told him to look up Ernest Tubb, and he did just that. Tubb listened to Don sing and invited the young man to appear on the Ernest Tubb Record Shop radio show, which followed the Opry on Saturday night. Don thought he was ready to break Music City wide open.

He wasn't. He struggled for months until he met some musicians who helped him get work as a guitarist in the bands of George Jones, Ray Price and Faron Young. Then Tubb arranged for a contract with Decca Records. Don took the stage name Donnie Young, in honor of Faron Young, whom he admired and respected.

Eventually, Donnie recorded several singles. They were country, yet rock-influenced somehow. Rockabilly. Nobody paid much attention, though, even after he cut such good rockabilly records as "Shaking The Blues." So he stayed country.

Donnie continued to back the well-known country singers in every rough-and-tumble honky-tonk and dusty fairgrounds in America. In those uncaring places he perfected his strong, melancholy delivery and his right hook. His nose was smashed twice in fights with unappreciative patrons. By 1965, he decided he needed another name, one nobody could forget, so he called himself Johnny Paycheck, after a boxer he had admired as a boy. The critics said the name reminded them of some hillbilly in a rhinestone suit.

Johnny didn't care. He continued to record for the independent labels and finally he brought home a hit. He followed "A-11" with more hits: "Heartbreak, Tennessee," "The Lovin' Machine," "Motel Time Again" and "Jukebox Charlie." They were all honky-tonking songs sung by a honky-tonking man.

Finally, Johnny was getting the attention he thought he deserved. He traveled all over the nation but always took the time to stop in Greenfield to perform at various benefits for sick children or for the annual Toys For Tots show. Yet, he had an incomprehensible darker side, which led him on more erratic paths. Working in the honky-tonks didn't help, either. The relationship between Johnny and the honky-tonk was a symbiotic one. He had to perform in them to earn a living, and he liked the applause. He *always* liked the applause. But soon he fell victim to the clubs and the business, and the hits suddenly stopped.

Then, after fighting his way back from personal troubles, Johnny signed with Columbia Records in Nashville. Producer Billy Sherrill cut a top ten hit, "She's All I Got," a former rhythm and blues hit, for Paycheck. But it was "Take This Job And Shove It" that really pushed Johnny into the public eye. With one record, honky-tonk Johnny became the anti-authority figure of country music. He grew a beard. He moved to Austin, Texas, where the outlaws congregated, and adopted Austin as his middle name.

As "Outlaw's Prayer" and "I'm The Only Hell (My Mama Ever Raised)" rushed up the charts, Johnny earned big money and the praise of country fans. But trouble pursued him like some determined fan. The Internal Revenue Service. Courts. And more.

"His problem," says performer-songwriter Bobby Borchers, "is that Johnny began to believe all that press stuff about the outlaws. There were some of us into that country music outlaw thing a few years ago, but I was smart enough to know that it was my music that was renegade, not me."

The jury deliberates. Out in front of the courthouse, Johnny sits on a bench and reminisces about the old days of Donnie Young. "Yeah, I cut some good records back then," he says. "I don't know how I ever developed such a soulful style, though. Just happened, I guess. I didn't listen to black artists as a kid. Just country ones. Some people say my early stuff was rockabilly. I don't know about that myself. I was always country, man, country. That's me."

Johnny walks up to the front of the courthouse. A thin woman approaches him. "Do you remember me?" she asks.

He looks at her nervously, laughing and trying to change the subject. The woman persists. "Don't you remember me, Johnny? We went to school together."

He thinks for a moment and puffs on a cigarette. "Uh, I'm from Greenfield."

"So am I. Now, who *am* I?"

"Well, I don't. . .oh, darlin', you look familiar, but I see so *many* people. You know what I'm sayin'?"

"Yeah," she says hurtfully. "You don't know me."

"Do you remember Alice Scott?" asks a little girl.

"Oh, sure," Johnny replies.

"Well," says the girl, "that's *her*!"

"I swear!" Johnny shouts. He hugs the woman. "Thirty years is a *long* time."

They embrace momentarily as Johnny's private investigator — a man with slick black hair who looks like a young Wolfman Jack — takes their picture.

Johnny sighs and feels in his pocket for a cigarette. He heads for the stairs to take a smoke.

In front of the door, six elderly women are lined up, pointing Polaroids and instant cameras toward the door. An advance scout runs to the women, shouting, "Here he comes!" Johnny unknowingly walks right into their line of fire. Shutters click and little color photographs pop out of the Polaroids. Johnny just stands there, frozen. He throws up his hands and says, "Why, thank you darlin's. Thank you."

The word guilty flies through the courthouse like a stray cannonball. Johnny stands straight, with no expression, as the judge sentences him to nine and a half years in prison.

Johnny says he will appeal, of course, and, until the case is resolved, he'll be free on bond to pick up the rest of his life. He's got a record deal again, and a nice chart record, too. He'll be out there on the road again in the night, traveling to some town where folks still appreciate an aging rockabilly man who can sing those cheatin', drinkin', losin' songs. But this time, Johnny Paycheck, the only hell his mama ever raised, will sing those songs a little more soulfully. For everything is still changing but Johnny.

"Sugaree" Revisited

RUSTY YORK LOOKS THE WAY we would expect an accountant to look, not a rock music singer. His soft Appalachian drawl hints that he could sing sad country songs, perhaps, but nothing — from his neatly coordinated three-piece suit and tie to his silver, computerized wrist watch — suggests that gaudy part.

Today, he is a businessman in his early fifties and the owner of a thriving recording studio and a city block of Mount Healthy, Ohio, a town in suburban Cincinnati. The days of singing "Sugaree," his small rockabilly hit on Chess Records in 1959, seem gone. York has made the transition from singer to producer-businessman and, during the last three decades, managed to keep a smile on his face and a Cadillac in his garage. A late-model black Seville, in fact, is the first thing a visitor sees at York's Jewel Re-

Rusty York in his Jewel Recording Studio. (Photo by Randy McNutt)

cording Co. on Kinney Avenue, a street filled with small businesses and residences. The automobile is a symbol of financial solidity in the wacky and competitive music business.

York usually sits inside the carpeted studio, turning knobs and muttering such foreign commands as "EQ" and "mix-down." On this afternoon, however, he happened to walk into his office and pull out a tattered scrapbook from a desk drawer and remember July, 1959. As he turned the yellow pages of his career, he laughed softly at the stories and photographs: Rusty and Frankie Avalon, Rusty and George Jones, Rusty and Jan and Dean. In each picture, a slick-haired Rusty looked bewildered in that year of fins and chrome.

The scrapbook is about as close as York will come to being any kind of singer these days. If the money is right, he might perform at so-called oldies concerts, but he is not really in demand on the nightclub circuit anymore. And he doesn't want to be. His only big record — it rose to only number 79 on Billboard's top 100 chart — was called "Sugaree," two minutes and thirty seconds of unrestrained wailing. It propelled him into rock's dark sky, where most of the stars shine six months and burn out. So it was with him. But that's all right, he will tell you, because he lived in exciting 1959, a great time to sing and be a kid in Cincinnati, Ohio.

They called Rusty both country and rock then, but now, in this era of electronic

The Cajuns, about 1959: Rusty York, Jim Lundy (drums), and Hap Arnold (bass).

music, he is simply rockabilly. Strangers send him checks for an album of his old songs, and his record is faithfully reviewed in music publications in England and Sweden, where rockabillies are still appreciated. York just stays home, meanwhile, and operates his recording studio and Jewel Records label. He's a businessman, not a bar singer. And he's no rebel.

But the bars of Cincinnati are where he started his musical career. During a break one night a friend suggested that Rusty cut a record, but he had written only one song. When somebody else brought up a song called "Sugaree" by Marty Robbins as a b-side, York didn't even know the words. He never bothered to learn them, either.

"I recorded over at the King Studios and just made the lyrics up when I couldn't remember the lines," he said with a laugh. "First thing I knew, I was in demand for record hops and television shows. We pressed 10,000 records here in Cincinnati. That's great for one town this size. Then a man purchased the master and put it out on his Note label in Columbus. Then Chess Records heard of it and bought the master. The record immediately got a lot of airplay, and I said to myself, 'Man, this is really nice of the Chess people to put me up in these fancy hotels and all that stuff.' Of course, I didn't know that when it came time to get my royalty check, all of that money would be taken out. When the record first hit, I was working downtown at Jim Skinner's record shop on Fifth Street. I spun records and played the guitar and turned the knobs as the engineer there. At night, I played music in lounges. They got mad at me at Skinner's because I wanted to leave to promote the record. Somebody said, 'How can you do this to us?' I said, 'Do *what*, man? This is my big chance.' So I went on to Dick Clark's show and I played at the Hollywood Bowl along side of the Everly Brothers, Anita Bryant, the Coasters, Jan and Dean, Santo & Johnny, Jerry Wallace, Lou Rawls, Frankie Avalon. So many people out there. All around me. I must have looked like an ant standing down there on stage.

"When I got back home, the record was starting up the charts. People stopped me and said they really dug the vocals and the words. I didn't want to tell them that I didn't even know all the words to the song, and that I just made them up as I went along! But you know, Marty Robbins once told me that he got a big royalty check as writer for that cut, one of the biggest checks he had ever received. I know I didn't get much. I guess I did seem pretty countryfied to the big-city people at Chess at Chicago. They called me up there for a meeting, and these guys were expecting a teen sensation like Frankie Avalon. Instead, they got *me*. I'll never forget them pointing to me and my argyle socks. One said, 'See, I told you so....' I was expecting a big royalty check, but I got less than $1,000. I said, 'Man, where's all the money?' Some guy said, 'Remember your plane trips to California? Your hotel rooms? You blew it., kid.'"

Yet for six glorious months, Rusty kept smiling all across America. He played in every major city and traveled first-class. "I remember driving up Hamilton Avenue here in Cincinnati and hearing 'Sugaree' on one station on the radio. At a traffic light, I saw a girl in a car next to me listening to the song on another station."

York is grinning now. The era has come alive for him through conversation. He can't stop talking. "The Bandstand was the high point. We taped the show back East, and a week later it was played on national television. Well, that night I went to a gig around here and a guy in another band said, 'Hey, Rusty, baby, we caught you on The Bandstand, man, and you were cool. But, man, how'd you get back here so fast?' Well, I had a flunky then named Cleemont, a boy with no teeth who called everybody dad and drove me to gigs in an old Cadillac. Well, Cleemont looked up at this guy and said, 'Hey, dad, we hopped a *jet*, man.' The other looked shocked and said, 'Into Hamilton, Ohio, on a jet? We are standing here on a stage in Hamilton, aren't we Rusty?' I just looked cool and told him, 'Yeah, well, we landed in Blue Ash. . . .'

By the early '60s, the rockabillies had to either adjust or fade out. Rusty was trying to perform in Cincinnati and operate a small recording studio he had built in his garage. In time, the schedule was too much of a strain. He was playing music until 3 a.m. then coming home and sleeping in his studio so that he could start a session at 9 a.m. He finally quit playing music.

The studio grew larger each year. By the late '60s it occupied a site on Kinney Avenue. He couldn't believe he had tried to sing and operate a studio at the same time. He vowed to never do it again. He could do without memories like Detroit, early '60s: "I had laryngitis. I needed the money. So the drummer sang and I mouthed it, and nobody ever knew the difference. We both got paid."

Sometimes, though, he likes to get out those old records. He grabbed one from a shelf and put it on the stereo. In monaural, the record scratched its way to the song "Sugaree," and guitars blasted like jackhammers. Rusty York smiled and shook his head. "I don't know," he said quietly. "Maybe it's just me. Maybe it's because I was a lot younger then, but things were great in '59. Things were *exciting*."

"When rock 'n' roll first hit, I really hated it," Rusty York said. "I liked country. People kept asking me to play 'Hound Dog,' and I couldn't understand why. But one night my band played 'Mystery Train' and the club went wild. Then I thought that maybe I was wrong about this music. But I always wanted to keep rockabilly pure. I believe rockabilly faded though because people thought it was too country. Then the string sections took over and that was about the end of it. . . ."

Story Of The Rocker

I SPENT THREE YEARS AND FIFTY dollars in telephone calls trying to find Mr. Billy Lee Riley. When I finally located him at his home in Murfreesboro, Tennessee, he seemed unimpressed with my search. "Hey, I've been here a long time," he said, as if I should know.

I went to so much effort to find him because Riley is a rocker. Not just some weak-voiced country singer trying to swing, but a soulful, powerful, *rockin'* man.

Indeed, there is something different about the music of Billy Lee. Something that pushes the novice and veteran rockabilly enthusiast to a frenzy. His music is explosive, unchecked, rebellious, hard-edged. He forged it in Memphis in the mid-1950s, when he was hired as a session player at Sun Records. Riley thumped the bass on Jerry Lee Lewis' "Great Balls Of Fire" and on numerous other records. He even played drums, guitar and other instruments. But he did not make his name from behind the scenes of the record business. He made it as a performer.

"My band *was* the Sun sound," Riley told Associated Press reporter Joe Edwards in 1984. "We've never gotten credit for that, but it's a fact. I was doing what Elvis was doing before Elvis did it: mixing blues and hillbilly, putting a laidback, funky beat to hillbilly music."

In those days, Riley was rather extroverted. His stage antics became local legends. When company owner Sam Phillips needed another rockabilly for his Sun label, Riley was a natural choice. One day, when Jerry Lee had reservations about recording a song with possible hell-fire connotations, Phillips launched into a philosophical discourse on religion with the young singer. Billy Lee listened to both sides of the discussion and said, "Let's cut it, man. . . ." That casualness, that impatience, spilled over into Riley's music. He had no national hits as an artist, yet he is one of the more popular rockabilly performers of today. Why? Perhaps he, unlike so many other singers, was a talented performer, vocalist and musician, whose ability comes through even today.

Riley probably should have had a hit record in those days, but he didn't. Many artists of lesser talent did, but then that's the nature of the record business.

Riley, a native of Pocahontas, Arkansas, came to Memphis as a part of the great second wave of artists who were attracted to Sun Records as though it were a big yellow magnet. Sun had, after all, made Elvis Presley a regional star, and led him to national success with RCA, so the artists believed that Sun could do the same for them. The only trouble was, Sun was limited in its financial, promotional and recording resources. It could accommodate only so many artists, and, of those, it could afford to push just a few.

So Riley recorded and performed in the South in 1956 and 1957, gaining a reputation as an exciting performer. His records received substantial local attention, but, nationally, not much happened. That was the case for most rockabilly records, even in rockabilly's heyday. It simply was a local phenomenon that sometimes broke loose upon the nation.

In those days, his hair was dark and slick. In photographs he appears as a man with a sly smile. On stage, he pranced nervously. He had a rocking good dance band, The Little Green Men, who turned Southern audiences on their heads. His records, "Red Hot" and "Flying Saucers Rock 'n' Roll," are perhaps most remembered today. The songs are rockabilly at its most turbulent peak.

Yet Riley said history has distorted many things about those records. For example, he said, "Red Hot" was written by fellow Sun artist Billy "The Kid" Emerson, and "Flying Saucers Rock 'n' Roll" by singer Ray Scott – not by Riley. "Many people think I wrote them," he said. "Sometimes people write and say things that happened, and they know they're not the truth. If somebody says something about me that's bad, I don't care. Long as it's right."

Recording engineer and session player Roland Janes remembered Riley as an excellent singer. Janes, another Arkansas native who came to Memphis in 1955, said he played on Riley's early records and helped Riley put together a band. "The name Little Green Men came about because of the title of Billy Lee's flying saucer record," Janes said. "I mentioned that this would be a good name and Sam Phillips agreed, and so it happened. I played guitar in the group. In fact, it was a trio for quite a while – guitar, bass, drums. Our band was so good due to our desire to be creative and to having a certain amount of creative talent in each of us. We also strived to be different. I consider Riley to be one of the greatest talents of that era, both musically and on stage. He could be classified as an Indian on the warpath; he had a lot of energy and charm. He was very, very good."

Malcomb Yelvington, another Sun artist, said Riley was a wild young man. "He played bass, drums, guitar, harmonica – about everything. Billy was a nice guy, but one with an I-don't-care attitude. I mean, he was carefree. But he was a solid musician."

And a good singer. His raspy vocals were the opposite of many of the thin-voiced rockabilly and country performers of the period. "Billy was simply a great entertainer," said Carl McVoy, another Memphis recording artist. "He used to back me up. He had one of the tightest bands around."

Dickey Lee, a high school band leader and former Sun artist, said Riley used to hire him to sing for the Little Green Men as a second vocalist. "I recall that he used to do a lot of instrumental stuff," Lee noted. "His band just *rocked*. Those guys were fantastic pickers, and they lost the mold when they made Riley. He was a wild man on stage. He had the greatest rock band that ever came out of Memphis, but he was overshadowed by Jerry Lee Lewis and some of the other artists who got more publicity at Sun. Billy Lee, well, he was your authentic rock 'n' roller."

But being good and being booked for gigs are two different things. Riley continued to record for Sun with no national success, so in 1961 he left Memphis and headed to Los Angeles. He performed on many records as a session player, made some records of his own, and kept trying to make his name known. When the Beatles hit in the mid-'60s, Riley recorded an interested album for Mercury called "Billy Lee Riley...Harmonica...Beatlemania." On the back cover are two photographs: Billy Lee blowing a harmonica with two others in his hands, and Billy smoking a cigarette and laughing uproariously in the studio.

By 1973, he had returned to Arkansas to become a contractor doing painting and interior decorating. "I was just an old rock 'n' roller from Memphis — half hillbilly and half rock 'n' roll. I just couldn't relate to heavy metal," he once said.

Only one year earlier he had landed on the charts for the first time in his career with a record called "I Got A Thing About You Baby." The Tony Joe White song was produced expertly by music mogul Chips Moman, but the record stayed on the Billboard charts only two weeks, peaking at number 93. "We had big hopes for that one," Riley said, "but it just didn't happen. What can I say?"

In 1979, he was invited to perform at a Memphis music festival, and 30,000 people heard him sing. He was asked for three encores. He wanted more.

So he moved close to Nashville and made some records on his own. He traveled to Europe to play for affectionate audiences. He even started writing a book about the rockabilly days.

"The thing that I did was contribute," Riley said. "I didn't get credit for it."

He will not rest until he gets that credit, either. He will sing until he can sing no more.

Let this, then, be the epithet of Billy Lee Riley: May he forever rock and roll.

July, 1987.

Billy Lee Riley (center) and his band, about 1957.

And now the long awaited debut of
BILLY RILEY & His Little Green Men

SHOWTIME!

9:30 TO 9:45 INTERMISSION

With Tall TEX MASON
and His Bullwhip!

TOMMY MITCHELL
Opens up the final segment

Then LES GILLAM
"New Love" — "Crazy Arms"

And now — Tonight's
"SEARCH FOR STARS" WINNER!

Next JOE POOVEY
"No Thanks, Bartender"

Talent winner
LONNIE SMITHSON
"All Alone"

Back Again — BILLY RILEY & BAND

And then — THE RANGERS QUARTET

And, the finale — JERRY REED

Next Week — The Five Strings & Jerry Lee Lewis

March 23, 1957

By the spring of 1957, Billy Lee Riley's reputation as an outstanding performer had reached Texas. He appeared on the "Big D Jamboree" that year, and the show's program proclaimed: "Billy Lee Riley and His Little Green Men make their long awaited debut on the Big D tonight. They record for Sun and they are said to be show-stoppers all the way. They feature rock and roll numbers. . .but they are well-versed entertainers who should fit right into our show."

All For A Song

RAY PENNINGTON WALKED INTO HIS office at Step One Records near Nashville's Music Row, and sat down at a cluttered desk. It was a potpourri of his life: phonograph albums, liner notes, artists' photographs, a gold album, notes, reel-to-reel tapes, and a comfortable old pipe.

Pennington was not about to apologize for the condition of his desk, for it meant that he was busy. Step One had recently been recognized by one of Music City's independent music journals as one of the city's most successful small labels. And Ray Pennington, former rockabilly crooner, was the reason.

Success did not come quickly, however. Pennington has worked in town since the early 1960s, starting as a low-level publishing company employee and eventually working up to the position of staff producer for RCA Records in Nashville. The early to mid-'70s were his golden years. He produced and wrote songs for many of the label's artists, including Waylon Jennings and Willie Nelson.

But, after years of fighting the record industry bureaucracy, Pennington decided to continue his writing and producing for many of the independent record companies. That was in the late '70s, and the hits have not stopped since.

"I got active in the music business in Cincinnati in 1953," the Kentucky native said as he lit his pipe. "I played in bands locally and worked at various jobs throughout the decade, including that of staff producer at King Records, disc jockey at a country station, and a owner of a record store. I worked constantly. When I played country at the Venice Pavillion, I was Ray Pennington. When I played rhythm and blues and rockabilly, I was Ray Starr. I don't know why I did that. Hiding from bill collectors, I guess. But we were just people who wanted to make records and didn't know what to do with them when we made them. My rockabilly was different. I played it sometimes, then added something else. When country music hit a depressed state about '56, I added drums. Then horns. I was always mixing it up. I played country, R&B, and whatever the crowds wanted. There were many old road houses out there. Go past them now and you can probably still hear me playing inside."

Pennington played within a 200-mile radius of Cincinnati by night. By day, in the mid- to late-'50s, he produced records at the King studio in Cincinnati. "I was looking for something, I didn't know what," he said. "Then I found my niche in the studio. We'd use some of my musicians and mix them up with some black players even then. All the time, I'd keep bands and play, play, play. I didn't know any other way. Heck, when you are the son of a sharecropper, you want something better."

At King, Pennington got the opportunity to work with most of the top country acts in the nation. And, he got to write for many of them, too. An early success for Pennington was "Lonesome 7-7773" by Hawkshaw Hawkins. Pennington produced the record. But as he took on additional studio work, his singing had to be curtailed. The days of cutting fine rockabilly and country sessions for Lee Records of Cincinnati and King were coming to an end.

Pennington did, after all, have a fascination for writing songs. He seemed to enjoy writing as much or even more than singing. He wrote his first one when learned to play the guitar at the age of thirteen back in Clay County, Kentucky. When the family moved to Cincinnati two years later, Ray continued to write and play.

In the early '60s, he quit his job at King and produced and wrote for its artists as an independent producer. He also became music director for WCNW Radio in Fairfield, Ohio, and he performed when he could get the time. Then, in the early '60s he went to Nashville and got a job as a song-plugger for Pamper Music. His friend and fellow vocalist Bobby Bobo, formerly of the "Midwestern Hayride" television show in Cincinnati, started Boone Records in Nashville about this time, and Pennington was enlisted to produce Kenny Price and Tex Williams. "We got lucky and had two top-five songs on Kenny and other hits," Pennington recalled. "By the late-'60s, I was producing and writing at Monument Records, and also recording as an artist. I left in 1973 to go to RCA. I could only handle that for 3-1/2 years. I didn't feel there was any room to create. You did what you were told."

Despite what he felt were the restrictions, he was successful. His old song "Ramblin' Man" was a big country hit for Waylon Jennings. Other hits followed. Pennington was in demand and he was putting that sharecropper's life far behind him.

He blew a ring of smoke from his pipe and leaned back in his chair in the office and reflected on the last thirty years. They seemed to pass before him in an instant.

"I wrote 'Ramblin' Man' while playing at a place called The Black Orchid in Kentucky in 1958," he said, shaking his head in amazement. "The song was an R&B piece at first. Like Jimmy Reed. I changed it later to fit the country thing. You know, in those days I wanted to be a great singer. All this other stuff just seemed to happen. I thought of singing the way some men think of painting. I was a guy who wanted to be a great singer, like a great painter."

By this time, Pennington had a small audience — his office staff. Three people were sitting in overstuffed chairs, listening intently to what the boss had to say about the old days. They were engrossed. Suddenly, a young man said, "I can't believe that *you* played rock 'n' roll!"

Pennington laughed good-naturedly and replied, "David, I was rockin' before you were born."

Then songs moved before his eyes like ghosts: "Mercy Have Pity" and "Stay Away From My Baby" by Ted Taylor; "Don't Stop In My World If You Don't Mean To Stay," by Bill Walker; "Don't Cheat In Our Hometown," by Ricky Skaggs. Pennington wrote them and others. The hits were many and varied.

"So tell us about those rockabilly days," the young man said.

Pennington smiled. The look on his face was that of a man who was fondly remembering a moment in time when he was young and the world was a much more simple place.

"We'd play places that were used to having country music," he said. "As fate would have it, though, there were people our own age there who wanted to hear a beat. I guess we were young and wanted to hear our own kind of music. I was playing rockabilly before Bill Haley had his early hits, about '53 or so. We'd take the old country songs and jazz 'em up. The people were no different than they are today. They were looking for something to dance to, and some excitement. Then when Elvis came out, we had to do his stuff in the clubs. Now, it's hard for me to believe that the young kid up there on that stage was really me.

"I guess I was really influenced by that rock 'n' roll. It is a part of me, somehow. Man, that was a great era to live in. *Great.*"

July, 1986. Additional interview, August, 1985.

Ray Pennington (standing left, with guitar) and his Western Rhythm Boys in the late 1950s. Below, Pennington in his Nashville office in 1986. (Photograph by Randy McNutt.)

Dickey Lee and his group...early days.

Teen Rockabilly

DICKEY LEE WALKED INTO HIS office at Welk Music on Nashville's Music Row and gently placed an acoustic guitar in a corner. In this huge rectangular office of glass and steel, Lee is treated with the respect reserved only for the successful. And he is successful.

Yet his rugby shirt and jeans contrast with the pin-striped suits and wing-tipped shoes of some other men in the building. They come here for many reasons. Lee comes to write. That's what he does. He writes songs for a living.

It is his greatest talent, for Lee has written numerous pop and country hits, including the giant "She Thinks I Still Care," by George Jones. The song will be a country music standard for decades.

His office does not reflect the image of a high-powered songwriter, however. It is of only moderate size for a personal office, with a couch, desk, two chairs, and a few framed awards on the walls. Lee is a modest man who jokes to friends that he made it just in time for the 1950s but he hasn't done anything special. The facts show a different story.

Lee — that's his legal name, changed from the original Lipscomb — grew up in Memphis at a time when radio and music were changing. Young Dickey was most influenced by Elvis Presley and The Hilltoppers, and his early music reflected those styles. As a teenager, he played the guitar and wrote songs. And dreamed.

"In those rock 'n' roll days of the mid-'50s," he explained, "you could turn on the radio and hear anything. What a great musical spectrum. You could hear Chuck

Berry, Marty Robbins, Little Richard — everybody and everything." Dickey listened to the radio and bought 78 rpm rock records and watched the local performers at every opportunity.

"Disc jockey Dewey Phillips had this show called 'Red, Hot and Blue' on WHBQ Radio, and the program was the hottest thing going in Memphis," Lee said. "He'd play all different kinds of stuff. I listened to the man for two years and still thought he was black. I knew if I was ever going to do anything myself, Dewey Phillips was the man to see."

So Lee took some songs to Phillips at the station one day, and Phillips liked what he heard. He recorded a single, "Dream Boy," backed with "Stay True Baby," right there in the WHBQ studios. When Lee was twenty-one years old, he was handed a copy of his first 45 rpm record on the Tampa label. He was rather disappointed. "I said, 'Wait a minute. This is not a *record*. I want a real record, a 78 disc.'"

By mid-1957, his local record, plastic though it was, had reached the number two position in Memphis and threatened to knock Elvis Presley's "Teddy Bear" from the number one position. That never happened, but Dickey Lee did get the attention that he had been seeking. His band, Dickey Lee and the Collegiates, performed all over the area. By this time, he and other band members were attending Memphis State, where Dickey majored in commercial art.

In 1958, after recording a few unsuccessful selections, Phillips convinced Sam Phillips at Sun Records to sign Lee. Two singles, "Dreamy Nights" and "Good Lovin'," resulted. "Not much happened with Sun," Lee said. "In fact, I think Sam took me on the roster as a favor. To him, I was a tax write-off."

But those two records on the legendary label were enough to give Lee a reputation as a young rockabilly sensation, a reputation that persists among rockabilly collectors. He has been asked to sing at rockabilly reunions in Memphis, and he has often accepted, but he believes he was different from his contemporaries in those early days. "I was really into country and rock 'n' roll, like the others," he explained, "but I think I was a misplaced Philadelphia boy living in Memphis. All of us had some hillbilly in us, and it came through in our music. But I was more influenced by some of the northeastern music. And it showed."

He analyzed other records and tried to incorporate interesting sounds into his act. He was not afraid to experiment with the sounds of commerciality. Those times were exciting in Memphis. Lee could hear all the major artists in his hometown, record at one of the hottest independent labels in the nation, and go to college at the same time. He even got to work as a singer for other vocalists' bands, such as Bill Justis and Billy Lee Riley. All the while, he heard an eclectic blend of rhythm and beat on the radio.

Dickey Lee (left) and Randy McNutt in Lee's Nashville office in July, 1985. (Photo: Wayne Perry)

"You haven't heard radio unless you heard it then in Memphis," he said. "Today, radio is so boring, so segmented. But then, we heard all kinds of music. And Dewey was a wild man. One night he told the kids to honk their car horns at 10 p.m., and they went crazy. So the police chief called Dewey and reminded him of the noise laws and so forth. Well, Dewey came back on the air and said, 'The chief doesn't want me to tell you guys to blow your horns at 11:30, as I was about to do. So remember, don't go blowing your horns!" Well, at 11:30 the city exploded in horns. That's the way it was then. Things were fun."

By 1960, however, things were changing. Top 40 radio was killing the creativity of programming, Lee said, and the sun was setting on Sun Records. Lee recorded something for Dot Records, but nothing happened. "Then Jack Clement, the producer and engineer in my Sun days, got a song called 'Patches.' He let me have it. It laid around for five months but we finally cut it in Beaumont, Texas, where Jack was recording. At first, nobody wanted to play it when it came out on Smash Records. I guess that was because it was one of the first teenage death songs. I finally gave up on it, but the promoter continued push it and it eventually jumped into the national top 10 hits."

"Patches" was not a rockabilly record. To Lee, those days were gone. He became

Publicity photo of Dickey Lee from the mid-1970s.

commercial pop-rock singer. He succeeded with "I Saw Linda Yesterday," a top 15 record, but despite numerous other chart hits, he was tiring of the constant tour schedule. The hard rock days of the mid- to late-'60s pushed him into the background of the music business, so he started writing and producing for other artists in Memphis with his good friend Allen Reynolds. He had played in bands with Lee years before.

"About 1969, Jack Clement suggested that we come to Nashville, so we did it," Lee said. "By then the rock 'n' roll thing had fizzled, and I wanted to write and work in the studio. We cut some demos for me — pop stuff — and then I recorded a record called 'Charlie,' which did nothing. I realized that if you worked in Nashville, you were branded a hillbilly. I finally told Chet Atkins at RCA that I'd like to cut some country stuff. I didn't think he'd let me do it, but, to my surprise, he said, 'Let's give it a shot.'"

That "shot" ultimately resulted in about fifteen chart records out of twenty-four releases in the country field. An impressive percentage of hits for any artist, especially a former pop artist. He even had four top-ten hits during his career at RCA, from 1970 to 1980. By the end of the decade, however, radio was changing again. So were the record labels. Lee went back to the songwriting and he was successful with hits for Reba McEntire and George Strait.

"I was disgusted with radio and with record executives who made records for an audience that no longer existed," he said. "You can't make records between pop and country. People are tired of hearing the same twenty records on the radio. Many

Dickey Lee...mid-1960s

who have controlled country music over the last few years have had no idea what country is all about. All music progresses. I think we need good, honest music with good singers. I try not to take this personally, but for a time there country music almost was nonexistent. Everything was a pop record. Country artists would go on the road, however, and sell thousands of albums to the fans. They still loved country music. Look at Slim Whitman. He couldn't buy a record deal. But he sold a lot of records in other ways. I had one guy tell me a couple of years ago that radio stations wouldn't play his record because it was too country. That scares me to death."

Lee performs occasionally but now his occupation is songwriter. "It's fun to make records, but I'm into my writing and I want to continue it. And if I record again, I'd rather be on a committed independent label than a major if it won't do anything to promote you. The secret of my songwriting success is surrounding myself with talented co-writers. There's a lot of talent in this town."

Although Lee enjoys country music, he still can't stop thinking of those rockabilly nights in Memphis, when the world seemed young and vibrant and the music was exciting.

"I feel so lucky just to have been a part of it then," he said. "Records had a real edge to them. We didn't cut reference vocals then. We just went into the studio and *attacked*. I look back on it all now and I think I took it for granted."

Nashville, Tennessee; July, 1985 and August, 1986.

Dickey Lee and his group, early 1960s. The boys were indeed true to their school.

Dickey Lee, mid-1960s. Over, Dickey Lee performs with acoustic guitar in the early 1960s. He let his country roots show even then by wearing a cowboy hat.

Dickey Lee performing in the mid-'60s.

No Regrets

MALCOMB YELVINGTON IS ONE OF the most well-known unknowns of the record business. He was there in that tiny Memphis recording studio before Elvis came to be recorded by Sam Phillips, and before country music helped spawn a hybrid called rockabilly.

But fate worked its capricious ways, and Elvis was later transformed into the ultimate American myth and a tragic hero of epic dimension. Malcomb was to be no such thing. He lived to become a factory worker and grandfather, and an everlasting part of our musical lore. An odd footnote to rock 'n' roll history.

Today Yelvington is neither popular nor influential in the music business. He rarely performs or records. But he is a fascinating eyewitness to rockabilly development and a true American picker.

He was reared in Covington, Tennessee, a small town that had three movie houses and a strong country music tradition. In 1942, when Yelvington was twenty-three years old, a man from California came to town and bought the theaters. He said he wanted to offer something more than just the usual films. He wanted music. So Yelvington, an amateur country musician who had grown up singing songs for nothing with a black friend, offered his services at The Gem one day.

"The owner hired me without even hearing me play," he said. "I never will forget the first Saturday I performed at the theater. The place was packed. All these little kids just sat there in their seats, staring up at me on the stage. I thought my knees would break. I sang a song called 'You're My One Rose,' a ballad, and then I felt all right. Things sort of went on from there, and I put together a little country band. Then came the honky-tonks. I wouldn't set foot in one today. I haven't played with any consistency for the last twenty years. But, I'm *happy*."

In 1953, he moved to Memphis to get a job as a welder. He worked in the factories by day and in the nightclubs by night. He eventually formed a band called Malcomb Yelvington & The Star Rhythm Boys to play at dances and in

Malcomb Yelvington and his band, early 1950s.

the clubs around Memphis.

At 706 Union Avenue, meanwhile, Sam Phillips was feeling frustrated. He had been recording many blues artists for national companies, including Chess Records of Chicago, but he wanted something more. He wanted, as legend has it, a white man who could sing the blues. On this man he could earn a fortune, Phillips figured.

In walked Malcomb Yelvington. He could not sing the blues. He was not a handsome man, either. In fact, he would later be described by writer Greil Marcus as "a Memphis country singer endowed with false teeth and the best rockabilly name outside of Elvis."

Yelvington can laugh at that comment now. A few years ago, however, he would not have been smiling.

"A friend of mine told me one day that a little studio was operating down there on Union," he recalled. "He told me I ought to go down and talk to the man. Well, I did, and he turned out to be Sam Phillips. I didn't know what was going on there at the time."

Yelvington walked into the office and said, "I hear you're looking for singers."

Phillips looked up at the tall, lanky stranger and asked, "Well, what kind of music do you do?"

"Country," Yelvington replied.

"I'm not really interested in country right now."

"Well," Yelvington said, half irritated, "what kind of music *do* you want to hear?"

Phillips paused. "I don't know," he said, finally. "And I won't know until I hear it."

Yelvington was persistent, however, even though he knew that Phillips seemed more interested in rhythm and blues than country music. Phillips finally agreed to record the band, if the material could be found that pleased him. The two men continued to talk during the next few weeks, and then one day Phillips said, "Malcomb, I think I've got something. A kid with a good voice, a guitar and a style. His name is Elvis Presley."

Yet Yelvington continued to hope that Phillips would find the Star Rhythm Boys worthy of recording. One day in 1954, when the group was practicing in the Phillips studio, trying to find that elusive piece of material, the musicians suddenly started playing 'Drinkin' Wine Spodee-O-Dee,' a song more R&B than anything else. "Sam was ready to go home," Yelvington said, "and then he turned to us and said, 'Where'd you get *that* song?' He laughed and said, 'Let's cut it!' We worked it over for two hours, then cut it with another song called 'Just Rolling Along.'"

The record was an incongruous mixture of hard country – steel guitar and nasal vocals – and R&B. Country with a beat. Not country boogie, that rhythmic hillbilly boogie that had flourished in the 1940s and early '50s, but a real country beat music; the orgin of rock 'n' roll. This is what Phillips had unwittingly been seeking, even though it was crude. This was *rockabilly*.

So Phillips went on to release two records by that Presley kid, the Hillbilly Cat with quick moves and boyish good looks. Sun Records number 209, "That's All Right," and "Blue Moon Of Kentucky," and then number 210, "I Don't Care If The Sun Don't Shine," and "Good Rockin' Tonight." Next came number 211, "Drinkin' Wine Spodee-O-Dee," by Malcomb Yelvington and the Star Rhythm Boys.

Yelvington was everything that Presley was not: a family man in his mid-thirties, who sang with a typical country twang. Soon, Presley's records started jumping up the country charts. Whenever he played, the crowd of young people went into a great frenzy. Yelvington continued to play his odd brand of country music in the local honky-tonks.

"One day a woman from the front office at the plant called me in and said, 'Malcomb, did you hear your record on the radio?' I said, 'My *record*?' I didn't even know it was out. So me and the band took off to promote the record in the Arkansas and Tennessee area, where it was getting some airplay. The record eventually sold from 6,000 to 8,000 copies, but it was not really a hit. I can't blame Sun Records and Sam Phillips. The label had Elvis then. I just happened to be number two. After that, the rockabillies seemed to start coming in from all over. All those young fellows. There was Warren Smith, a good-looking guy with a full head of hair who could sing so nice. And Billy Lee Riley, a guy who could play about any instrument and sing too. Then, there was *me*. They didn't call me Pop, but they could have, because I was about thirty-four years old by then. The companies all seemed to be looking for good looks, hair, youth. And I didn't have *any*."

Yelvington laughed loudly and walked into a bedroom of his attractive Cape Cod house on a quiet street in suburban Memphis. He picked up some yellow-labeled Sun recordings, the one sent to him by a collector in Sweden, where the name Mac Yelvington on a piece of vinyl still means something. Yelvington put "Drinkin' Wine" on the turntable of his son's old stereo and listened intently as the stylus hugged the record. The record was crude by today's sophisticated recording standards. It was something country, yet rock. A musical dinosaur. He said the voice coming over the speakers seemed to be somebody else.

"I wish we wouldn't have put that steel guitar on the record," he said, sitting on the bed and shaking his head. "I *hate* that. Sounds too tinny. We needed more of a rock feel. The funny thing is, when I was growing up, I always listened to country music, not R&B. Later, I had to be exposed to other things, and I enjoyed R&B. But I'm a country performer at heart. That's all I *ever* was. I never even liked rockabilly, to tell you the truth. Only the *beat*. I grew up on Wayne King and that stuff, not hard country, but I took up country later because I liked to play the guitar. When the rockabilly thing came in about '54, I did that because it was offered. I mean, a lot of guys like myself did it because it was the only thing we could get invited to do. It was happening and we were not. We did it to get a start. We figured if we got big enough, we could always switch back over to country. Some of the guys – Johnny Cash and Jerry Lee Lewis come to mind – are still doing basically the same thing today that they did in the '50s."

Now, however, all those Memphis rockabillies are as scattered as the November leaves. Most have settled comfortably into middle age. They think more about pension benefits than royalty checks.

Yelvington sings in church once in awhile. He said he doesn't miss the performing life. He is amused that some of his records – ones that didn't succeed in the '50s – are now selling for as much as $65. Such attention amazes the personable performer who is more popular in Europe than he ever was in the United States. Perhaps his reputation comes from the magical association with Sun Records, or perhaps it comes because he, unlike many other early rock artists, was his own musical self. He was not simply another Elvis imitator.

Yelvington recorded fewer than six singles in his career, with "Rockin' With My Baby" being the most commercial, in his opinion. He said he wrote it as an uptempo country song with a rock beat. "After my first record came out," he explained, "I decided to try a little more rock 'n' roll, at least as much rock as this country boy could get. So I cut 'Yakety Yak,' but Sun never released it. Bill Justis, the producer, didn't like it. So I cut my own song called 'Rockin' With My Baby' in 1956, after Elvis' contract had been sold to RCA-Victor. The song intentionally contained the titles of hits. Mine never made it, though. Looking back on all of this, I can honestly say I didn't make it because I insisted on being too country. I'm not disappointed, though, because I had the opportunity to headline shows with Johnny Cash in the mid-'50s and to have a lot of fun. I cut some good records, too...."

Frazer, Tennessee; September, 1985.

Malcomb Yelvington, 1985.

Malcomb Yelvington, early '50s.

WHEN the rockabilly thing came in about '54, I did that because it was offered. I mean, a lot of guys like myself did it because it was the only thing we could get invited to do. It was happening and we were not. We did get a start. We figured if we got big enough, we could always switch back to country music. Some guys. . .are doing bascially what they did back in the mid-1950s.

— Malcomb Yelvington.

Rockabilly Soul

WHEN GENE SIMMONS was a teenager in Tupelo, Mississippi, in the early 1950s, his two sisters brought home an old guitar. He could not stop smacking its strings. In a few months, he was strumming them sweetly and performing on the radio and at dances with his brother in the Simmons Brothers band.

Simmons' career has taken him from Tupelo to the world, from obscurity to fame, and from fame to relative obscurity again. Yet the man who started recording for Sun Records as a rockabilly artist in the '50s finally succeeded with "Haunted House" on Hi Records in 1964. He is still performing, writing and producing, and enjoying every minute of it.

"One day, I guess it was about 1954," Simmons recalled, "I was visiting a cousin of Elvis Presley. I didn't know who this Elvis fellow was at the time, but everybody said he played the guitar, so I handed him one. He just smiled. He was real shy. He said, 'I only play by myself.' Personally, I thought the guy looked weird. Greased back hair, tight pants, all that. Yeah, this guy was 'weird' all right; hipper than we country boys. Well, one day a short time later I had the opportunity to hear his first record on the radio. I said to my brother, 'Hey, is that the guy I met? I'd sure like to hear more about this record deal.' So a few weeks later a guy named Bob Neal called and said he wanted to book Elvis back in his old hometown of Tupelo. Neal asked our band to play with Elvis on his date. That's really how my career got started."

Eventually, Simmons approached Presley about getting in to see Sam Phillips, the owner of Sun, about a contract. "I can arrange an audition," Presley told Simmons, "but I'm afraid that's all I can do for you boys. The rest is up to you."

Phillips apparently liked what he heard, for he took Simmons into the little Memphis studio to record eight sides. But Sun was too involved with other artists and projects at the time, and Jumpin' Gene Simmons – called that because of his antics on stage – got only one release.

"So I just left to go on tour all over the country," he recalled. "In Canada I met a woman who later became my wife. When I brought her to Memphis with me, vocalist Ray Harris got me on the Hi label. At the time, in the early '60s, Bill Black's group needed a vocalist, so I started singing for him. In all, I had releases on Hi in '61, '62, '63 – but no hits. I looked around and saw my buddies having hits, and I started to think that maybe this was just not meant to be for me. By '63, I was ready to hang it up. Then I found a guy named Domingo Samudio – you'd probably know him better as Sam The Sham – playing in the clubs with me. All the pickers laughed at me for saying so, but I thought Sam had such a different stage presence. I cut the first record on him on a Tupelo label, a record called 'Betty Ann Dupree,' but nothing happened. About that time Sam was singing a song that had been recorded unsuccessfully before called 'Haunted House.' I liked it. Sam got a wild reaction when he played it in the clubs. Well, the folks over at Hi asked me to ask Sam if he would record it for them. Sam didn't like Hi for some reason, and he said to tell them that he would make the record on his own. Anyhow, the man over at Hi said, 'Look, Gene, we're gonna make that record anyway. Would you like to cut it?' I said, 'Hey, why not?' My contract with Hi had already expired, though, and they had to make arrangements for me to record again. But what Sam turned down I had a hit on. It was all so unlikely."

Simmons said the session was not like his others in that everyone involved had fun. The label president called his distributor in New York City and said Hi was putting out a new Gene Simmons record.

"Man," the distributor complained, "we've got that guy's records stacked up to the ceiling now, and they aren't doing a thing."

"Well, get ready for a stone smash," the president said.

By August, 1964, "Haunted House" had rested at number eleven on the Hot 100, and the Hi executive seemed to be a teller of fortunes. In a time when disc jockeys seemed obsessed with English bands, "long" hair, and a new sophistication in music, a Memphis label came along with a novelty record about a man who refuses to leave his new house just because it's haunted.

"Actually, the English thing helped me," Simmons said. "The DJs were sort of tired of all that stuff, I think, and my record was a refreshing one because it had a funky beat that you could dance to. I was just happy to be on the charts. Later, I got tagged as a novelty act. I couldn't find anything nearly as good as 'Haunted House' and I never had another big national hit."

He didn't mind all that much, however, for he had always wanted to be a country singer. Yet Simmons was not like his contemporaries in country or rockabilly because he could sing a variety of music and sing with soul. He was an excellent vocalist in an era when many singers were mediocre. "I started out singing country and I was happy with it," he said.

In recent years Simmons has been performing as a country-rockabilly artist and producing, writing and publishing music. He even recorded a less frenetic version of "Haunted House" on a local label called Deltune Records.

But the big national hits have stopped coming for now, and Simmons has moved from Tupelo to the Nashville area to work for a music publishing company. He said he will keep singing country music as long as somebody wants to hear him.

"That's where my heart is," he said.

*From Tupelo, Mississippi;
February, 1987*

Gene Simmons as he appeared about 1964 (above, left), when his single "Haunted House" jumped on the charts; with Bill Black laughing and playing "bass" and Ace Cannon on sax at a party to celebrate the success of "Haunted House" (above, right); and Simmons with Carl Perkins in the early 1970s (right).

All photos courtesy Gene Simmons.

Gene Simmons, 1987.

"Mr. Frantic"

Although Ronnie Self found only limited success as a recording artist in the 1950s and '60s, he wrote hit songs for other vocalists and became the epitome of rockabilly: wild, untamed, erratic. He was born in 1938 in Tin Town, Missouri, and lived a rural life with his family until his parents decided to move to Springfield when he was still a boy. Self was a respectful child who learned to appreciate music at an early age. He took up the guitar, and discovered the joys of country music while still living on the farm. He listened to the recordings of such country artists as Hank Williams and Jimmie Rodgers, but when Elvis got popular in the mid–'50s Self found a new kind of music with which to identify. Like many of the early rockabilly performers, he successfully merged the two musical styles and fashioned his own music. According to Self legend, he got into a rock 'n' band while still in high school. Seems that Ronnie got a little upset with one of his teachers at school one day, and went after the teacher with a baseball bat. So much for the three Rs. Ronnie went into rock 'n' roll. He was always a little wild. Not bad, though. His music was a bit wild, too. When he tried out for a radio talent contest once, the station rejected him because his act was too strange. Later, he set out for Nashville, where he recorded for a number of major labels, including ABC-Paramount, Columbia, Decca, and Kapp. He also wrote for Cedarville Music, a big Nashville publisher. His manager billed him as "Mr. Frantic," presumably for Self's restless energy on stage. In the late '50s, he recorded a number of strong rockabilly sides, including "Big Fool," "Date Bait," "Ain't I'm A Dog," and "Bop-A-Lena." It seemed that Self was eighteen, cocky, and a little crazy, and headed for the top. But his one hit – and it reached only number 63 in 1958 – was "Bop-A-Lena," a song by Mel Tillis and Webb Pierce. Self did go on to write "Sweet Nothin's" and "I'm Sorry" by Brenda Lee in late 1959 and early 1960. But he sunk into personal troubles and frustration with Nashville. He even burned his gold records in front of the BMI office there. He was a perfectionist. He could not tolerate those who were not. Ronald Self died in August, 1981. He was 43 years old.

"Hellooo...BABY!"

He came wailing out of Texas, singing "Hellooo...Baby!" Yes, this was The Big Bopper speaking. Jiles Perry Richardson (called Jape by his friends) was born in Sabine Pass, Texas, on October 24, 1930. When his family moved to Beaumont, Richardson took an interest in entertainment, and eventually received a diploma from a technical school in radio and television broadcasting. After a stint in the U.S. Army as a radar instructor, Richardson returned home and got a job at KTRM radio as a disc jockey.

He later earned the coveted 3-6 p.m. shift and took the name The Big Bopper. His program, "The Big Bopper Show," fared well, and he was also appointed program director of the station. He was a wild radio man. In 1957, he set the world's record for continuing broadcasting by playing 1,821 records during six days and nights. The 240-pound Bopper lost 35 pounds but gained much publicity for his "Discathon."

But Richardson was not happy with being only an air personality. He wrote songs and sang, and he wanted to achieve some success with them as well. He did not have to wait too long, either. By the late 1950s, he had written "Running Bear" for his good friend Johnny Preston of Port Arthur, Texas. The record shot to number one. (That's Richardson chanting the Indian mumbo-jumbo in the background.) The

Bopper also wrote "White Lightning" for George Jones.

For all his writing, however, J.P. Richardson is most known today for a cheap little novelty record called "Chantilly Lace," from which the immortal introduction "hellooo...baby!" came. Richardson cut the record as The Big Bopper for the D label of Dallas, and it attracted attention locally. The record was a basic production — rhythm section, rocking saxophone, Richardson half singing and talking the vocals in his deep, radio-trained voice. Bells were used to simulate the ringing of a telephone. This record was not a big-budget session.

Yet it was picked up by Mercury Records in the summer of 1958 and pushed to the top ten nationally. Richardson followed the record with "Big Bopper's Wedding," but it was only a moderate hit by January, 1959.

Richardson, meanwhile, took a leave of absence from the station to perform in The Winter Dance Party with several other rock stars, including Buddy Holly. The group of rock performers sang at the Surf Ballroom in Clear Lake, Iowa, the night of February 2, 1959. When they had finished, Holly arranged for a local pilot to fly several performers to Fargo, North Dakota. Richardson had been feeling ill, and didn't want to endure the long bus ride, so he asked to fly.

J.P. Richardson died that night in a plane crash, along with Holly, Ritchie Valens, and pilot Roger Peterson. One of The Big Bopper's biggest hits as a songwriter, "Running Bear," was successful after his death. His son was born after his death, too. But The Bopper's musical history lives on as an example of novelty rockabilly done energetically and enthusiastically.

CHANTILLY LACE
Big Bopper—Mercury MG 2040

The late artist's LP (actually his first) will help to perpetuate his image among his many fans. "Chantilly Lace" and "Big Bopper's Wedding" are included along with 10 other tunes, also written by the Bopper (J. P. Richardson). With a good cover that jumps out, and coming in the wake of a million seller single, this can be expected to pull brisk action. Jocks will likely go for some of the not previously released sides.

In 1957, Bobby Helms was a country singer with a moderate pop hit called "Fraulein." His label, Decca Records, followed with "My Special Angel," which has become an often-recorded classic. Helms' record featured heavy echo, a fat chorus and the Anita Kerr Singers in the background. Although he was not a rockabilly in the strict sense, Helms is known as a rockabilly ballad singer to some extent. And he did it on the strength of "Angel," which rose to number 7 on the Billboard charts in October, 1957. Helms later hit with "Jingle Bell Rock" — five times, in fact, from 1957 to 1962.

Above: Bobby Helms, early 1960s and, insert, about 1967. Right: Sheet music from the 1957 hit "My Special Angel." The record had the feel of a rockabilly ballad at a time when rockabilly music was prominent on the charts across the nation.

When George Hamilton IV was 19 years old and a student at the University of North Carolina, he found a part-time job at WTOB television. He recorded "A Rose And A Baby Ruth," written by another staff member, Johnny Dee (John D. Loudermilk). An appearance on Arthur Godfrey's television show brought national attention to the record, which had been released on Colonial Records. As a result, the disc sold 100,000 copies in two days, and eventually reached number two on Billboard's top 100 pop singles. That was in November, 1956, and the relaxed style of the young singer caught on with the public. His label, ABC-Paramount, which had obtained the master from Colonial, continued to release records on Hamilton throughout the remainder of the decade. Other hits included "Why Don't They Understand" (number 10) and "Now And For Always" (number 25). By the early 1960s Hamilton was singing country music and recording for RCA Records. He scored on the pop charts with "Abilene" (number 15) in June, 1963. His country hits continued for many years, and his friend, songwriter Loudermilk, continued to write hits for artists all over the world. Loudermilk was an accomplished vocalist himself, but his rockabilly and country recordings never achieved the recognition they deserved. But who will ever forget his haunting "Tobacco Road"?

Eddie Cochran was a top studio guitarist who became a smooth rockabilly vocalist with "Sittin' In The Balcony," "Summertime Blues," "C'mon Everybody," and other songs. He was born in Oklahoma and raised in Minnesota and California. His personal manager, songwriter Jerry Capehart got Eddie on Liberty Records and in the film 'The Girl Can't Help It." His smooth licks ended April 17, 1960, in England, when he died in an automobile crash.

Jim Lowe's "The Green Door" went to number one for three weeks in 1956.

Lowe was from Chicago. He went to New York City in the mid-'50s and met singer Bill Carey, another Chicago boy. They shared a room. They were of the northern country-rock variety, with leanings toward folk and country.

Top: Sheet music from 1956. Below: Lowe in a publicity shot.

ROCKIN' GUYS FROM MEMPHIS

They rocked the city and the world: Ray Smith, top left, scored with "Rockin' Little Angel" on the Judd label; Eddie Bond, top right, performed all over the South on the strength of Sonny Fisher's song "Rockin' Daddy" and other regional hits; Jack Clement, bottom right, produced many hits for Sun Records in the 1950s, and also wrote and performed on his own.

Above, Jimmy Bowen sings; below, the Rhythm Orchids: (l-r) Bowen, Dave Alldred, Buddy Knox and Don Lanier. The band featured Knox and Bowen as dual lead singers.

Buddy Knox hit with "Party Doll" in early 1957 on Roulette Records of New York. He followed with such hits as "Rock Your Little Baby To Sleep" and "Hula Love." The Texas boy is now based in Canada. He performs all over the world.

RAL DONNER

Ral *who*?

Ral Donner, that's who. He might have had a little later start with his hits, but once they rolling, they were impressive. Donner was one of Gone Records' semi-rockabillies. His discs sounded like they were sung by Elvis Presley, and for this reason Donner has been ignored by many music journalists.

But Donner was successful. He first hit the national charts in the spring of 1961 with a record called "Girl Of My Best Friend," with a band named The Starfires. That record reached the top twenty and led such hits as "You Don't Know What You've Got (Until You Lose It)" and "She's Everything (I Wanted You To Be)."

By early 1962, however, the hits stopped. And Ral Donner became another notation in the book of musical memories.

Charlie Gracie, a boy from South Philadelphia, was an unlikely rockabilly. Although he wasn't strictly a rockabilly singer, many of his songs straddled rockabilly's borders. "Butterfly" went to number one on the Billboard charts in 1957. His first goal was to buy his family a house.

Marty Robbins was country — smooth, mellow country. Yet some of his early recordings drifted near the rockabilly border, and Robbins became one of country music's top performers over the years. His Columbia single "A White Sport Coat (And A Pink Carnation)" reached number two on Billboard magazine's pop chart in April, 1957. Until his death in December, 1982, at the age of 57, Robbins continued to perform regularly and to achieve success on the country charts. Many rockabilly collectors remember him best, however, for some of his earlier recordings, including "Maybellene" (the Chuck Berry song) and "Pretty Mama," both in 1955.

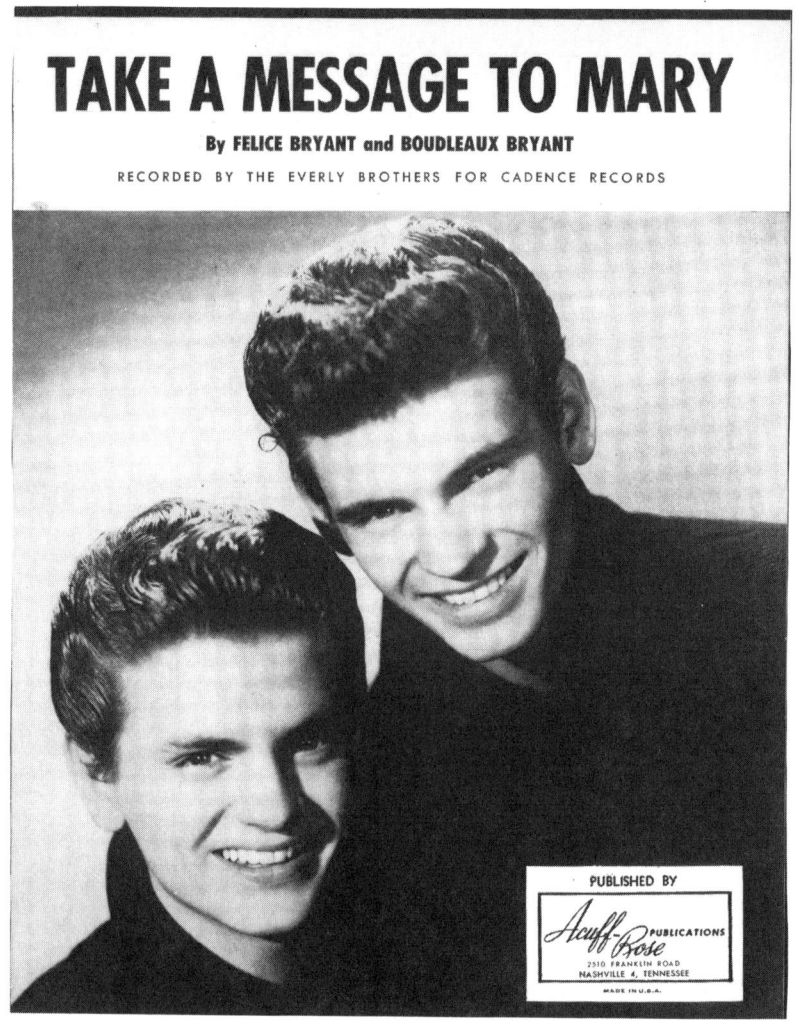

If rockabilly music was considered the domain of wild rural young people who could only moan and jump wildly, then somebody was mistaken. The Everly Brothers proved that this new music could be tamed and harmonized. Don and Phil Everly, from Kentucky, recorded numerous hits for Cadence Records from 1957 to the early 1960s. In between, they recorded other hits for Warner Brothers. Top 10 hits included "Bye Bye Love," "Wake Up Little Susie," "All I Have To Do Is Dream," "Bird Dog," and "Cathy's Clown." Whatever they did, the hits just kept coming. The Everly Brothers were not a rockabilly beat act, but they did retain the sound and feel of that music. Perhaps they can be called middle-of-the-road rockabilly.

"Young Love," a ballad co-written by rockabilly artist Ric Cartey, propelled singer Sonny James to number one on the Billboard top 100 pop chart in December, 1956. The young man with the black string tie from Hackleburg, Alabama, was another country ballad singer who easily slipped into country music in the 1960s. He calls himself the Southern Gentleman. As a boy, he performed with his family as the singing Loden Family. When his sister married and his parents retired to operate a clothing store, Sonny dropped his surname and performed as Sonny James on such shows as "Big D Jamboree" in Dallas and "Ozark Jubilee." Later, he went on the Ed Sullivan television show, where he was introduced nationally. But his heart was in country music, not rock 'n' roll, and James is still performing to enthusiastic crowds across America.

Some rockabilly purists maintain that Rick Nelson was a manufactured pop-rock star, not a pure rockabilly artist. Perhaps he was a suburban rockabilly. Yet his early recordings — and some of his last — were indeed rockabilly. Rick got his start, of course, with his family on radio and television in "The Adventures Of Ozzie And Harriet," from 1949-66. Rick, who was influenced by some of rock's early guitarists and singers, started singing on the show himself in the 1950s and achieved success with many records. "Be-Bop Baby," "Stood Up," and "Believe What You Say" were among his first top 10 hits in 1957-58. As the years went on, however, Nelson's music took on a softer edge, and some of his hot players, such as guitarist Glen Campbell, left to pursue their own careers. After numerous hits, Nelson seemed lost during the English band invasion of the mid-'60s. He resurfaced as a country-rock performer in the late '60s, however, and went on to have a number six record in "Garden Party" in 1972. Some interesting rockabilly-style tracks recorded in Memphis late his his career have been released. Nelson died in a plane crash near De Kalb, Texas, on December 31, 1985.

The late Norman Petty didn't achieve the fame of some of his rockabilly artists, but he was an influential creator of the rockabilly sound in the late 1950s. His group, a middle of the road ensemble called the Norman Petty Trio, had two chart records in 1957, "Almost Paradise" and "The First Kiss," but it was records that Petty produced for other artists that are remembered today. Petty and other members of the group used royalties from an earlier record to start a recording studio in Clovis, New Mexico in the mid-'50s. Soon, other artists came to be recorded, and in time Petty produced – the term "producer" was not used much then, but that is what Petty was – Roy Orbison, Buddy Holly, The Rhythm Orchids (with Buddy Knox and Jimmy Bowen) and other groups from the West Texas and New Mexico area. NorVaJak Studio was the top place to be by 1958. In addition to Holly's immortal hits, Petty recorded "I'm Sticking With You" by Bowen and "Party Doll" by Knox. Both were lead singers for their band. Petty may not be remembered today for his own hits, but he helped give rockabilly music direction and depth in those unstructured days of the late '50s.

Bob Luman, The Rocker, died at the age of 40 in 1978. He left us a wonderful little song called "Let's Think About Living," a top ten pop hit on Warner Brothers Records in 1960. Luman was born in Texas and spent his boyhood listening to country and blues music. He emulated Elvis in the mid-'50s but developed his own smooth rockabilly style over the next few years. He later went into country music and scored numerous hits, including "Ain't Got Time To Be Unhappy," "Lonely Women Make Good Lovers," and "Still Loving You." He became an Opry performer in 1969.

Lawrencine May "Lorrie" Collins and her little brother Larry were rockabilly's child performers. They came from Oklahoma and became novelty singers who were later taken seriously for their talent. They appeared on numerous country music shows and were signed to Columbia Records. Larry played a double-neck electric guitar – he learned to pick from the hot lick man himself, Joe Maphis – and Lorrie sang and played acoustic guitar. They often dressed in wild western outfits and grew into first-class entertainers. Although their records were popular to a certain degree in the '50s, the Collins Kids, as they were billed, never had a big national hit on the pop charts. Lorrie went on to become a wife and mother. Larry became a songwriter, composing "Delta Dawn" and other hits.

Before he had a moderate pop hit and a country hit in 1968 with "The Ballad Of Two Brothers," Autry Inman sang many kinds of songs. He recorded some rockabilly and country in the late 1950s and early '60s, and he is most well-known among record collectors. But he also recorded party records. He could go on tour in the Midwest and sell 300 albums in one night.

Marvin Rainwater used to dress up in an Indian costume — well, he was only depicting his heritage — during the late 1950s. He was rockabilly's resident Indian. But his real talent was not in theatrics but in songwriting and singing. By May, 1957, he reached number 18 on the Billboard charts with the single "Gonna Find Me A Bluebird" on MGM Records. "Whole Lotta Woman" and "Half-Breed" reached the sixties on the charts in late 1958 and early 1959. Rainwater's many compositions are recorded to this day by country performers.

Jack Scott, a Canadian whose real name is Jack Scafone Jr., scored with nearly twenty chart records in the U.S. from 1958 to 1961. His powerful, deep voice is still outstanding. He recorded several songs with women's names in the titles, including "Geraldine." He recorded for several labels, but his most successful singles were released on the Carlton and Top Rank labels.

LET'S BOOGIE

Buck Owens played on many sessions in California in the 1950s. His guitar-playing was suitable to the country and rockabilly sounds.

Roy Clark is known primarily as a guitarist who who sings and tells jokes, but in the 1950s he was in great demand as a session guitarist in California. Like Buck Owens, he played on some of Wanda Jackson's hot Capitol sessions.

Country singer Jimmy Velvet — isn't that a smooth-sounding name for a hillbilly singer? — made an occasional foray into rockabilly in the 1960s.

The Sparkletones

Joe Bennett and the Sparkletones are better trivia answers than anything else, but the band did have two chart records in 1957: "Black Slacks" and "Penny Loafers And Bobby Socks." Although they recorded in New York City for ABC-Paramount Records, the boys in the band were rockabillies from Spartansburg, South Carolina. They were (and this is left to right on the photograph): Wayne Arthur, upright bass; Jimmy Denton, drums; Joe Bennett, lead vocals and lead guitar; and Howard "Sparky" Childress, rhythm guitar. In 1955 their ages ranged from twelve to sixteen, which caused some legal confusion for booking agents and talent scouts. Nevertheless, the youngsters wrote and performed with the precision of their older counterparts, and soon the Sparkletones found themselves in depand for television shows and concerts. Bennett and Denton composed the band's first hit, "Black Slacks," which pushed up to number 17 on the Billboard Hot 100 charts. Bennett's song "Penny Loafers And Bobby Socks" reached number 42. Although the band split up in 1958 so that its members could finished their education, the Sparkletones will always be an example of youthful rockabilly enthusiasm.

RONNIE HAWKINS

Ronnie Hawkins blew out of Arkansas in the late 1950s and moved into Canada like a big warm front. If the United States was filled with Southern rockers, he thought, then he would set up shop in Canada, a place usually being left behind by native singers. In Canada, Ronnie billed himself The King of Rockabilly, and he and his band, The Hawks, played in every dive and auditorium they could find. He filled the Canadians' heads with tales of the blues and cottonfields, and of his own rockabilly prowess. His band included guitarist Robbie Robertson and drummer Levon Helm, who were to win acclaim in the late 1960s as an important part of The Band. Hawkins never did achieve lasting fame, although he did have success in America in 1959 with his singles "Forty Days" and "Mary Lou." By 1970, however, John Lennon had discovered him, saying Ronnie's music sounded "partly now and partly then." A new label, Cotillion Records (a part of the Atlantic family) undertook an impressive advertising and promotion campaign for Ronnie's new single called "Down In The Alley." It reached only into the 70s on the top 100 in the United States.

BILLY "CRASH" CRADDOCK

Billy Craddock was born of poor parents in Greensboro, North Carolina, where he used to go into the family barn to pretend to play a broomstick guitar. He imagined he was standing on the stage of the Grand Ole Opry. "Being on that stage—just one time—was my great ambition," he once said. At age eleven, he learned to play a real guitar, and by the time he was in high school, Craddock and his brother were performing in a local band. Their group, The Rebels, played the area clubs and school dances. The singer earned the nickname "Crash" by consistently smashing through the opposing teams' offensive lines. One night a Columbia Records official saw The Rebels play, and, after the band had broken up, he offered Craddock a record deal. So in 1959 the young, handsome vocalist went to Nashville to record. He achieved minor success with a record called "Don't Destroy Me," which reached number 94 on Billboard's top 100 chart. (Oddly enough, however, he had a hit in Australia, and then other hits there.) But the American charts seemed elusive. "They tried to make another Fabian out of me," Craddock once said. "You've got to realize that back then there was pop and then there was country. There was no blend of the two like there is today. They wanted me to be a pop singer, but there was a great deal of country in my style. I just didn't work." Later, he returned to North Carolina to race cars and work in a cigarette factory. He performed only sporadically. Then one night in 1969 he stepped onto a nightclub stage in streetclothes and got a standing ovation. Craddock thought about his singing that night and decided he needed to continue it. He was eventually signed to a new independent country label, Cartwheel Records, and several country hits followed, including the No. 1 record

"Knock Three Times," a pop hit by Tony Orlando and Dawn. Craddock has said the signing with Cartwheel was timed just right because he had decided to quit the business. "I'd gone to a show one night and got on a real downer," he explained. "There were several established stars on the bill and I kept asking myself, 'If they can make it, why can't you?' Afterward, I went home and told my wife, 'That's it — I quit.'" After a few hits with Cartwheel, Craddock was signed by ABC Records when that major company purchased the smaller label. His country success continued, but this time he also got some pop attention. "Rub It In" reached number 16 on the pop chart, and Craddock later reached that coveted chart with two more releases. "Now I can do country rock or good ol' rock 'n' roll and everybody accepts it," he said.

5

Wild, Wild Wimmen

ROCKABILLY MUSIC WAS NOT necessarily an equal opportunity employer in the mid-1950s, but some women were daring enough to try it anyway.

Rose Maddox, who had performed with her brothers for years as a country boogie act, was one of the first women to wail in the rhythmic new music. She was never a pure rockabilly artist, however, even though she helped open the field to other female vocalists. Rose was simply a mixture of the boogie, country, rockabilly and whatever else she was influenced by in those days.

Her counterparts were few. Rockabilly was the domain of the macho males, leaving little room for women. Who remembers such singers as Sparkle Moore (real name: Barbara Morgan), Patsy Timmons, Glenda LoVett, Joan King, and Laura Lee Perkins? Yet their attempts at cracking through the emerging rockabilly market helped other female rockers be accepted later by the public and the music industry.

Although the female rockabillies were engaged in making serious music, many leaders of the male-dominated record business didn't seriously consider the women as performers. To some executives, and even to some male performers, the women were nothing but novelty acts, incomplete imitations of the real thing.

"Nobody took us seriously in the mid-'50s," said Memphis singer Barbara Pittman. "We had to make our own way the best we could. When somebody suggested that I could have a hit if I went on Dick Clark's show, the people at my label (Sun) sat back and did nothing. Sam Phillips once said he didn't know exactly what to do with Barbara Pittman."

Considering the sentiment of the time, this reaction is not altogether that strange. After all, the public was debating the merits of Elvis Presley's gyrations. Charges of rocking juvenile delinquency were thrown about frequently, suggesting that the new music was overly rebellious and encouraging anarchy. Women were not going to get a favorable reaction by singing such controversial music.

"Back then," Rose Maddox said, "women were expected to get married and have children. That's *all*. Well, I just wasn't made that way. I wasn't married and music was all I thought about in life. So I plunged into it. The whole thing was such a terrific challenge. You had to give yourself support every day, because nobody else was going to do it."

Somehow, the small but vocal female contingent kept on singing, even after rockabilly had declined in the late '50s and early '60s. By 1963, after the deaths of Buddy Holly, Eddie Cochran, and The Big Bopper, and after the fall of Jerry Lee Lewis, many women rockabillies continued to cling to their old music. In time, however, most of them returned to country music, where they had come from a few years earlier. Such rockabillies as Jean Chapel, Skeeter Davis, and Wanda Jackson became country artists easily. A few others — Jackie DeShannon comes immediately to mind — drifted into pop music.

From the beginning, the rockabilly movement seemed like an exclusive male club. The music was developed by men, sung by men, made by men. There were female rockabillies from the start, of course, but overall they made up a tiny percentage of the recording and performing artists. Perhaps this was a reflection of the music itself — tough, rough-edged, wild. Only a minority of women singers would be inclined to enjoy such music was performers.

Rockabilly's sexuality — tame as it was from today's perspective — was overt and suggestive in 1955. The image of Presley moving his hips shocked adults and inspired the young people.

Rose Maddox sang the way she felt, adult reaction notwithstanding. She was not a kid herself by the mid-'50s. She was an adult, too. For years she had moaned and wailed with her brothers in what can only be described as upbeat country music. When rockabilly arrived in '54 and '55, she incorporated some of its energy into her performances and recordings. She sang "Hey Little Dreamboat" and other wild, driving numbers for Columbia.

In those early days, two girls from Kentucky, Betty Jack Davis and Mary Frances Penick — she took the name Skeeter Davis — also recorded their upbeat country for RCA-Victor as the Davis Sisters. In 1953, they had a country hit called "I Forgot More Than You'll Ever Know About Him," backed with "Rock-A-Bye Boogie." The duo never showed its rockabilly promise, however. Betty Jack was killed in an automobile accident, and Skeeter went into pop-country.

The title of Rockabilly Queen was left unclaimed until Wanda Jackson opened her mouth to sing a rocking song. The girl could *wallop* a song. There were several excellent female rockers, including Janis Martin and Lorrie Collins, but Wanda Jackson will always be considered the strongest voice of female rockabilly.

Like many of her contemporaries on the female side, Wanda led an expedition from country into the dark territory of rockabilly, then returned to country. In between, we have roughly seven years of remarkable music, both country and rockabilly.

Wanda grew up in Maud, Oklahoma, but her family moved to California when she was young, and there she heard some fine country music. At six years old she was strumming the guitar, and later she tried the piano. Then her father moved the family back to Oklahoma, and Wanda eventually got her own show on KLPR Radio while she was still a junior in high school.

Country singer Hank Thompson, a resident of Oklahoma City, liked her enough to offer her a tour with his band. She also got a record deal with Decca in 1954, recording fifteen sides by herself and with Billy Gray of Thompson's band.

By the time she was graduated from high school in 1955, Wanda had joined Red Foley on the "Ozark Jubilee" touring group. She also met Elvis Presley along the way, and he encouraged Wanda to express her country music more fully with rockabilly flare.

In 1956, she was signed to Capitol Records, and the company wondered what to do with the dynamic, strong-voiced singer. She was not the typical country singer because her vocals were overpowering and her stage presence was mobile. All labels seemed to be looking for a youthful rock 'n' roller in '56, so Wanda became one. Yet the label did not want to take her away from her country roots, so label executives slanted her both ways.

By 1957, Wanda was recording top rockabilly songs for Capitol, including "Honey Bop" and "Hot Dog That Made Him Mad." The records just kept coming over the next few years: "Fujiyama Mama," "Let's Have A Party," and "Cool Love."

But Capitol was too timid. It had a fireball on its roster and didn't know it, or at least didn't know how to sell her records. Her version of "Let's Have A Party" was even more explosive than the ones recorded by Presley and The Collins Kids, yet Capitol allowed it lay in the vaults for a couple of years before releasing it in 1960.

Wanda recorded a country ballad, "Right Or Wrong," which, at number 29, became her highest chart record in Billboard's top 100, at least until her next release, "In The Middle Of A Heartache," reached number 27. That was October, 1961. She would start to concentrate her energy on country music now.

The 1960s and '70s found her firmly in the country camp. Later, she recorded numerous gospel records. Although Wanda's rockabilly records were arguably some

Wanda Jackson in the early 1960s and (left) in 1967.

some of the better ones of her era, they generally did not hit on the charts. "Let's Have A Party," the record Capitol was forced to release due to demand from radio stations and the public, was her biggest rockabilly hit, and it reached only number 37 in 1960. Yet those rockabilly discs are remembered because of their sheer explosiveness.

Wanda could sing well as a girl and she can still sing well. She has style. Her voice is delicate enough to sing country ballads and coarse enough to rip through a rock number. And her 1950s recordings, made by some of California's top session players, were technically superb.

So what happened to Wanda Jackson's rockabilly career? That cannot be answered with certainty. Maybe she did not become a big rock star because she was *too* good. Perhaps the public was not ready for a girl who sang that she was about to "blow her top" as a "Fujiyama Mama." Most likely, however, her records just were not promoted enough to make Wanda Jackson another rockabilly star, one that could sustain hits through the years.

Country was another matter entirely. She achieved considerable success in that field throughout the '70s. Wanda and her husband, Wendell Goodman, became Christians in the early '70s, and Wanda mixed gospel and country music with her records and stage act.

Then in 1987 she recorded an album of rockabilly songs for an independent

Left: Wanda Jackson, early 1960s. Right: Janis Martin, about 1957.

label. The "Let's Have A Party Girl" had finally returned to the music that had brought her fame throughout the world.

But Wanda Jackson was not the only woman adored by rockabilly admirers. Janis Martin had a chance in the '50s, too, when RCA-Victor promoted the young woman as "the female Elvis."

Martin started singing on "The Old Barn Dance" program in Richmond, Virginia, and was soon propelled into the Nashville music scene. RCA-Victor had just purchased Presley's contract from Sun Records of Memphis, and RCA executives were intrigued with the idea of creating a female Presley.

So Martin recorded such songs as "Ooby-Dooby" and "My Boy Elvis," and from 1956-58 the label promoted her to disc jockeys nationally. Her only big hit, however, was "Will You Willyum," which reached number 50 in Billboard's top 100 in 1956.

The Nashville tracks were slickly produced by Steve Sholes, and included such top session players as Chet Atkins on lead guitar, Grady Martin on rhythm guitar, Buddy Murray on drums, and Floyd Cramer on piano. Meanwhile, the company's promotion people got her records played and the publicity agents got her interviewed by magazines and newspapers.

By 1960, however, her records had stopped selling and she retired to be with her family. In later years, she resumed her career, but the times had already changed.

Goodbye, rock 'n' roll woman.

JEAN CHAPEL

When I was growing up in Neon, Kentucky, I always loved spirituals. My parents sang them, and I was into that king of music. Anything that *moved*. Even today, let me rock. I love it. I used to sit on the steps at home and sing for hours as a child. I had rhythm. I performed at elections and singing conventions — anywhere I could. Well, eventually I left Neon and met a man named Murray Nash, who became my manager. We recorded some things and took them to Sam Phillips at Sun Records in Memphis. When Sam heard the tapes, he flipped. So he arranged a session to record "I Won't Be Rockin' Tonight" and "Welcome To The Club." Sam then put a record out on me, but I don't think it got much distribution. Not long after that he sold my contract to RCA-Victor, just like he did with Elvis. Steve Sholes, the RCA executive, labeled me his "female Elvis Presley," and I never could get over that. This all happened in '56. So *much* went on. Alan Freed brought me to New York to perform at the Brooklyn Paramount Theater with his big rock 'n' roll show. There were so many wonderful performers. But I had no big hits, and I eventually dropped out of the business to stay home with my little girl. I sang at a few clubs once in awhile, and I started writing songs. This started another career for me, as my songs were recorded by Jerry Wallace, Eddy Arnold, and many other singers. But you know, I still love to rock. I never was after the the money in the early days. No, I just enjoyed it.

ROCKIN' WITH MISS WANDA JACKSON

WANDA JACKSON
star of
Ozark Jubilee
ABC-TV

"Hot Dog"
backed with
"Silver Threads & Golden Needles"
No. 3575

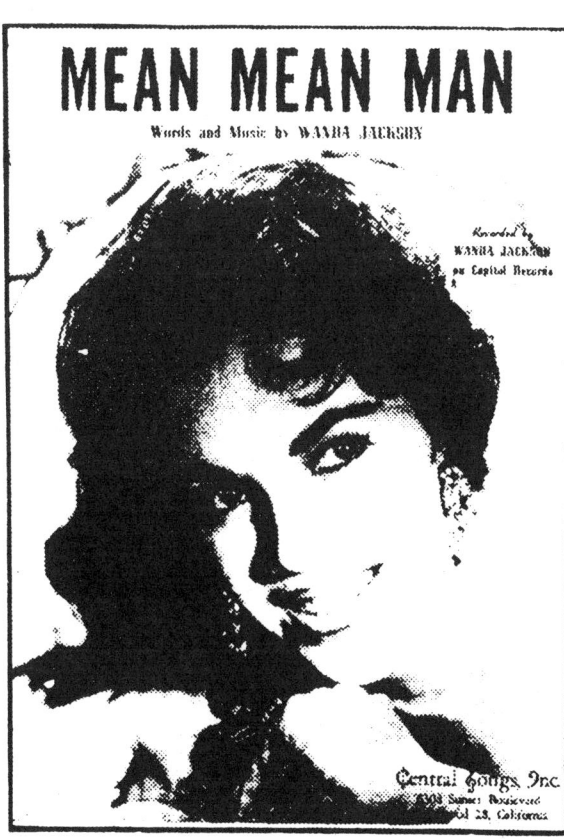

In the rockabilly days of the 1950s, a fan magazine conducted a poll of its readers to determine the best new female vocalist. Those readers must have been rockers because none other than Wanda Jackson, a wailer of country and rockabilly from Oklahoma, won by a wide margin. Her competition? Oh, just some women named Janis Martin (291 votes), Patsy Cline (211 votes), and little Brenda Lee (140 votes). Wanda received 1,010 votes!

ROSE MADDOX: MISS BOOGIE

This is my fiftieth year in the music business. I started in 1937 in Modesto, California, with my brothers. Our family moved from Alabama to California during the Depression, so I was really raised on the coast. I was only eleven years old when I started singing professionally with my brothers, who were all older than I. We were called hillbilly singers – not country – then. No, none of this country music then. People just called us hillbilly. It took people in our field years and years just to get to the point where we were called country singers. After recording for Four Star Records for about six years, starting in 1946 or '47, we went over to Columbia Records, which offered us a good deal. We recorded many things with Columbia in the '50s, and the label offered me the opportunity to record as a single, too. Naturally, I accepted the offer. When the band broke up in '57, I stayed on the label by myself. People tell me that I was one of the first women to sing what I sang – country boogie. I guess I was. There was no rock 'n' roll in those early days, before 1955. Only country boogie. My brothers also played that way. We called it country then. In the mid-'50s, I threw a little rock into the act. We did all our recording in California, except for my first session as a single, which was done in Nashville. And sometimes we recorded in Texas. But California was our base for recording for The Maddox Brothers and Rose. I was always a different kind of singer. Nowadays, all the girl singers sound alike. I sounded like nobody else, and I guess that's why I was so dinstinctive. When I go to Europe to perform, the crowds all yell for my song "Wild, Wild Young Men." It's better known today than it was in the '50s. It was never even released as a single then. I got the song from a recording by a colored gal singer, who had an R&B hit on it. I figured I'd try it in the country field. The cut was put out on an album, but that's all,

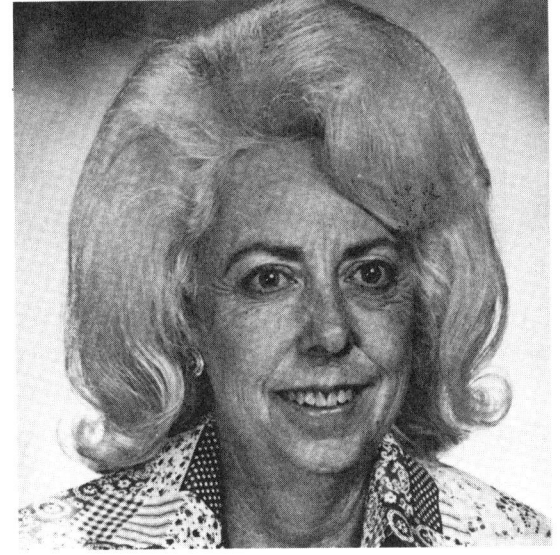

Top: Maddox Brothers and Rose, 1950s. Right: Rose Maddox, 1987.

and, to tell you the truth, I even forgot the words over the years. Then the crowds all wanted it in Europe, so I had to relearn the words. I think that's a little strange, but that's the way this business works. I've been at it a long time. I'm still performing, too, but these days I stick mainly to the west coast. But everybody knows who Rose Maddox is.

BARBARA PITTMAN

I was born in Memphis. I was a dancer and singer in high school. All my life I've been singing. My mother and Elvis Presley's mother were friends, and I used to go over to his house all the time. My first professional singing job was with Elvis, in fact. A girl bet me twenty-five cents that I couldn't get a job singing with Elvis at the Eagle's Nest. Well, I did, but he went on to Victor and I got fired for being under the legal age. After that, I went on the road with Lash LaRue for a year. What a year it was! I sang on shows that he put on all over the country with all of his old matinee cowboys. Like an old cowboy named Panhandle, and others. So many others. We lived in cars and washed up in filling stations. I was a baby sitter for his kid, too. Lash didn't go first-class. Strictly back roads. He kept firing me for doing stupid things. I was still just a kid myself. So I came back to Memphis in 1956 and got a job singing over in Arkansas because I was still too young to sing in bars in Memphis. Then I met Stanley Kesler, and he asked me to cut a demo of a song that he wanted to get to Elvis. Stan knew that I knew Elvis, so I sang the demo and gave it to him. In return, Stan got me in to see Sam Phillips at Sun Records. Only a year before I tried to get Sam to record me, but he told me to come back when I was older and when I had learned to sing. This time, Sam didn't remember me. He signed me to a long-term contract, making me the only female vocalist under contract to Sun. We cut "I Need A Man" in '56. I bought a copy. My mother bought a copy. Seriously, it didn't do much. In all, I recorded eight sides for release for Sun, but I also cut many other sides that were not released at the time but have been put out today on various labels. I got a big thrill when one of my records knocked Elvis out of the number one spot on the Memphis charts in 1957. But recording for Sun in the '50s was, for a woman, being a part of a man's world. It was tough just to get heard then by the label and I guess I was one of the lucky few. My records were not promoted, though. Not like the men's. They didn't think they should spend any money on a girl's records. One time when a promoter told Sam that my record could break out if I would go on "American Bandstand," Sam just said no. His only excuse was that he didn't know how to treat Barbara Pittman. You see, I was always a well-endowed girl, and the guys used to tell me that they didn't know how to fit a 42 into a

33-1/3. Anyway, by 1957 I had been taken off of Sun and put on Sam's other label, Phillips International. He asked me which label I preferred, and I said I'd rather be on Phillips because it looked prettier. I cut the most expensive session ever for the label that year: $5,000. "Two Young Fools In Love." Sam was sick with the flu and he managed to get out of bed that day to come to the studio to see how his money was being spent. When my contract was up, I went to California to get into the movies. I did eventually get into some of the motorcycle films of the late '60s, but mostly I performed in clubs — jazz and blues, mostly — and recorded for a few labels. I had a ball. I really wasn't interested in furthering my career that much. I did some shows with the Righteous Brothers and Johnny Rivers. Had a good time. I really always have been a blues singer. In the beginning, of course, I sang rockabilly, but then I got into the blues. I grew up on Beale Street, you see, listening to B.B. King and other artists practice when I was a child. So here I am, thirty years after Sun, singing rockabilly again.

Memphis, Tennessee; July, 1987.

Barbara Pittman, 1987

At the Sun piano, in American studios, Memphis.

1986.

Barbara Pittman and friends: bassist Marcus Van Story to her immediate left; Paul Burlison behind them; Glenn Honeycutt between Van Story and Burlison; drummer J.M. Van Eaton to the left of Van Story in checkered shirt; guitarist Roland Janes behind Van Eaton. Singer Sonny Burgess, far right. 1984

Barbara and Carl Perkins 1986.

All photos from early 1980s. Courtesy Barbara Pittman.

Barbara and Jerry Lee Lewis. 1985.

At the age of sixteen, Jackie was a recording artist for Fraternity Records.

Jackie Dee

They called her Jackie "Dee" Shannon and she was just a kid — fifteen years old in 1959. She sang in a rock and country kind of way, and became one of rockabilly's youngest proponents. She toured the Midwest with Rusty York and the Cajuns, before Rusty left to promote his record "Sugaree." "Man, that girl could *sing*," York recalled. "We'd travel around to these little record hops and television dance programs, and she would say that she wanted to be a big-name singer. All I can remember is that she wore these bright gold pants. . . ." She ended up in California, where she wrote songs and sang. She wrote "Dum Dum" and "Heart In Hand" for Brenda Lee, and "The Great Imposter" for The Fleetwoods. When the English rock band invasion took place in the mid-'60s, she was on the charts again as a songwriter with "When You Walk In The Room" and "Needles And Pins" by The Searchers. She had recorded both songs herself with little success. In 1965, she finally arrived on the international charts with a Burt Bacharach-Hal David song called "What The World Needs Now Is Love." She has continued to record over the years for various labels. In the early '80s she wrote Kim Carnes' hit "Betty Davis Eyes."

TRANSFORMATION: Skeeter Davis' appearance has changed drastically over the years. Top, left, circa 1960; bottom, left, early '60s; top, right, 1972; bottom, right, 1975.

Rockin' Gals

Top, Brenda Lee. the dynamic child vocalist; below, Jean Chapel, 1979, and right, 1957, before she became a successful country music songwriter.

Jean Chapel
Recording Artist
From Becky's To Paramount Theater in New York City!

JEAN CHAPPELL
Songs And Personality

December 4, 1957

JEAN CHAPEL — "the female Elvis."

The Female Elvis Opens Week At Slipper

Jean Chapel, singing star of this week's Silver Slipper floor show, just can't imagine why people insist on calling her "the female Elvis Presley," unless it's because she plays a guitar and "just can't keep still when I'm workin'."

A Nashvillian, Jean has made one record for Sun ("Welcome to the Club" and "No Rockin' Tonight"), which RCA-Victor bought, along with her contract, and subsequently re-released. She is proud to say she is the first performer to "stop the show" for Alan Freed at the Paramount in New York.

Did she ever meet Elvis? "Once, before he was famous. He asked me if I wanted to kiss him and I said no. I wouldn't say no now."

JEAN WILL APPEAR AT BECKY'S CLUB CHARMING ON THE SHOW EVERY NIGHT THROUGH AUGUST 9th!

Daddy-O

Bonnie Lou, early 1950s.

BONNIE LOU

I had some national country hits on King Records in the early 1950s, including "Seven Lonely Days" and "Tennessee Wig Walk." Got them into the top ten in '53. But when the rockabilly thing got popular in '55, King directed me that way. "Daddy-O" was my big one, in '55, but there were other records, too, like "La-Dee-Dah" with Rusty York. The people at King always got the songs for the artists. They told us what to record. King had a lot of country and rhythm and blues artists then, you see, and sometimes both black and white would play on the sessions. It was so hard to keep the records country; some players wanted to do a Detriot-type of thing. I think that's why I had no further success. Anyway, "Daddy-O" was a cute song. The King people told me to keep the inflection — the yodeling feel.

Photos: Bonnie Lou, mid-'50s. Record: One of her rockabilly efforts — and an unsuccessful one — on Harry Carlson's independent Fraternity label in Cincinnati.

So I did, but I think the record was ahead of its time. We cut it in the King studios in Cincinnati. I did all the background vocals. But the sound on my later records was too mixed. Part country, part R&B. It got the artists and the public confused, I believe. You've got to do one thing or another. People won't accept it unless you focus. You can't have a mixed bag. Myself, I was always a

Top, left: Bonnie Lou, mid- to late-1950s; top, right, 1945; bottom, right, mid-1980s.

country singer. I grew up singing country music as a girl in Bloomington, Illinois, where my parents used to take me to festivals and lodges just to perform. I learned to yodel from my grandmother, who came from Switzerland. As a child, I was known as The Yodeling Sweetheart, Mary Jo. I sang on the radio in Kansas City at the age of 17, and a short time later I was hired by WLW Radio in Cincinnati. A station executive named me Bonnie Lou. At one time, I was supposed to sign with RCA-Victor but instead I went with Fraternity Records just because it was local. I should have had more sense. I've always wanted to stay in Cincinnati, though, because of my family and profession. There is a loyalty in country music that you don't find in other fields, you see, and, besides, country was *me*. So I remained in town, doing radio and television, and I have never regretted not moving to New York. People still call and say they love my work. It's gratifying. I've always admired and respected my public.

Cincinnati, Ohio; October, 1987.

BOBBY BARE

This buddy and I came down to Cincinnati from Ironton, Ohio, to cut some demos. That was 1959. We went into a little studio and cut them, and that was that. We really didn't think too much about it at the time because the U.S. Army was waiting for us, man. From there, I went to Fort Knox, Kentucky, to basic training. One day I turned on the radio and heard this familiar voice singin' a familiar song: "All-American Boy." I said to myself, "Bobby, what is goin' on here?" Yeah, that was *me*! What a feeling to turn on the radio and suddenly hear yourself singing your first record. The shock came at the end of the song, though, when the disc jockey said, "That's a big hit by a newcomer named Bill Parsons. . . ." Bill Parsons, heck! That was me! What I didn't know at the time was that Harry Carlson, owner of Fraternity Records in Cincinnati, had heard the demos that my buddy and I cut up there. Harry loved "All-American Boy" and wanted to release it. The studio guy got the tapes mixed up, though, and somehow Harry thought that the record was by Bill Parsons. Harry went ahead and pressed the record up with Bill's name on it. Well, the record was an overnight smash. By the time the confusion got straightened out, the record was sitting high on the charts and I was in the Army. Bill started getting all these offers to perform and to appear on Dick Clark's show. Well, that just about scared Bill to *death*. He knew that it was my record, and he also knew that "All-American Boy" was a rappin' record. You could hardly lip-sync it. It was my story, too. And on that record and a few others on Fraternity I eventually built up a good following. I also made a good friend in Harry Carlson. He was a like a father to me. The hardest thing I ever did was leave Fraternity for RCA in the early 1960s.

From Detriot, Michigan; February, 1986.

EDDIE BOND

I cut several records in Nashville for Ekko Records in California before I cut my first big one — "Rockin' Daddy." Sonny Fisher wrote and recorded it, and I liked the song and decided to cover it. I had a three-year contract with Mercury Records at the time, 1956, and we went in and recorded the song at the old WMPS studio. The record did well in Little Rock, Memphis, and cities about that size. In fact, it *still* sells extremely well for an old record. When I go to Europe, that's the one the crowds all yell for. About 1959 I started in radio. I had 64% of the Memphis audience, and I quit traveling to places to play music. Through the years I continued to record, though. I wrote "Walking Tall," a tribute to Sheriff Buford Pusser. Now I own my own radio station here in Hernando, Mississippi. I still live in Memphis, too. I enjoy radio because it's a lot more profitable than playing music. And the work isn't so hard. But I will keep on recording.
Hernando, Mississippi; July, 1987.

Eddie Bond enjoyed a long and fruitful singing career in the 1950s and early 1960s. On the publicity photograph on the previous page, a sponsor had written: "Eddie Bond...Goodwill Ambassador For Coleman's B'Q's." Right, Bond singing, probably in the late '50s or early '60s. Below, Bond and his Western Swing Band in the mid-'50s. "We played everywhere," he said.

When I was in junior high school in Tyler, Texas, I formed a band called the Four Roses. We used to joke that the drummer was the fifth. I was raised on classical music, but it bored me. Then, in high school, along came Jerry Lee Lewis. I *loved* him. I went to a party once where he was, and I watched him intently. While the other kids danced, I studied him. I knew that if I saw him play, I could figure

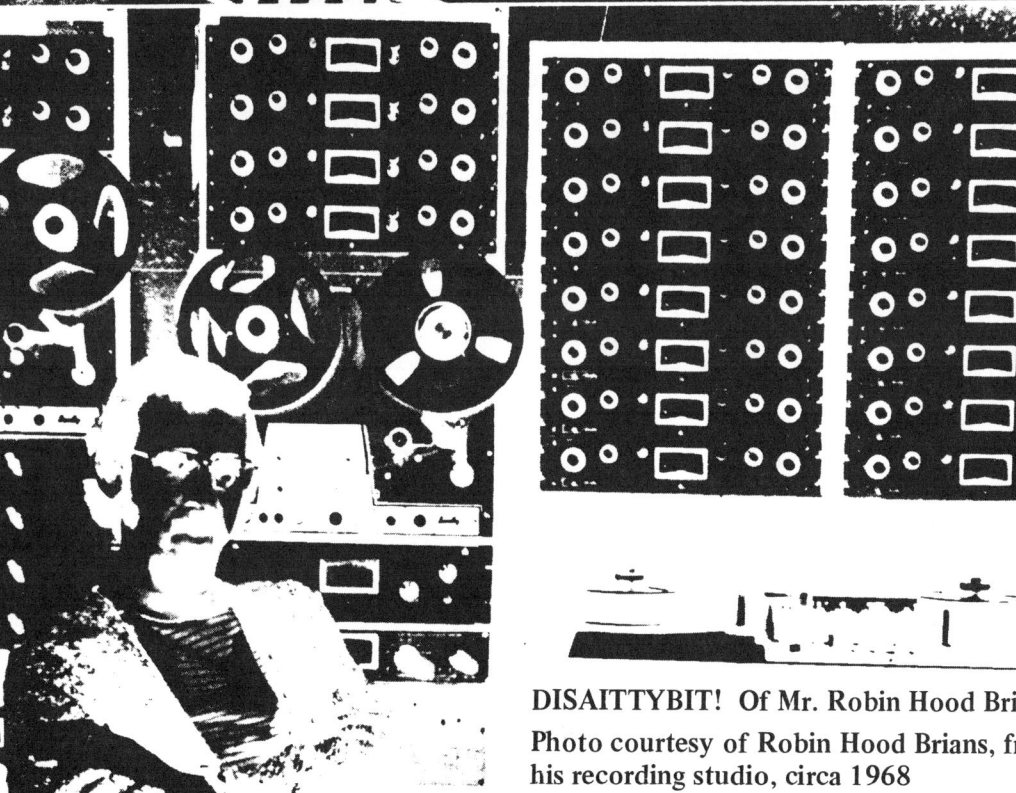

DISAITTYBIT! Of Mr. Robin Hood Brians
Photo courtesy of Robin Hood Brians, from his recording studio, circa 1968

out how he got that sound from the piano. My parents always encouraged me with my music, and I gradually progressed. We had two grand pianos in our house, and each Monday we'd have at least ten strings broken. It got so bad that my dad said to a friend, "My son is the only kid who studied piano at a karate school." When I formed another band, Robin Hood And His Merry Men in high school, we'd play at school dances, parties or at any place that would have us. By the time I was a senior, I had cut a tape with the band in a radio station. It was my own song, "Dis A Itty Bit." Well, a jukebox operator in Tyler sent the tape to a distributor in Dallas, who in turn sent to on to Harry Carlson of Fraternity Records of Cincinnati. Harry called me and said he liked it, and wanted to release it. But first, he said, he thought we really should recut the song in Nashville. I agreed. I arrived at Owen Bradley's studio one day in late 1957. I showed up and learned that Harry had booked four hours of studio time, with Bradley's quintet playing on the session and the Anita Kerr Singers doing backup vocals. The arranger was Lew Douglas, a man cut right out of the Dorsey era. Well, they took a guy named Dale Wright first to record. He was also there to also cut a session for Fraternity. The only trouble was, he took three hours to get his record finished! That left one hour for me. Somebody said I could come back some other time, but I didn't have that much money, so I said we could do it all in an hour. First thing, Owen Bradley said he was going to play piano. After a few minutes, though, I said to him, "Hey, don't do that lick, man." That's when Bradley, one of the giants of Music Row, laughed and said, "No, this one certainly isn't my style." So I ended up playing piano that day. We also cut the flip side, "Without You," sort of a Bing Crosby style song, which shows you that I had not yet developed as an artist. One side was wild rockabilly; the other, Bing. Anyway, Fraternity did release the record in early '58. It was banned in a few places, I suppose because of the lyric: C'mon, baby, dis a *itty* bit. Most radio stations ignored it, though. But that little record, cut on the second take, launched me in the music business. I could ride around the streets of Tyler, Texas, listening to my record on three stations. I believe that if I had been discovered in New York, and had found a good manager, I could have continued my singing career. But I was like most of the young rockabilly singers from the country — I had no guidance. Those early rock performers had a lot in common that way with their black counterparts. The black stuff was very horn-oriented, pushing rock in one direction, while country was pushing rock from another. Both rhythm and blues and rockabilly were coming at you from a similar vein, but with a different slant, and usually without much artist management. I really don't miss those days, however, because I had so little time to perform. I started my own recording studio by the time I was twenty-four years old, and over the years we've cut some of the biggest groups, from John Fred & The Playboy Band to ZZ Top. Remember the Five Americans? Dale Hawkins cut them in our studio. Right now, I'm still involved with it, but I'm doing a lot of commercial work for national accounts. Whatever I'm doing in this business, I love.

Tyler, Texas; October, 1986

Sonny Burgess (on guitar) in the '50s.

SONNY BURGESS

My song "We Wanna Boogie" was inspired by what we did in Newport, Arkansas, on a Saturday night. Elvis played the clubs there, near Memphis, and so did I. Back then, you could go up to Elvis or anybody else and just *talk*. The crowds really got into the music then. They were there to have a good time. I was playing country music back in the '50s, as well as stuff by Joe Turner and Jimmy Reed. So much feeling there. And I did Hank Williams' songs, too. Nobody could beat them, not even today. Of course, Elvis came along and we all decided we also wanted to be rockers. We had three clubs in Newport then. I first saw him at Porky's Roof Top, playing with Scotty and Bill. Man, they knocked me *out*! "That's All Right" had just been released on Sun Records about that time, when our band was playing songs by Moon Mullican, Merrill Moore, and Hank. So we sat down and decided to start playing rock, about '56, I guess, a little after Elvis' first records came out. He was real hot by then. A group of us formed The Pacers and I wrote "Boogie" and "Red-Headed Woman." We were considered pretty wild and animated then, but we would be tame today. We had what I would call a three-ring circus on stage. We laid down on the big old bass, straddled each other, and did the bug dance. Ever hear of it? It was fun. The bug dance is when you're itchin' and scratchin', and each musician acts like he's throwing a bug on another guy. Then he throws it into the corner, into the crowd. Then the band jumps into the crowd and sings.

Sonny Burgess in a publicity photograph from the early 1960s.

One time, we did the bug dance and my guitar hit me right in the mouth. What days those were. So much energy; so much fun. That is a time in history that we will never see again, in my opinion. That's before things got so wild. We had fun, but it was the right kind of fun on stage. We guys on Sun Records were just poor boys, so playing music was fun for us. Getting paid, well, that was the

Sonny Burgess, behind bass.

icing on the cake for us. In those days, the one thing I was really good at was picking musicians. Man, I had some *good* ones, too. Most people don't realize that I played my own guitar. I'd play rhythm, then switch to lead. On record, though, the guitar part dropped out while I made the quick switch. These days, people ask me what it was like to be on Sun in those crazy times. They remember me, for some reason. Everybody talks about my red hair, about my red this and my red that. How that happened was I had a candy apple red guitar, the first ever made by Fender,

211

a Stratocaster. Then I had a red suit and black tux pants. My red hair came about when we toured with Johnny Cash, Roy Orbison, and whoever else we happened to hook up with. One day I tried to put peroxide on my hair to turn it white, and for some reason my hair came out red. So I was stuck with it for a time. That image of me has somehow stuck over time, too. Anyway, in those days we didn't even know how to record. Nobody ever told us what to do. We just played as if we were playing for a crowd. We thought we were big record stars then, but we were really only known in our home areas. Sun did have a few stars; the rest of us were just a bunch of local players. Now, after we're all past the prime of our lives, we're getting some attention. In 1960, I got out of the business altogether. Some vocalists wanted the band to go to California. I didn't want to. Since then, I've been working at a company — well, since the '70s — and playing a little music on the side. We tour with some other Memphis fellows in the Original Sun Rhythm Section. We may never be big stars, but then, who knows? We made a little money and had a good time.

Newport, Arkansas; February, 1987.

Sonny Burgess, far right, on guitar.

PAUL BURLISON

Left to right: Johnny Burnette, Dorsey Burnette, Paul Burlison (on electric guitar).

My family moved to Memphis from a small town in Tennessee when I was only seven years old. As a young man I played the guitar and worked as a journeyman electrician at Crown Electric, where Elvis Presley worked. He was just another kid in the neighborhood then, in the early 1950s. Along the way I met up with the Burnette brothers, Johnny and Dorsey, and eventually we formed a band called The Rock 'n' Roll Trio. We started playing country music about '53, I believe, and we went on to appear on Ted Mack's *Amateur Hour* television program, and that led to meeting former President Harry Truman and to signing a lot of autographs for a lot of folks. After winning the top slot on that show three times, we signed with a manager, Henry Jerome, a New York band leader and producer. In '56, we signed with Coral Records. We moved into the Edison Hotel in New York, *the* place for the hip people to stay at the time. The Andrews Sisters and Mickey Mantle lived there, too. Anyway, we used to practice upstairs! I can't believe that. Upstairs. We made our early recordings in a place called the Pythian Temple in New York. There was a big ballroom upstairs, as I recall. Bill Haley cut there. We made our first record there, "Tear It Up" and "You're Undecided." We had a thirty-two piece orchestra at the session, and we weren't cutting country by this time. The conductor of the session said, "OK, fellas, we don't know anything about rock 'n' roll music, so you tell us what to play." We just laughed and told him we played only what we felt. So he dismissed everybody in the band, but we asked the drummer to stay. I told him, "Man, play *louder*!" He tried. The poor man tried. I kept yelling, "No, play louder, not better!" So he finally put his drums away and said he was afraid he'd break them. He ended up playing on the black plastic drum case. That was rock 'n' roll, early-style. Well, about '57, after being together for nearly four years, the group changed. Dorsey wanted to sing by himself; he was tired of being a bass player. When he left the trio, we split everything 50-50, Johnny and me. I decided to get out, eventually. I wanted to be at home with my wife and kids. I started my own electric contracting business and I've done all right with it. I've also raised five children. Every time one of them was in a ball game or a play, I was there to see them. Their awards and trophies mean more to

The Original Sun Rhythm Section, with Paul Burlison, front row, bottom right.

me than any gold records. I didn't make much money in the record business, but I've made more in the last couple of years than I did in the entire early part of my career. Now I'm playing with some of the old Memphis gang in a band called The Original Sun Rhythm Section. We play about one weekend a month and we love it. My wife has faith in me. That's what's important. We in the band just have fun these days. My kids call us The Polyesters. We can laugh about it all now because we don't have to worry about feeding our families. Or making the house payments. But we like the music and we like to see people being happy when we perform. Our big honor came not too long ago: we played at the Smithsonian. I guess we're a part of history now. The odd thing is that I'm doing all this and I'm the only guy in the group to never record for Sun Records. But I am a Memphis player. Guess I'll always be one.

Memphis, Tennessee; January, 1987.

RAY CAMPI

My family moved from New York to Texas — Austin — in 1944. One of the first things they did was buy a Bob Wills album. At the age of twelve I started picking up the guitar, and in high school I started a band with some friends called Ramblin' Ray and the Ramblers. I started cutting some discs in 1949 on a friend's disc-cutting machine. I was so intrigued with the music of Austin. I got introduced to some of the black artists around town, and, of course, I noted what the country musicians were doing. I even listened to big band albums my family had brought from New York. In 1951, when I was still in high school, I cut a session with a band at the University of Texas studio. Our group had steel, fiddle, drums, two guitars. A couple of us sang. We played dances and whatever we could find. In '53, the year I started college, I bought a tape recorder to cut demos and other things on. I still have it. In '54, I went to see the film *Blackboard Jungle*, featuring Bill Haley's "Rock Around The Clock." I was impressed. I had always done hillbilly boogie, so it wasn't difficult for me to start rocking and to eliminate some of the slower songs. By this time, it was pretty evident to me that this music was something I would really enjoy and excell in. That year, I wrote a rock song. Well, I continued in school, at the University of Texas' Drama Department, where I had started in '53. The band changed from cowboy shirts to white sport coats. One day about '56, I saw a record label in a store, a label and address for TNT Records of San Antonio. They recorded Roy Head and the Traits. I went on down there and the head of the label listened to my songs and said, "Come on back next week and we will record you." I went, of course, and recorded my songs "Caterpillar" and "Play It Cool." I was writing all of my own songs by this time. The A-side, "Caterpillar," came to me one day when I was inspired by Charlie Gracie's "Butterfly" record. I just wanted something crazy. My TNT work never hit nationally, however, and in '57 my cousin in New York got be acquainted with the head of Roosevelt Music, one of the top rock publishers in America. She was his babysitter. I went up to New York City and got a deal with Dot Records and a guest shot on Dick Clark's show through the label folks.

Rambin' Ray Campi and the Ramblers, mid-'50s. Ray is second from left, on guitar.

Unfortunately, I never did get that elusive hit record. I went to other labels and other states, including California, but not much happened. In '64, I went back to California and got my teaching certificate. I started teaching English. I stayed in Los Angeles and taught and played my music on the side. And, I recorded. My records have been released and re-released all over the world, even though they never have sold extremely well as singles in the United States. I've toured Europe. I don't know what it is, but there seems to be a resentment against the early rockabillies because we were first. Resentment from the big labels, that is. The people, well, they have always liked our music. Some new bands like The Blasters and The Stray Cats have helped open rockabilly up to the world. They made it a viable musical form. I came back to Austin some time ago to record a new album. I will return to Los Angeles and keep on teaching until my retirement. Then I intend to record and continue my singing career. It's that same old struggle: Try to convince the world you have talent.

Spicewood, Texas; September, 1987.

JOHNNY CARROLL

As a kid, I appeared on local radio shows in Cleburne, Texas, and in high school I started singing in bands. Somehow, I blundered my way onto shows with big names. We were doing rhythm and blues and country on the same shows then. Of course, Elvis, bless his heart, he broke the ice for the rest of us. A bunch of us were doing that mixed bag around here in the mid-'50s. Anyway, Ferlin Husky let me do the first fifteen minutes of his show in '56. There was a promoter who then came to ask us to record. We went to Nashville to cut some stuff, but I was a minor then so Decca Records wouldn't let me record. After the band got that settled, our promoter got me in the movie *Rock, Baby, Rock It*. He produced the film. Meanwhile, I had done some shows with Presley, so I knew Scotty Moore and Bill Black. When they left Elvis, they asked me to front a band for them. Bill got me on Sun Records. That didn't lead to much at the time. Rockabilly died in 1960. I stayed out of everything until '75. But it has always been music with me. I've done this for a living. I managed clubs and engineered in recording studios when I wasn't performing. After being out of the performing thing from '60 to '75, though, I sang one night and I said, "Oh, yeah. *That's* what I want to do." I thought I was over the hill, but, at the age of 49, I find out now that I'm not. In fact, if I had to quit on a high note in my career, it would be in France recently. June, '87. The crowd was great. I've teamed up with country singer Judy Lindsey now. We play country in the U.S. and rockabilly in Europe. Rockabilly is so popular over there. That place is a fantasy land for old rockers.

Owen Bradley and Johnny Carroll, June 4, 1987

I cut *two* versions of "Wild, Wild Women." I wrote the song after hearing "Wild, Wild Young Men." No plagiarism involved. I told the publishers what I had done, and they said that everything was all right because the songs were so different. Anyway, I cut the first version at Owen Bradley's studio in Nashville about March of '56. For Decca. We cut three singles in two days. The musicians were: Harold Bradley, electric rhythm guitar; Owen Bradley, piano; Grady Martin, electric lead guitar; Bob Moore, bass; Buddy Harmon, drums. Now those were some *good* pickers, some of the guys who also played on the Brenda Lee sessions. I was pleased with the sound they gave to the record. That first Decca session was the only time I ever used session players on my records. They gave the tracks a pretty good sound, I think. It didn't sound like Presley and mainstream rock 'n' roll. But after thirty years, those records have held up well. They have definition. I used my road band to record "Wild, Wild Women" number two — and the tracks for the movie *Rock Baby Rock It* — at Sellars Studio in Dallas, not long after the originals were cut. Decca didn't want us to use their masters in the film, so we recut stuff. I think that second recording gave us yet another sound. Both were good. On the Nashville sessions, though, I recorded Johnny Cash's "Rock 'n' Roll Ruby." I was kicked in the stomach — well, at least I *felt* that way — when I first heard Warren Smith's version of the song on Sun. That was my first record on Decca and, while it sold pretty well, and, incidentally, better than Warren's original, I wasn't all that happy with it because I liked Warren's record better. We cut it from the original Cash demo. Three or four people released the song at the same time. I didn't even know that Warren Smith had recorded it when we cut it. But I soon found out.

Godley, Texas; July and August, 1987.

BRUCE CHANNEL

Bruce Channel, mid-1970s.

My family moved from Jacksonville, Texas, to a little placed called Grapevine, between Fort Worth and Dallas, when I was young. I grew up listening to the Louisiana Hayride and, when I could pick it up, the Grand Ole Opry from Nashville. Living near the big cities, I'd always hear some rhythm and blues records on the radio. I loved Fats Domino and Brook Benton. By 1955, I had my own band. But it took me longer to write a song. I remember that for certain. It wasn't easy. I remember I finally wrote my first one when I was sixteen. I then had one published by a man involved with the Louisiana Hayride, which I worked at for six months. When I left there, I got any gig I could find. I sang in all the honky-tonks, using their house bands as I performed. I wrote "Hey, Baby!" then, about 1959, with my good friend Margaret Cobb. I had played the song in the clubs, although at the time I put more of an R&B feel to it. Somehow, over the years, the song just evolved. Then one day I went into a studio in Forth Worth to record some demos for Major Bill Smith, a local producer and promoter who was a Texas legend. I had cut some unsuccessful records before, and this time I was hoping that I could really do something big. The Major asked me if I had any more songs to record that day. "Well," I said, "I do have one called 'Hey, Baby!'" He answered, "Let's try it." So we cut it. Delbert McClinton's band played on it, with Delbert on harmonica. The record was first released on the producer's local label, and then on Smash Records nationally. "Hey, Baby!" just happened. Went to No. 1 in March, 1962. I think people liked it because it was just good-time music. I went on the road after the record hit. Toured all over America and even went to Europe, where I met the Beatles. Stayed on the road about ten years; seemed like forever. In 1969, after things had died down for me, I cut some records down in Tyler, Texas, at Robin Hood Brians' studio, with Dale Hawkins producing me. We had one single, "Mr. Bus Driver," go into the bottom of the charts. Another, "Keep On," went to No. 12 in England. Both songs were written by Wayne Carson Thompson, who wrote "The Letter." He was going to give those other two songs to the Box Tops, but I got them instead. In the late-'70s, I decided to come to Nashville to try to be a songwriter. I got a job with a publisher as a staff writer, and I've been a whole lot happier just writing and hanging out with my friends. I've been fortunate to get some good cuts here. I tell you, I was on the road a long time. Too long.

Nashville, Tennessee; August, 1985.

JOE CLAY (AKA, Claiborne Joseph Cheramie)

When I was twelve, my parents used to take me to a country music club on Sundays. I wanted to sing so much! The band finally set up three Coca-Cola cases for me so that I could reach the microphone. My mother and father must have thought that their boy was finally getting a chance to express himself musically, because I had always tapped my feet and played the spoons and sang around the house. When I was about thirteen, I started playing drums in public, and, later, I started singing country music. Then, I got into rockabilly. I did that to break into country, really. About 1954, when I was sixteen and living in Harvey, Louisiana, I was doing that rockabilly thing and watching people's reactions. I was the only guy doing that around here in those days. By 1957, I was playing in a band that performed on a country music radio show every day. One

Saturday I walked into the studio — I performed by myself on Saturday — and the disc jockey said, "We got a letter from a new label up in New York called Vik Records that's looking for talent. You interested?" Well, in no time I cut four songs at the station and sent them to the label. In about a week the label guys came down and got me and took me to Houston, Texas, to record me. It seemed like in no time I was up in New York to record and perform on *The Ed Sullivan Show.* Man, everything happened so fast, I went *crazy*. I was only eighteen years old then, and I had my own record and was appearing on national television. I sang "Duck Tail," as in "Buddy, don't mess with my duck tail. . . ." I was so *happy*. The record started to get a lot of airplay. The song was written by a guy from Houston named Rudy Grayzell, and I thought it would click. Especially after the television appearance. But then, everything stopped. The company wanted me to go on tour, but my manager, who had me under a strong contract back in Louisiana, wanted me to stay more around New Orleans. The label stopped pushing the record and that was the end of that. I never recorded again. I felt that it just wasn't to be. When my two-year contract expired with Vik, the company didn't retain me. In all, I had eight releases, including "Cracker Jack," but no real hits. But I had some good times. I remember performing with Elvis on the Louisiana Hayride before he made it. And I played drums in back of him one night at an amusement park in New Orleans in 1959. His drummer, D.J. Fontana, got sick that night, and I said, "That's no problem at all. I can play drums, Elvis." So I backed up Elvis and Scotty Moore and Bill Black that night. It was the first time in my life that I got paid twice for one show — to sing *and* play. Those days faded, though. I got a job driving a school bus. I wasn't active musically for a long time. Then one day I got a call from an Englishman named Willie Jeffrey, who wanted me to come over there to sing. He said he had been searching for me for *four years*. Well, man, I just didn't know what to think. I arrived at the airport in London and the agent said, "Joe, I want you to meet your bodyguards, Mark and Dave." I just laughed and said, "Ha! What is this, some kind of publicity stunt?" He chuckled and told me I would soon find out. Well, I arrived at the club and there were all these '57 Chevys and '58 Caddys out in front. People from nineteen to twenty-six were all dressed in old '50s clothes, with crew cuts and duck tails and all that. As I played, the crowd went crazy. They rushed the stage later. Man, they're really into rockabilly over there, like you wouldn't believe. Not just England, but all over Europe. I just have to laugh, man. I really do. I couldn't even get the disc jockey fellas in New Orleans to play my 45s back in the '50s. Some life, isn't it?

Gretna, Louisiana; February, 1987.

Previous page: Joe Clay at the height of his career.
Right: Joe Clay, 1987.

MAC CURTIS

When I was in high school, I heard a recording of "That's All Right Mama" by Marty Robbins. and I liked it. Then a fellow took me to town and played me Elvis Presley's version on Sun Records on a jukebox. I said, "Man, *that's* what I've been looking for." Until then, our band had done mostly upbeat country. One record changed that approach. When I was a child growing up in Olney, Texas, I took up the guitar. I continued to play it for my grandparents, with whom I grew up. When my grandfather bought a farm near Fort Worth, in 1954, I was a sophomore in high school. I played in a local band. Then one day a man named Bill Thompson from Fort Worth got us on the "Big D Jamboree." Things started happening. KNOK Radio asked us to appear at a car show in town, and in between sets we got to perform on the air. We had one fantastic time. About a week later, somebody from the station called and said we ought to go to Dallas to audition for Ralph Bass, an executive with King Records out of Cincinnati. So we went there and played for him in a motel room. After we had played only two songs, he said, "Yeah, I want you." At the time, you see, every label was looking for an Elvis. So I got a record deal as a high school kid in the winter of '56. In all, I cut 17 songs for King, and only one, "Blue Jean Heart," was not released by the label. In those days, I never did consider being a writer, even though I did write "Little Miss Linda" and "Don't You Love." The record company thought of you as a singer. It thought of writers as writers. There were so many of us doing our thing then – what did somebody call us? Oh, yes, "obscure Southern rockabillies." Well, I recorded all the King material in Dallas and Fort Worth. My first single was "If I Had Me A Woman," and my second was "Granddaddy's Rockin'." The records did well for me. In the '50s, if you got a review in the trade magazines it was almost as good as a hit record, and I got good reviews. I got stacks of mail from all over the world. Unbeknownst to me, Alan Freed had started playing my records on his radio show. In the fall of '56, Freed's people contacted me and I played the Brooklyn Paramount rock shows. I didn't know *what* to think of it: all around, a eager sea of humanity. We couldn't even leave the hotel room until two in the morning because the kids wouldn't leave. I met George Hamilton IV then, and we became good friends. About this time,

I came back to Texas to finish high school. All this time I had been on a leave of abscence. As a senior in high school with a record deal, I was pretty unusual, I guess, and the manager of a local radio station asked me if I wanted to get into radio. So I did. Had my own show. Then I went into the Army, and I studied broadcasting and went to the Armed Forces Radio Network in Korea. I came to Dallas when I got out of the Army, and by that time I had redeveloped a love for roots country music. The rockabilly thing had faded by then — 1960 it was — and there was little demand for the kind of thing we did. Buddy Holly had went on to New York City and the string section. Then, of course, he was killed in the plane crash. Rockabilly was not doing well. Probably what happened was evolution as much as anything. The green country kids learned the techniques of the big-time New York producers. Suddenly everything had a big sound, with voices. As with anything, the spectators became the participants. The same thing happened with country music. Evolution just happens. But I know that in '56 we, as kids, had our own kind of music. When the film *Rebel Without A Cause* with James Dean came out in those days, we knew it was all right to dress and act a certain way. The movie reconfirmed what we already knew. When rockabilly went out, I got into pure country music, like that of Hank Thompson, and I got heavily involved in radio and performing. Over the years I moved to stations in other states, but I wanted to return to Texas. So I did. My official title now at KPLX near Arlington is creative production director. I love to write and deliver commercials. I'm happy to say that I've had two careers — radio and records. I still perform sometimes. I'm fortunate to have another shot at it, with the popularity of rockabilly and country being what it is. I can do more now than I did in the '50s. Somebody told me once that show business is two words. You must present a show and work on your career like a product. You've got your show and you've got your business. I'm really lucky to have had two careers that I have loved so well.

Euless, Texas; August, 1987.

Mac Curtis, 1956.

Mac Curtis, mid-1960s.

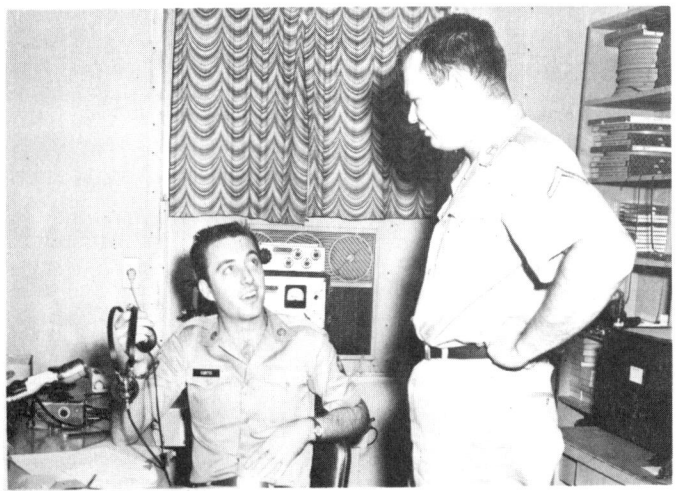

Left, top: Mac Curtis, 1957, with his "model rebel haircut"; top, right, 1967, WPLO award presented to Waylon Jennings by Mac Curtis for Most Popular New Artist poll; bottom, left, Sp. 4 Mac Curtis (sitting) discusses radio with Pfc. Fred Anderson of the radio broadcast school, 1959-60; bottom, right, Curtis (center) with The Country Cats, Ken Galbraith, bass, and Jim Galbraith, lead guitar. From 1956.

SONNY CURTIS

As a kid growing up in Meadow, Texas, I was greatly influenced by the music of my own uncle, Ed Mayfield, an outstanding bluegrass picker. He influenced me a lot. Unfortunately, he died at an early age after becoming ill on the road with Bill Monroe. I was slow to catch on to the rock 'n' roll thing. I met Buddy Holly and starting playing with him and Bob Montgomery back in high school. After playing around Lubbock, Texas, for a time with Buddy, I joined Slim Whitman's band, and then I went to Nashville to become a part of the "Philip Morris Country Music Show" with Carl Smith, Ronnie Self, Red Sovine, and others. We toured all over the country by bus. That was 1957. About this time, I wrote hit song for Webb Pierce called "Someday," and I knew I wanted to be a writer. I had already written songs before. "Rock Around With Ollie Vee" had been recorded with Buddy. I was told by a fellow in the early days that I had better learn to write because that was the only way I could make it in the record business. So I tried writing. At first, I just wanted to write a rock 'n' roll song, so I sat down and composed "Ollie Vee." A black man who worked on my father's farm had a wife by that name, so I used it, but she had nothing else to do with my song. From there, I drifted to California, New York, Colorado — all over. I tried my hand at writing and almost starved. I did get a record deal with Dot Records when I hung around New York. Meanwhile, The Crickets had split with Buddy because he wanted to live in New York and they wanted to live in Texas, so they asked me to come back and play with them. I did. Then I went into the Army, and that's when I wrote one of my early hits, "Walk Right Back" by The Everly Brothers. I loved their smooth sound. Then I wrote "Fool Never Learns" by Andy Williams and "I Fought The Law" by The Bobby Fuller Four. Things were going pretty well for me, and I finally decided that my songwriting career was no fluke. So I quit the road and devoted all my time to writing. I thought I had recorded some pretty good records over the years myself, but for some reason or another they never did click. Well, I eventually ended up writing the television theme for "The Mary Tyler Moore Show," and that was a good thing. It was a prestigious lick for me. It pays well, and it has given me recognition. After writing it, though, I did a weird thing. I wrote jingles for the next four years. My partner and I were extremely busy, but in 1976 I decided to move my family to Nashville. Two of the Crickets had already moved here, and when I came Waylon Jennings invited us to go out for the weekend. It ended up being for five years. We did that till about '83, when I cut three albums for Elektra Records. Since then, I've been performing in Europe and other places and continuing to write songs. I've also

kept up my recording. Looking back on my career, I guess I was always a little different. A lot of the other singers were heavy into the early rock thing, but I was slow to catch on to it because I always did love country music and bluegrass so much. Later, I liked Grady Martin and Chet Atkins. They were influential. I guess I've been a part of history.
Nashville, Tennessee; September, 1987.

Sonny Curtis' first publicity photo, Dot Records, about 1958. Taken in New York City.

Top, left, Sonny Curtis, 1987; top, right, school picture, 1953, when he was a junior in high school; bottom, left, Sonny with his two older brothers, Pete (center) and Dean (right). Pete and Sonny played guitars, Dean the fiddle. About 1951. And, bottom, right, photo of Sonny at United Recording in Hollywood, 1964, as he recorded an album called "Beatles Hits Flamenco Guitar Style" for Imperial Records.

CHARLIE FEATHERS

A lot of folks talk about the early days, but not many were really around then. But I *know* what I'm talkin' about, man, 'cause I was *there*. Memphis, '54, '55. Hey, Carl Perkins used my band when he come to Memphis. I cut before he did. I worked on a lot of the Sun Records artists' records as an arranger and player. I started out as a kid who liked Bill Monroe. He was my favorite. I *love* bluegrass. My first instrument was a mandolin. I tried to play like Bill Monroe. A lot of bluegrass music is done fast. Back years ago, people had an upright bass and a fiddle around the house. They'd start poppin' that ole bass. All they done down here, see, was that poppin'. The cat-gut strings had a unique sound. Gives you plenty of bottom. Sounds great. Then somebody put that cotton-patch blues with bluegrass and created rockabilly. Guys slipped away and picked. Dee-dee-dee-dee-dee. Most beautiful music I ever heard in my life. But what really made those early rockabilly records was slap-back, man. I don't like gimmicky things done with the voice, drenched in echo. No way. Now you listen to those early records. As far as I'm concerned, man, Elvis died in '55. It was unbelievable that sound he got earlier, on "Mystery Train" and other records. Slappin' bass. Slap-back. No drums. What a sound! Right off the floor and onto the record. What a presence! Those records sound so "out front." They really explode. Yeah, man.

Memphis, Tennesse; June, 1987.

NARVEL FELTS

When I was growing up near Bernie, Missouri, in the late 1940s, I used to listen to country music. Later, I heard Ernest Tubb's "Walking The Floor Over You" and I wondered what his girlfriend was doing on the floor while he was walking over her. I couldn't understand. I first started in show business myself in 1956, when I was in junior high school. I entered a talent contest and sang "Blue Suede Shoes" and "Baby, Let's Play House." I won. A guy in the audience was from KDEX Radio in Dexter, Missouri, and he heard me sing that night and wanted me to perform on a program for the station, but he didn't know how to contact me. The next day I was listening to the radio and the announcer said, "If Narvel Felts is listening, please call the station immediately." I said to my father, "Quick! We've got to get to town!" We jumped in a pickup and drove eight miles to the nearest telephone. I got on the radio. In December, 1956, I joined a band, which later became known as Narvel Felts and the Rockets. A few months later, I managed, with the help of a local man, to get an audition with Sun Records of Memphis, Tennessee. Jack Clement told me to go back home and practice and write some more

songs. I did what he told me, and then he brought me back for a few sessions. I met Jerry Lee Lewis, Johnny Cash, Roy Orbison, Harold Jenkins — he was not yet Conway Twitty then. What an exciting time to be in the studio! Jack said the sessions came out fine, but he might not be able to release something for about a year. Well, that sounded more like an eternity to me then, so I later accepted an offer to cut ten sides for Mercury Records. They took me up to Chicago. I believe my first release was a record called "Kiss-A-Me-Baby." Not too much happened, though, and I eventually went to Memphis to record some sides for the Pink label. My first release, "3,000 Miles," got a good reception, and my next record, "Honey Love," did even better, and hit the national charts. That was early 1960. "Honey Love" got banned in a lot of places. People said it was too risque. There were a lot of protests against it. While I was getting action on Pink, some people at MGM Records called and said that if I could do this well on a small label, just think what I could do on MGM. So, I went on to sign with them. They never did release a record for me, and I ended up going into the Army. When I got out, I recorded for many labels — ARA, Rene, Starline, Groove, Hi, to name a few. But it wasn't until the early '70s that I finally hit big with "Drift Away," a country record on the independent Cinnamon Records in Nashville. I followed that one with "All In The Name Of Love" and others. Then, I went to number one with "Reconsider Me" on ABC-Dot in 1975. Producer Johnny Morris and I had other big country hits after that. In all, I've had the good fortune to have twenty-three big singles and eight albums. And I'm still at it. I still live in Missouri and I've managed to survive in this competitive business for thirty years. It's still fun for me, too.

From Nashville, Tennessee; January, 1987.

Narvel Felts in the studio, about 1960.

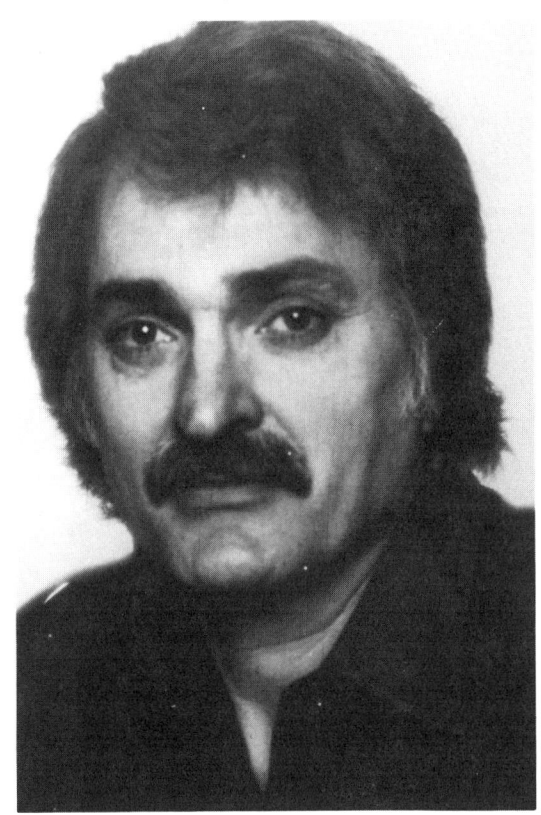

Top, left, Narvel Felts about 1967; top, right, about 1975; bottom, right, 1987.

EDDIE FONTAINE

My 200 single releases were many things to many people. Some pop. Some rockabilly. Some old-time rock 'n' roll. I was born in Jersey City, New Jersey, in 1939, and I went to high school there. After I got out of the Navy, I cut for RCA's Label X in 1955. My first record, "Rock Love," sold more than 300,000 copies. Those were legitimate sales. Nowadays they give gold records for that many sales. Anyway, I was a nightclub performer since I was fourteen years old. I went on to Decca Records in 1956, the year I did the film "The Girl Can't Help It." I think I got $20,000 for singing in that movie. I bought a Buick Century with a part of the money. Oh, what a time! We shot the movie over at 20th Century-Fox in Hollywood. I stayed on the set for two days. Elvis was on the next lot over doing "Love Me Tender." He had just hit it big. So I went over there and watched him. Somebody said, "Go ahead, introduce yourself." I said, "I can't do that," and I left for Las Vegas, where I was to perform. I was one of the few rock 'n' roll artists who could perform his own hits. I still can. I'm a *singer*. I still sing in supper clubs and at rock festivals in Europe. Here's an interesting story: In 1957 I wrote "Nothin' Shakin'." I made a demo in New York City and, to my surprise, my publisher leased the tape to Argo Records. Meanwhile, I had recorded another version of the song for Sunbeam Records. I competed with myself as artist on the same song. Isn't this some business? When my singing career started to get a little soft in the early '60s, I got an acting job on the television series "The Gallant Men," and later I appeared on many other programs. I played Fonzie's father on "Happy Days," you know. But I'm still a singer. I think I am one of the grandfathers of rock 'n' roll. I *worked*. I earned $150,000 a year for years. That was an immense amount of money then. The music was wild but it was clean. It was durable, too. Then the drugs came in the late '60s. There were so many of us who performed in the '50s, who were successful. We still sing. I myself had many big records. Sometimes it bothers me that nobody knows about that. Or cares.

Reseda, California; August, 1987.

GLEN GLENN
(AKA, Glen Troutman)

My family moved from Joplin, Missouri, to California when I was thirteen years old. Me and my long-time guitar player, Gary Lambert, were school buddies in California, and we appeared on a television program called "The Country Barn Dance" and other shows. About 1955 I went to Springfield, Missouri, to play with my cousin, Porter Wagoner, on "The Ozark Jubilee," but I got homesick and returned to California to appear on television in Los Angeles in 1957. I was the front man and singer for The Maddox Brothers and Rose. I got a lot of exposure that way, and in January, 1958, I cut a record called "Everybody's Movin'." I cut the master myself over at Gold Star Studios, using my band, and then I pitched the tape to a number of companies. Era Records, an independent, signed me and used the tape as a master recording. Then I was drafted a few months later. That hurt because I couldn't promote my record. I couldn't go on "American Bandstand" and other shows; all I could do is perform on the Army base in Hawaii, where I was stationed. Here I had a pick hit of the week, and I couldn't even take advantage of it. Eddie Cochran was lucky that he didn't have to go into the service. Eddie and me were about the only two rockabillies in California. I think there were so few of us out this way because we never heard Elvis out here on the radio in the early days — 1954, I guess. The stations around Memphis and in the South were playing his Sun records in those times, and the other performers got to hear what was going on. But we never even heard of Elvis Presley in California before "Heartbreak Hotel" came out in '56. I knew about him before, though, because of the Maddox Brothers and Rose, who kept telling me about this young "cat" — that's what they called him — who recorded for Sun. So I ordered a Sun record that he had made. I said, "Man, he *is* different!" I've had a lot of records out over the years, and I've had a lot of fun. I've been on tour in Europe and the United States. For years I have worked in a plant here in California. So I've been able to enjoy the best of everything.

Ontario, California; August, 1987.

Oh! Suzy-Q

DALE HAWKINS

I had a little band in '57. Played in the clubs around Shreveport, Louisiana. I was just a kid then, working part-time in a record store in town. I was into a lot of blues, and I liked what Scotty Moore was doing on guitar with Elvis. But we sort of had our own sound in Louisiana that came from our heavy blues influence. Our band had the riffs for "Suzy-Q" for some time, and we kept putting them together until one day I finally said, "That's it." It was just sheer *sound*. And, it worked. We went into the studios at KWKH Radio in Shreveport to cut the song. I know that sounds unusual today, but they used to do a lot of recording there. We cut the session one night between midnight and one a.m., when transmitters were changed. We sent the tape to Chess Records in Chicago, and Leonard Chess said he wanted it. After some weeks went by, though, we got tired of waiting for the record to come out. I sent a copy to Jerry Wexler at Atlantic Records, and he put out the word: Chess had better do something or get off

the pot. Two weeks later, our record was released. It broke in different parts of the country at different times. We got instant calls. We knew it was a hit after only a week and a half, man. At that time, the independent labels were coming on strong because the big ones weren't into that stuff so heavily yet. And our little record, it just sounded so much like Louisiana. James Burton and I played guitar on the session. The special sound of the guitar came from a reverb thing done in Chicago. The overall sound was our own, though, from our area of the country. Just a little bit of the blues, man.

North Little Rock, Arkansas; December, 1986.

Glenn Honeycutt (center, with guitar) performs in the early 1980s.

GLENN HONEYCUTT

I was born in Mississippi but my family came to Memphis when I was seven years old. I started playing guitar when I was about fifteen, and when I got out of the service at the age of twenty-one, in the mid-1950s, I started playing professionally. I played the clubs with one band mostly, Slim Wallace and the Dixie Ramblers. Jack Clement was a drummer with the group for a time. Slim had a little studio at his house, and he and Jack used to record people. They cut some tapes on Billy Lee Riley, then made a deal with Sam Phillips over at Sun to take Riley as an artist. Sam recut the tapes that were made at Slim's place. Well, Slim liked some of my material, so we recorded "I'll Be Around" and "I'll Wait Forever," and the tapes were taken over to Phillips and a deal was made. I recorded only about three songs over there at Sun that could be considered records; the others were just things that I sung as demos and when the tape was rolling. The funny thing is, today many of those songs have turned up on albums put out in Europe. You know, I had only one record out on Sun Records — "I'll Be Around," I believe it was in '57 — but I've gotten a lot of attention regarding that. I'm a letter carrier, and one day I was asked by a man to autograph a record that he had ordered from Europe. I looked at it carefully and saw that it contained songs that I barely remembered recording. So the business has been interesting to me. I can still sing a song. About the last thing I performed at was in Memphis, about 1983. Lately, my interest has been in writing, as it has always been. My sister and I have written some spiritual songs that have been accepted for a church hymnal. That's a dream come true for me. If one of those songs catch on, they could be around forever. I've never made a lot of money in music, but, if I had one wish from the music, it would be to have a song accepted for a hymnal. Back in the

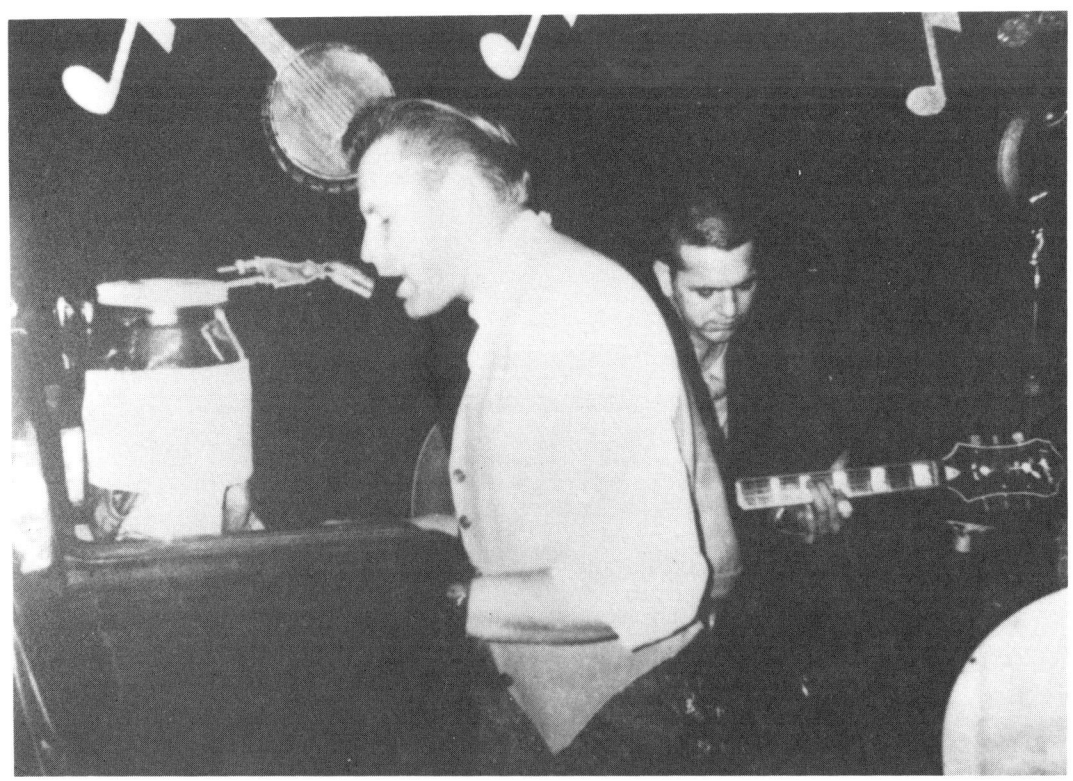

Glenn Honeycutt, early 1960s.

'50s, I had a lot of fun with music. I wouldn't classify myself as 100% rockabilly because the band played a little of everything, from country to rock to pop ballads to polkas. We never were asked to leave a place, so I guess we entertained pretty well. Of course, I played a lot of country music. And I kept on writing songs. I wrote and recorded "Tombigbee Queen," named after a riverboat and the Tombigbee River, on Fernwood about 1961. I also wrote a song called "All Night Rock" that I recorded over at Sun in the early days. It was never released in the United States, but it was put out in Europe. So many of my tapes have been released over there, things I can barely recall. In fact, I heard one thing that I recorded many years ago. It was on an album from Europe. That got recorded when Slim Wallace called me up on the telephone and told me to get over to his place, because a guy wanted to pay me five dollars to sing a couple of songs. The band was there. The guy was there with his songs. I thought they were stinky. I sang, collected my money, and left. Now I hear that song on an album. Interesting, isn't it?

Walls, Mississippi; August, 1987.

ORANGIE RAY HUBBARD

I probably cut one of the first rockabilly records. Yes, sir. That's hard to prove, but who knows? My mother, she was a Pentacostal singer, and I guess that's where I picked up that spirited type of music. I put a beat with it. That was in Barberville, Kentucky, about '53. Man, I got a bad memory for dates. A man came to town from Nashville and staged a talent contest with the local radio station, WBVL. The winner got to cut a record for Dixie Records, a subsidiary of Starday. Well, I won. Took 'em a year to put out "Sweet Love," the record I had cut at the station. It was rockabilly, man. The record went big in my part of the country. I was just a poor country boy who thought it was great to be recognized in his hometown. I was only about nineteen. Later, I moved to Cincinnati to work in the automobile plants, and I kept playing music on the side. The establishment didn't accept me, though. And I had bad luck. A record called "Big Cat" would have done something for me if Syd Nathan of King Records hadn't died just before it was to be released. Doesn't bother me now, though, 'cause I'm getting too old to worry about that stuff. What do you think about all this rockabilly stuff now? Everybody likes it. When I was recording in the '50s, nobody understood it. Heck, collectors are selling my "Sweet Love" for a couple of hundred dollars. Guess I'm finally discovered. I even had some folklore group come in and spend the day with me here at my son's gas station. They wanted to know of my experiences. Who will keep the music alive?

Cincinnati, Ohio; February, 1987.

SID KING

I was raised in Denton, Texas, where I got started on live radio. I played the guitar and sang. Then a fellow I knew in high school invited me up to his radio show, and I got to be a regular. Somehow, me and Mel Robinson, one of my players, ended up with the show on KDNT Radio. Then we brought in my brother, Billy King, as a guitarist, and we kept adding people. All we had was guitar players! That was 1952. The thirty-minute radio show gave us a showcase, but we inherited the name of the original band, The Western Melody Makers, which I personally never did like all that much. One day we were sent up to Beaumont by Starday Records to cut a song called "Who Put The Turtle In Myrtle's Girdle?" We cut in on an Ampex recorder in a living room of a house that was a studio. There was truck stop or something next door, and I went over and sat down and ordered a cup of coffee. A guy turned to me and said, "Are you fellows recording too? My name is George Jones." Anyhow, we didn't like the quality of the tape, and we went to Jim Beck's studio in Dallas to recut the song. It finally came out on Starday, and airplay was good on it, but not sales. Our association with Beck led us to a contract with Columbia Records. Don Law, the producer, knew Jim. In fact, if Jim had lived, I think the Nashville sound might have started in Dallas, because Don Law helped get it started in Nashville. After we got the contract, we changed our name to The Five Strings. We continued to do most of our recording in Beck's studio. When he died in '57, we started recording in California and other places. We cut "Gonna Shake This Shack Tonight" and "It's True I'm Blue" and others. The records just kept coming. Our band had roots in country, like the other performers from Texas did, but we were also influenced a lot by black music. We did some group vocals, too. Somebody told me we were the first rockabilly band in Texas, and that's probably true. At club dates, you couldn't play much rockabilly, unless you had a teenage crowd. The older people wanted you to turn the music down. We stayed on Columbia until '58, then I went to Dot Records as a solo artist and Billy went to California to play in groups there. By '65, I had gotten out of the business completely. There weren't that many people making rockabilly records then, and if

Above, top: Sid King, 1960; bottom, Cotton Club, 1955, Lubbock, Texas. Left to right: Billy King, lead guitar; Dave White, drums; Sid King, vocals and guitar; Ken Massey, bass; Mel Robinson, steel.

you didn't have a label behind you, you couldn't keep yourself current and popular. So I got into the hair-styling business. I had a family to support, and I thought the work was steady. At first, I played a little on the side. We never did do straight country, though. I had two black guys in my band. We had an organ added to the group by then. After a little while, though, I quit. I stuck to the hair-styling business. Lately, I find that there's a demand again for my kind of music. I don't know *exactly* what that is because we were always doing all kinds of music — rockabilly, R&B, country. All kinds of stuff. We were never exclusively rockabilly, yet we were a rockabilly band, I suppose. We were different.

Dallas, Texas; August, 1987.

SLEEPY LaBEEF

I've been doing it since it all started, since I was fourteen years old. Of course, I didn't have a Col. Tom Parker to manage me, or the good looks. But I played. The years passed, too. Somebody said to me, "Sleepy, how do you feel inside?" The others have made it, he meant. I told him this: "You really can't measure success or failure by the size of your bank account." To me, I'm successful. I love what I'm doing. I do 300 shows a year. I'm always on the road. Music has been good to me and my family because it has enabled me to do something for a living and have fun at the same time. I have not had any chart-busting records, but my music attracts an audience. I started playing guitar there in Holiness Church in Smackover, Arkansas, and at eighteen I went to Beaumont, Texas, to play for gospel shows. After three months I went to Houston to perform on the Houston Jamboree. That's when Elvis began to come by and we did a few things. They all came through: Carl Perkins, Buddy Holly, all of them. I recorded "Tore Up" in 1959. Earlier, I had recorded for Starday. The company insisted on original material. At times the artists would record a lot of sound-alike stuff in the Goldstar Studios — stuff that sounded like Elvis, Hank Williams, Hank Snow, Johnny Cash. We'd get $10 a day for doing it. Then the label would lease it to XERF Radio in Del Rio, Texas. The station would then sell records over the air. They didn't tell you it was a sound-alike, of course. Starday wasn't Sun Records, but it was great experience for me. I don't regret my association with them. When I first learned to play, you see, I did so because I loved it. I went out and traded a .22 rifle for a guitar. I must have had a lot of help from The Creator, too. You cultivate a talent and you sustain it. I'm just thankful that money wasn't the only thing on my mind.

On the road from Saco, Maine; June, 1987.

THE HILLBILLY TWIST

About 1963 I had just opened up a recording studio and Alley Records in Jonesboro, Arkansas. Bobby Lee Trammell came around and played me a few tunes, including "Arkansas Twist" and "It's All Your Fault." The record we eventually cut turned out to be a two-sided hit for us. At least a hit in that we were selling a lot of records. "Twist" was nothing but a rockabilly twist song and one of the last of the twist records. "It's All Your Fault" was a slow blues thing. I produced both of them and took the tapes to Memphis one day to be mastered by Scotty Moore at Sam Phillips' recording studio. You see, Bobby and I intended to press only about 300, to be mainly used as a tool to book him. Well, on the way back home that day, I stopped to see a jukebox man that I knew. He asked to hear the record. When it finished playing, he said, "I'll take 300 of them, please." I said, "But it's not even pressed yet." He said, "Just give me 300 and come on up to a meeting of the jukebox association members tonight. You can have dinner and play your record." I did just that, and they loved the record. They ordered 3,300 copies! So all in one day, I got a master cut, a steak dinner, and orders for a record that I hadn't even pressed yet. When we did press it, the record sold like crazy, too. People loved it. Both sides. The funny thing is, when we cut "It's All Your Fault," I told Bobby, "This is not going to sell because I can understand the words." I took him across the street to the drugstore and bought two packs of Doublemint gum and he crammed the sticks in his mouth and cut the vocal. That's how we got that "special sound."

—Joe Lee, record producer. Jonesboro, Arkansas, July, 1987.

Joe Lee, early 1960s.

Vic McAlpin and me wrote "I Got A Rocket In My Pocket" coming back from the Louisiana Hayride in Shreveport one day in 1958. Somewhere between Shreveport and Nashville, Vic, who also managed me, started saying something about the rocket age and rock 'n' roll. Then, somebody — must have been Vic — came up with the title to the song. Of course, we had to tone it down a little. Too risque. I cut the song for Roulette Records under the name Jimmy Lloyd because I was already recording country music as Jimmy Logsdon. Back then, rock music was not so readily accepted by everybody, you see, and I thought I'd better have the two names. Besides, I was cutting for Decca as a pure country artist. Anyway, "Rocket" took off to number one in Memphis and the Louisiana area, knocking off Jerry Lee Lewis on his own turf. I think it finally sold all of 50,000 copies. Looking back on the rockabilly thing, though, I'm kind of glad that it didn't happen for me. All I can remember is being on television in Memphis, and having to lip-sync "Where The Rio Del Rosa Flows," the record that I had out on Roulette before "Rocket." The kids were screaming. I was nervous. I was in pretty good shape then for a guy in his thirties, but all I could think was: What am I *doing* here? Can you imagine me with a hit record as a rocker? They would have had to wheel me out as the oldest living rocker. That's one reason why my rockabilly career was rather short. I decided to stay country. What's interesting is that today few people remember my country records, but many people have heard of "Rocket." Did you know, for instance, that they used the record in the movie *The Right Stuff*? Yeah, they sure did. That's me singing. Oh, and I'm still waiting for my royalty check, too.

Louisville, Kentucky; November, 1986.

Jimmy Lloyd, late 1950s.

CARL MANN

I started singing in my church as a boy in Huntington, Tennessee, and later I had a little show on the radio in Jackson every Saturday. Later, some friends got a band together with me and we played in the local schools. About two or three years later I met a fellow who had a local label called Jaxon Records, and I cut a single on one of my songs, "Rockin' Love." That was in 1956, I believe. The flip side was, "Gonna Rock 'n' Roll Tonight." So I started a new band with a guitar player named Eddie Bush. We called ourselves the Kool Kats. We toured the South. I had the pleasure of meeting drummer W.S. Holland, who had worked with Carl Perkins, and W.S. got me an audition over at Sun. I got to cut a record on the song "Mona Lisa" without ever seeing Sam Phillips. There's an interesting story here. While I was in the studio recording that song, Conway Twitty stopped in. He liked the song. At the time, though, I had not actually signed a contract with Sun. Anyway, W.S. told me a few weeks later that he had heard Conway tell Ronnie Hawkins that "Mona Lisa" was going to be on the next Twitty session, which was coming up soon. And he did cut it in Nashville, too, and in the same style as my record. Well, I got on the telephone and told Mr. Phillips about all this. He asked me how fast I could get over to his office to sign a contract. I said, "Right *now*." So my record was released a short time later on Phillips International Records. It got a lot of play locally, and in a few months it caught on nationally. June, '59. Later, I recut "Rockin'

Love." We did it on the order of an Elvis song, with two tempos. I went into the service in '64, but the music still interested me so I recorded "Serenade Of The Bells" and "Down To My Last I Forgive You" for Monument Records. But the style of music had changed, and I sort of drifted away from it all. I started writing more, and in '74 I got a contract with ABC Records and did four singles, all country. I had a few that charted, but none stayed around long enough to do any good. I always did enjoy country music a lot, and most of my '50s stuff leaned toward country. Of course, when Elvis came out with his hot records, everybody around here tried the same thing. I liked rockabilly, and I tried to develop my own rockabilly style. Lately, I've done some recording for European labels. I plan on doing some more, too. Once this business gets into your blood, you just can't get rid of it.

Huntington, Tennessee; July, 1987.

Carl Mann, center, with guitar, and the Jimmie Martin band. 1950s.

Potpourri of a career: The fan club and all — early 1960s.

Attention! Carl Mann in the U.S. Army, about 1964.
Below, Mann's first publicity photo, circa 1959.

CARL MANN   Exclusive recording artist for Phillips International Records

CARL McVOY

In the fall of 1958, a group of us musicians went from Memphis to Nashville to cut four songs: "You Are My Sunshine," "Tootsie," "Little John's Gone" and "Daydreaming." We cut them at the old RCA studio, with Chet Atkins playing guitar and the Anita Kerr Singers doing background voices. I sang. That three-hour session was the beginning of our company, Hi Records of Memphis, a label that eventually went on to do well for us. But, in 1958, we needed cash. Although "Tootsie" got some good play for us in some parts of the country, it wasn't a big hit and we needed the money. So I sold myself to Sam Phillips' company over at Sun. The money helped our label, which had expanded too fast, but, looking back on my decision to join the Sun label, well, I really didn't help myself as an artist any. I finally went back on Hi. You know, I never did want to get into the recording business anyway. It just happened. Entertaining was never my bag. At the time, my brothers and I owned a construction business, and I played music at VFW halls on Saturday nights to supplement my income. Played by myself. Well, I slowly added a drummer and other guys. A band. Then, the record that I cut started our label. I got so involved with production that I stopped playing my own music. This is odd, I suppose, coming from a guy whose family is filled with entertainers and preachers. (Jerry Lee Lewis and The Rev. Jimmy Swaggart are first cousins; Mickey Gilley is a second cousin. — The Author.) I was born in Louisiana but moved to Pine Bluff, Arkansas, at an early age. I played in the school band and listened to mostly big band stuff. Not country music. In fact, I first got into country in Brooklyn, New York, of all places, when I was only fifteen. My father had taken our family there to live, and I met some people who played country. I joined a band there and, later, after I had moved to Memphis, I played country and rockabilly. My career turned out to be mainly in publishing and producing, though. I am proud of "Haunted House," a record I produced for Hi by Jumpin' Gene Simmons. You know, I originally wanted to cut it for Sam the Sham, but he wouldn't hear of it. He thought our label wasn't big enough then. So one day Gene walked into the studio and I said to him, "Gene, I'm going to make you some *money*." And, I did.

Memphis, Tennessee; October, 1986

DOUG POINDEXTER

I learned to play the guitar when I was a kid growing up in Vanndale, Arkansas, but I didn't do anything much with it until I got into high school. I came to Memphis about 1945, when I was seventeen years old, to go to work for a baking company. That was my first real job. I played music on the side then. Somehow, I met Scotty Moore, a guitar player, and Bill Black, a bass player, and we started playing what most people called hillbilly music. Must have been about 1950. We played around Memphis as Doug Poindexter and the Starlite Wranglers. I remember we were sitting around one night, and somebody came up with that name. Had sort of a nice sound to it. We went looking for a record contract after a time. I knew a fellow who worked as a distributor for MGM Records, and he sent us over to Sam Phillips' studio. Sam auditioned us. He didn't know what he was looking for at the time, about '53 or '54, but when he heard us, we started turning his wheels. We had something — I don't know just what — that got him going. That was, let's see, April of 1954. I've lost track of the time. I know we went into the studio and recorded a song called "Now She Cares No More" and a song that Scotty and I wrote called "My Kind Of Carryin' On." We cut both of them with members of the Wranglers, all six of them, and I played rhythm guitar, as usual. When the record came out, it did all right regionally. There were few places to get airplay for such a record in those days, but there were a few areas the record would have gone big in if we could have pushed it more. People were sort of tired of country music then, and they were looking for something else. They had heard the same old stuff for so long. They wanted something fresh. Country had sort of peaked, with the death of Hank Williams, so here we come with this wild country thing. I went to Nashville to promote the record and when I was gone, Scotty and Bill went in and recorded with Sam's new artist, Elvis Presley. They tried to run me down in Nashville, but they couldn't find me. They wanted me to help play on the sessions. But really, I had gotten to the point where I had to make a choice. I could stay in music or get out. I decided to get out. Somehow I knew that Scotty and Bill were the only guys in the group who could develop careers. I told them to go on to the Louisiana Hayride with Elvis. I got out of the business. I've never regretted my decision. I still like good country music, though. Yes, sir.
Memphis, Tennessee; June, 1987

GROOVEY JOE POOVEY

My neighbors came over the other night with a magazine. The story told about how most of the rockabillies never made it. They said, "Gee, Joe, it's such a shame that nothin' happened. Aren't you sad that you wasted your whole life?" Ha! I told 'em that it's probably best that not much happened. I've had a lot of fun. Seriously, I've always tried to stay active in the music business. I was a singer in the '50s and then I began my disc jockey career in '62. Did that till '84, when I got tired of radio and got into the union business as a Teamster organizer. I still perform and write songs, though. As a matter of fact, I'm playing this weekend. I'm from Dallas originally. I was on the "Big D Jamboree" in '53. Later, I played it some more, and I followed Presley on stage one night. Do you know what it was like to follow Elvis on stage in those early days? Well, it was tough. Anyway, Elvis performed and the crowd went wild over him. Those were his early days on Sun Records. Then, I went on stage. The 6,200 people weren't interested in anything but Elvis. His performance just *stunned* them. Anyway, I went on to meet a producer named Jim Shell, who got me hooked up with Starday's Dixie label. The company liked me so much that it paid for my releases, which it usually didn't do on its custom label, Dixie. I was just a hot kid around town then, and I was too scared to be bad. I recorded those rockabilly sides from the mid-'50s to about '58, I think. Cut "Movin' Around," "Ten Long Fingers," and others. I continued to sing and to write songs and I got into country music, where I had some chart records in the '60s. I've continued to write, and I think I compose some pretty good country songs. But there's too much politics in the music business these days. I always say that you'd better enjoy the music business, because you can't make a living in it. I've enjoyed it, though. I have no intention of quitting. Of course, I have no intention of being a star, either.

September, 1987; Dallas, Texas.

"When my first record came out in the mid-'50s, I took it to a radio station," Joe Poovey recalled. *"The disc jockey slapped it on a turntable, switched on a microphone, and said, 'Well, folks, here's the latest from a new artist, groovy Joe Poovey of Dallas.' The name sounded right somehow. It stuck with me...."*
— *Groovey Joe Poovey, September, 1987.*

Photo: Joe Poovey, 1987.

BOBBY RAMBO (AKA, JOHNNY ROBIN)

I've played with them all. I've played all kinds of music. I did my first road gig to Texarkana and Beaumont when I was seventeen. Before that, I played around Dallas as a rockabilly singer and guitarist – a *young* one at that. Man, I don't know where to start. In the early days, you see, Elvis and the rockabillies really stirred me. I started a little rockabilly band with my brother, me on guitar and my brother on upright bass. Played the Big D Jamboree on Saturday nights. I played with so many people – Carl Perkins, Warren Smith, and a lot of other artists – as a member of that little band, Gene Rambo & The Flames. When I was a little older I toured with Gene Vincent and Jerry Lee Lewis as a guitar player, worked in a band called The Casuals ("So Tough"), and picked for Scotty MacKay. Vincent came through Dallas one day, heard me, and signed me up. I was nineteen. Maybe younger. Gene was a *great* vocalist, an exciting performer on stage. We used to call him "Step 'n a Half," because of his limp. When I played with him, he was into so much, so much distraction, that he was not in top form. But still, the man was exciting. He was crazier than a bedbug, too. I mean, he used to get drunk and pull pistols out and fire them. We used to hide them because we were afraid he'd shoot us. He was *wild*. But he was hot, man, performance-wise. He'd bring down house. Gene wore a brace on his leg, but he moved and threw the mic around, got down on his knees. He was a singing son of a gun. He never really liked to play the guitar on stage, though. It was more or less a prop to him. He was just too wild to play all the time. Oh, yes, I've seen them *all*, or at least heard most of 'em. Like Cochran. Eddie was cut out of the Presley mold, real exciting to see on stage. Small guy, but with a lot of energy. He moved around more like Presley too, and played the guitar real well. He was a former session player, so you know he had to be good. My own playing was heavily influenced by several people. In those days, I was just a guitar player. Scotty Moore was my idol. Then I toured with Buddy Knox and Jerry Reed, and I copied Jerry's style a little bit. The days at the Big D seem so distant now. I remember Warren Smith. He was really only a country artist who crossed over. The D paid $150 a night. Smith came on first. I really wasn't that hot on him. He seemed a little arrogant and I didn't think he was that cool. He lacked the spark of a Vincent or Perkins. He was just riding the wave. I went on to sing and write and play. I was a player for the Five Americans and Jon & Robin and the In Crowd in the late '60s. Earlier, I recorded records in the '50s and early '60s – rockabilly records – as Johnny Robin and Bobby Rambo. They never amounted to anything. Jimmy Boyd even cut one of my songs. The funny thing is, in the early days we recorded in garages many times. Today, bands are trying to get that sound again.

Dallas, Texas; January, 1987.

HOT ROD CHARLIE

"Hot Rod Lincoln" by Charlie Ryan and the Timberline Riders of Spokane hit number fourteen on the country charts and number thirty-three on the pop charts in *Billboard* in 1960. The record was novelty rockabilly, with Charlie's accelerating vocal and an interesting steel guitar imitating sirens and speeding cars. Ryan had been recording his own version of rocking country music for more than a decade when the record hit the charts.

TONITE
CORRAL - 8:30
★ ★ ★ ★ ★
1st SHOW OF THE SEASON
STARRING
CHARLIE RYAN
and his Hot Rod Trio
and the
"HOT ROD LINCOLN"
★ "COUNTRY JOHNNY" ★
MATHIS
★ THE GAYS ★
Extra Added Attraction
SIMON CRUM
TICKETS NOW AT
HEINTZMAN'S
(Mezz. Floor)
AM 3-2050
ADULTS $2.00 & $1.75
KIDS $1.00

The first record of "Hot Rod Lincoln" that we made was done about 1955, but I had written the song as early as '47. I suppose that dates me a bit, doesn't it? The song sort of evolved between '47 and '50 as I was playing in Lewiston, Idaho. I was in all kind of bands, including the Timberline Riders and the Livingston Bros. The first record, released on my own Souvenir Records in the Spokane area, did all right for us. A guy had sort of threatened me with a little court action if I didn't record it for 4 Star Records. So we recut, and changed the name on the record from Charlie Ryan and The Livingston Bros. to Charlie Ryan and The Timberline Riders. The second record was about 1960. When I wrote the song, we were riding in a '41 Lincoln with a 12-cyclinder engine. I still have that car, too. Anyway, real incidents led to some of the things talked about in the song, although some had to be exaggerated for the song's sake. I was a country and rockabilly artist then. I did a country and rock thing for a long time, even in the early '50s. After the second record hit big, we changed the name of the band again, this time to the Hot Rodders. I've done it all. Fifty years of music. I'm still at it, too.

Spokane, Washington, May, 1987.

Show of Stars IN PERSON

THE MOST COLORFUL SHOW ON THE ROAD

JIM REEVES
RCA Victor recording star in "He'll Have to Go" "I'm Getting ___" "Four Walls" "Bimbo"

JOHNNY HORTON
Columbia Recording Star in "Sink The Bismarck" "Battle of New Orleans" "North To Alaska"

FERLIN HUSKY
Capitol Record Star in "Wings of a Dove"

SIMON CRUM
in "Country Music Is Here to Stay"
Country music's craziest character

CHARLIE RYAN
and the Hot Rod Trio Four Star Recording Artists in "Hot Rod Lincoln"
SEE THE CUSTOM BUILT HOT ROD LINCOLN ON DISPLAY
First Time in Canada

THE SENSATIONAL GAYS
Decca Recording Stars
Voted the most promising new vocal group of 1960

"COUNTRY" JOHNNY MATHIS
AND 3 BIG BANDS

Thursday, Sept. 15
SASKATOON ARENA
Reserved Seats
Adults $1.50 and $1.00
Children accompanied by parents 75c
TICKETS ON SALE NOW AT THE ARENA

PERFORMING NITELY

CHARLIE RYAN

AND THE "HOTRODDERS"

DIRECT FROM SUNNY CALIFORNIA

This Dynamic Country & Western Group are Stars of Stage & Clubs
Plus Recording Artists & Composers of the Popular "Hot Rod Lincoln"

AT THE

MALEMUTE

226 4th AVE.   NO COVER CHARGE

"SIDE CAR CYCLE" (2:48)   "LIKE NOTHIN', MAN" (2:27)
[Fowler, 4 Star BMI—Ryan, Stevenson]   [Red River, Golden West BMI—Bond, Howard]

JOHNNY BOND (Republic 2010)

Having shared action on Charlie Ryan's "Hot Rod Lincoln," Bond again figures to offer Ryan competition with "Side Car Cycle." It's a solid version and could figure in the final take. Also of strength is "Like Nothin', Man," an infectious ditty with a cute lyric.

Cash Box—December 24, 1960

RAY SCOTT

People ask me how I ever came up with the idea to write a song like "Flyin' Saucers Rock 'n' Roll." I tell them this: I *saw* one of those things. Near Indianapolis in '54, I saw something shaped like a big cigar. It was visible to others, too. That's when the flying saucer and UFO thing was in the news a lot, so I sat down and wrote a song about flying saucers and rock and roll. Now I didn't do it right away and I didn't write about exactly what I saw. I talked about little green men in the song, and, of course, I didn't see any of *those* fellas. I wrote a lot of songs back in the '50s. I could sit down and write a dozen songs in a day then, if I wanted to. I was raised in Bicknell, Indiana, and I left the area for twenty-eight years. I was in the service in World War Two and I met a girl from Memphis when I was stationed at the naval station there. We got married, so we lived there. In all, I lived around Memphis from about '54 to '70, give or take a few years before and after. I guess about '54 I went over to Sun Records because I only lived a few blocks away. I hung out there with the musicians. I was always basically a country singer myself. I'm still country. I do a Jerry Lee Lewis type of rockabilly, but I'm country. I've played music for over forty years and I never even studied it in school. I got serious about the music business when as a kid I bought a guitar. It's been downhill ever since. I used to work a factory job five days a week, then play music five nights a week in a club. I have done about everything there is to do in my life. The hardest thing, though, was playing on the road. Maybe you've heard of my old band, Ray Scott and the Demens. That stood for *demented*. We played all over the Memphis area. I had a vivid imagination then. About '57. We cut "You Drive Me Crazy" and had a good time. In time, though, I wanted to come home to

Indiana. In Memphis, the music people always thought of me as a writer first. I guess that was because I wrote so many songs for other people. It was something that I could never overcome. When I got to Indiana, I continued to perform. I've played every club within fifty miles of home. But I also got into other things. I own my own taxi company. I'm a house painter, too. I do all sorts of work. Every once in awhile, somebody contacts me about a record of mine that is doing well in Europe. I've had some of my old recordings released again on albums over there. One guy said he had searched for me for fifteen years. Isn't that something? Well, I'm still here in Indiana.

July, 1987; Sanborn, Indiana.

Although Ray Scott is probably best remembered as the composer of Billy Lee Riley's bizarre "Flyin' Saucers Rock 'n' Roll," Scott was also a popular entertainer around Memphis in the 1950s.

TROY SEALS

My roots run back to stone hillbilly, to growing up listening to the Grand Ole Opry on the radio in Kentucky. Our radio had dry-cell batteries and we played it once a week, on Saturday night. When I was still a boy we left Kentucky but not our music. By 1955 I was doing a little bluegrass on the radio in Hamilton, Ohio, where our father had moved the family to get a job. Faron Young, Carl Smith, Hank Snow — they were the big stars then, in the day of country and early rock 'n' roll music. Rock had yet to be discovered then in Hamilton, but that didn't take too long to happen, so we added drums to our bluegrass band. I guess you could say I was rockabilly. As soon as Elvis and Chuck Berry got real popular, we started picking up on that. Cincinnati and Dayton became known as top dancing towns, and if you didn't play dance music you didn't play. We were playing at a club called the Blacksmith Shop near Hamilton when Lonnie Mack merged his band with mine. We had Dumpy Rice on piano, Lonnie on guitar, and me on guitar. And other members I can't recall. I do recall that I used to rob Ray Pennington's band back then. I'd take his good players! Well, I knew Ray had good musicians. One night while playing at a local club called the Dude Ranch, I met Conway Twitty. He was still doing his rock thing then, in the late '50s, I suppose, and for some reason he liked me. I eventually signed with his manager and went to West Helena, Arkansas, to cut twelve sides with them. Not much happened, though. By the early '60s my wife, JoAnn Campbell, and I had gotten into the R&B thing with some success. Horns, the whole thing. Isn't this business one to come full circle? Now I'm writing country songs in Nashville and loving every minute of it.

Nashville, Tennessee; July, 1985

Troy Seals wrote "Boogie Woogie Country Man" by Sleepy LaBeef and numerous country hits.

PHOTO BY RANDY McNUTT

RAY SHARPE

When I wrote "Linda Lu" back in the 1950s, I didn't think much of it. I had no idea that it would someday do something. A buddy of mine named Mike had asked me to write a song about his girlfriend, Linda, who used to come into the club to dance. Mike and Linda were on the outs at the time. I wrote the song to rib her a little bit. You see, she had a fascinating rear end, so to speak. When she danced, people watched. Well, I wrote the song and didn't pay too much attention after singing it in the club. Then in the winter of 1958 I went over to Audio Sounds recording studio to make a record with Duane Eddy's band backing me up. My producer, Lee Hazlewood, asked me if I had one more song to make four, and I was stuck. So I started playing "Linda Lu" for him. We cut it. When the record came out in the spring of '59, the A-side, "Red Sails In The Sunset," started getting some airplay, but the people at Jamie Records weren't satisfied. Somebody in L.A. turned the record over and "Linda Lu" broke out. I think the reason was because it's a catchy tune with good riffs. Every dude and his brother can do it. It's easy to play and sing. The repetition of the words is a nice gimmick too. The song was popular in the clubs because of the funky blues beat, and popular on the radio because folks thought a nice white boy was singing it. In fact, the most significant thing about that record to me was that so many people thought I was white. It's just that I had always wanted to sing the blues and hillbilly music, but nobody would let me sing hillbilly because I was black. So I mixed a little country stuff in with my blues. I'm still singing them, too.

Forth Worth, Texas; March, 1987.

MACY "SKIP" SKIPPER

I'm a *Memphis* man. The only difference between me and Jerry Lee Lewis and all those other guys is that I worked for a living and did my music on the side. That is the difference, see. I hung around Sun in the mid-'50s, and I cut a lot of stuff. Take after take. I wrote songs — good songs. I wrote "Who Put The Squeeze On Eliose?" I wrote "Bop Pills." I could and I still can turn out a tune a day. I have the talent that the writers had in the '40s and '50s. The songs just fell out of my mind. But it's a dumb business. I couldn't tell you how many hours I put in on these tapes and songs. Now I am sixty-seven years old and all this seems so trivial to me. Unless, of course, somebody wants to pay me for my trouble. I'm not going to work for nothing. That don't mean a thing to me. I'm retired from the federal government and I make sufficient money to live comfortably. I don't need this kind of business where nobody gets paid for a session! As far as I'm concerned, the music business is dead. Hear me? I'm not going to bother with it, either. I wouldn't send you a picture if I had it. You tell all those people to spin those records till they wear out, 'cause I don't care. It's a dumb business no doubt. I'd like to get paid for my trouble.

Memphis, Tennessee, September, 1987.

HAYDEN THOMPSON

I came from Booneville, Mississippi, to Memphis after getting bit by the music bug early in life. Right out of high school in 1956 I traveled with the Dixie Jazzlanders. We played at hometown theaters with the movie *Rock Around The Clock*. Then I started hanging around Sun Records and eventually recorded such songs as "Blues, Blues, Blues," "Mama, Mama, Mama," and "Fairlane Rock." I started singing country music, and when Elvis came out he was a big influence on me. I remember one time in '54 I put some rock into a tune and the band like to killed me for doing it. The players said rock 'n' roll wouldn't last. Well, so much for that. I thought Elvis was the greatest. I wrote a tribute to him a few years ago, "The Boy Tupelo," on my album called "The Booneville, Mississippi, Flash." You know, I only cut seven songs for Sun Records, but you'd think I cut seven million selling ones. I sure got a lot of mileage out of Sun. I've had more attention paid to me because of Sun in the last couple of years than I had in the last thirty. I left Sun and Memphis in early '58 and came to Chicago to work the clubs and record for some small labels. That went nowhere. I got away from recording. Then in '65 country music got popular in Chicago and I worked some more. I signed with Kapp Records and recorded three singles and an album in Nashville. Since then, I've recorded a little and worked the local joints. Nothing really ever caught on for me, though. In '76, I just got tired of it all and hung up the guitar and called it quits. Or so I thought. By '84 the rockabilly thing was going crazy in Europe, and I went over there on tour and recorded more records. It has been just great. Now, this is 1987 and I'm 49 years old. I'd love to be able to play my music full-time. I've driven a limousine for the last twelve years and I've been able to be with my family. So I don't need a million dollars or a big house. I'm too old to dream. But I would like to perform full-time. If I don't ever get to do it, I won't care. This

career has been fun. People tell me to get on a revival show, but I tell them that I never even had a hit. The people enjoy my music, however, and I enjoy playing it. So I will. I guess I just don't know when to quit.
Highland Park, Illinois; May, 1987.

Phillips International Records Presents. . .Hayden Thompson.

Phillips International publicity photograph from the heyday of Hayden Thompson – the 1950s.

Rockin' Hayden Thompson in the Memphis area in the mid-1950s, with Roland Janes on the guitar, far right. Notice the hairstyles of the young audience.

BOBBY LEE TRAMMELL

I haven't done much performing in the United States in the last ten years, but I have toured Europe. For so many years I couldn't understand why people would like a country boy like me. I had always sung in church, understand. Then suddenly people are lining up to hear me sing my songs. I got started a little later than most of the other rockabilly artists. Sam Phillips of Sun Records was going to sign me, though. He told me to wait a few months because he was going to record me. And I, being just a kid, told Sam Phillips that I didn't have time. Can you imagine somebody saying that to him? So I went out to sunny California and got signed out there. That was in 1960. I got a job out there with a Ford Motor Co. plant and was making good money. A man named Fabor Robinson, a big promoter, heard me and asked me to sign up with him. I went out to his big house and played him "Shirley Lee" and a few other songs, and we cut them right there in the studio he operated in that house. I remember that Bob Luman's band played on those sessions, with guitar player James Burton, too. The "Shirley Lee" record came out, and in a month I was appearing on the Grand Ole Opry, Louisiana Hayride and many television shows. Robinson had the pull to get me on those programs and shows. I traveled all around, and got banned and thrown off of a few shows. I was pretty wild as a performer back then. But I didn't drink or take drugs. I never did any of that. By 1963 I was back in my hometown, Jonesboro, Arkansas, and I recorded the "Arkansas Twist." I owned 50% of that record. I wondered about what it would do because I thought it was the worst record I had ever cut. I couldn't believe it when the record was a hit. I made a lot of money on it, selling it out of the back of my car! The pressing plant was busy day and night. Those days are gone now. I believe an artist has ten good years, if he's lucky. I'm involved in real estate today and enjoying that work. I still record about two albums a year. I still have a good time in the record business, but, hey, I'm not a teenager anymore. I've had my shot. I recorded so many records, I can't remember how many. I had fun, too.

Jonesboro, Arkansas; July, 1987.

MARCUS VAN STORY

I was the bass player. I came from Corinth, Mississippi, where my family taught me music. I never took a lesson, though. When I was a kid, we moved to Grenada, and the family eventually got to be on a local radio program. When it was over, we'd go back to the farm to work. I went to Memphis to live after I got out of the Army. I wanted to make it in the music world. I joined Sam Phillips as a staff musician at Sun Records in 1953. I played the bull fiddle – the upright bass. I was once voted the King of the Slap Bass. They called it slap, you see, because there weren't many drums on records and stuff then, and the bass players had to *slap*, man. Later, singer Warren Smith said he liked my playing and he asked me to form a band for him. So I did: myself on bass, Al Hobson on guitar, and Jimmie Lott on drums. The band played all over. The crowds used to go *wild*. The reaction was unbelievable – people wigglin', jumpin', dancin'. We used to tour with Carl Perkins, Roy Orbison, Johnny Cash and other artists, and one night we warned Carl that he'd better watch out for the crowds, 'cause they were particularly eager. If they ever got ahold of you, well, your clothes would come *off*. Well, out on stage goes old Carl, getting a little too close to the edge. The first thing you know, he's standing there in his pants! They ripped his jacket and shirt off. Those days were crazy. I remember you could book a country show and hardly anybody would show up. Book a rock 'n' roll show, though, and half the country would be there. Naturally, the country artists were somewhat upset about this situation. So they looked down their noses at the rock singers for a long time. That was a long time ago, but rockabilly music is coming back strong and I'm amazed. I know it is popular because I'm still playing that music. We get a great reaction. I always heard that history repeats itself, but this is too much. This time, the sidemen are benefiting. People know who we are. I enjoy every minute of it. I'm doing just what I did in the '50s – getting up on stage, having a good time, and letting my hair down.

Memphis, Tennessee; October, 1987.

Marcus Van Story (left), with Al Hobson and Warren Smith, far right. From 1956. Courtesy Marcus Van Story.

BILL WATKINS

Nobody knew much about me until a record collector put out an album of local rockabilly music in 1978. Suddenly I got offers from Europe to release some of my old tapes. When I cut them in the 1950s, I didn't push real hard. In fact, I had only one release, on the Lucky label in Cincinnati, called "Mess At The Workhouse" backed with "Time Will Make You Pay." I had a lot of fun with that one record, but I never made much money from it. All I wanted to do was make music anyway. Growing up in Corbin, Kentucky, I picked up a guitar and started playing. I never did take lessons. Then I went into the service and, when I got out, I headed up to Cincinnati to get a job. At night I played in the clubs. We played fast country music in 1953, and in a couple of years it got tagged "rockabilly." I recorded for Lucky in '57. I also cut other songs that were not released: "Red Cadillac" and "Big Guitar." Then twenty years later, people seem interested in them. I'm satisfied. Roy Acuff cut "Time Will Make You Pay" in 1961. I've kept my job, I've written songs. That's what I really enjoy — the songs.

Cincinnati, Ohio; October, 1987.

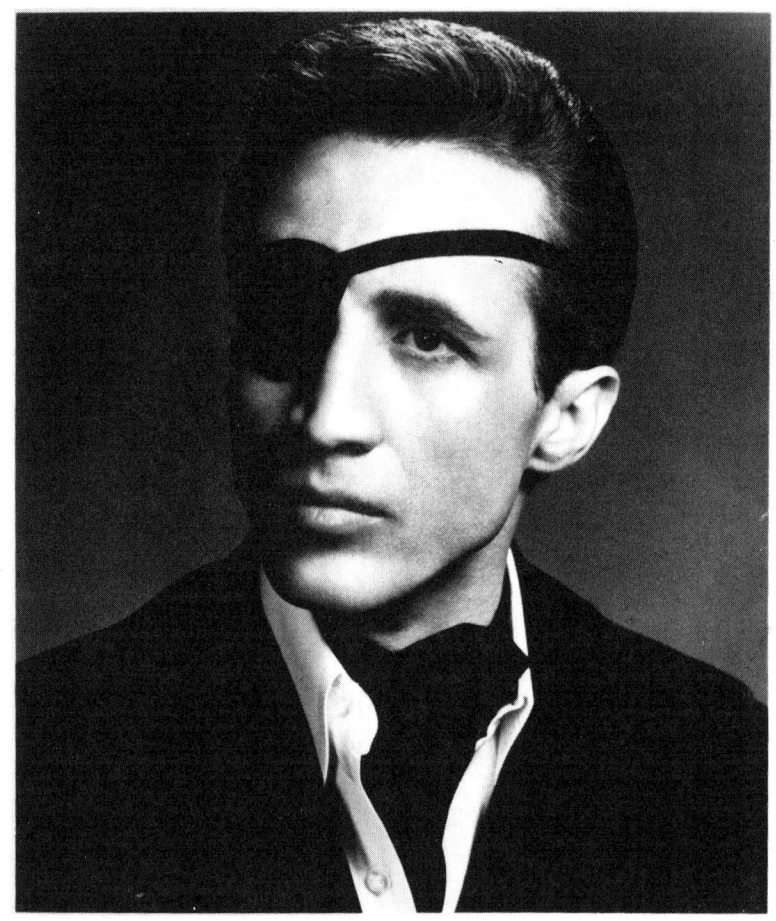

BOBBY WOOD

I grew up in Inogmar, Mississippi, a wide place in the road with a high school, a store and that's about it. I was raised on a cotton farm. As a boy, I didn't like country music. My family sang gospel, and black spirituals in the fields. A lot of the early rockabilly performers did the same. Jerry Lee Lewis, Elvis — their roots were in the church, too. Me, I was a Jerry Lee Lewis imitator in the late '50s. I was practically the guy's double. He was my idol. When I finally got some direction musically, though, the record company man said, "Bobby, we've already got one Jerry Lee Lewis in the world, and I don't think there's room for two." So I started doing my own thing with music, and, in high school, I even wanted to be an actor. An actor! I never did quite make it out to Hollywood. But, who knows? I did make it the 85 miles to Memphis, though, and I met Stan Kesler, who had written some songs for Elvis. Stan had a little studio at that time, in the early '60s, and I cut something called "The Day After Forever." The second record we did was a song he had written called "If I'm A Fool For Loving You," which I believe we recorded over at the Sun studio. I had recorded for Sun earlier, I know,

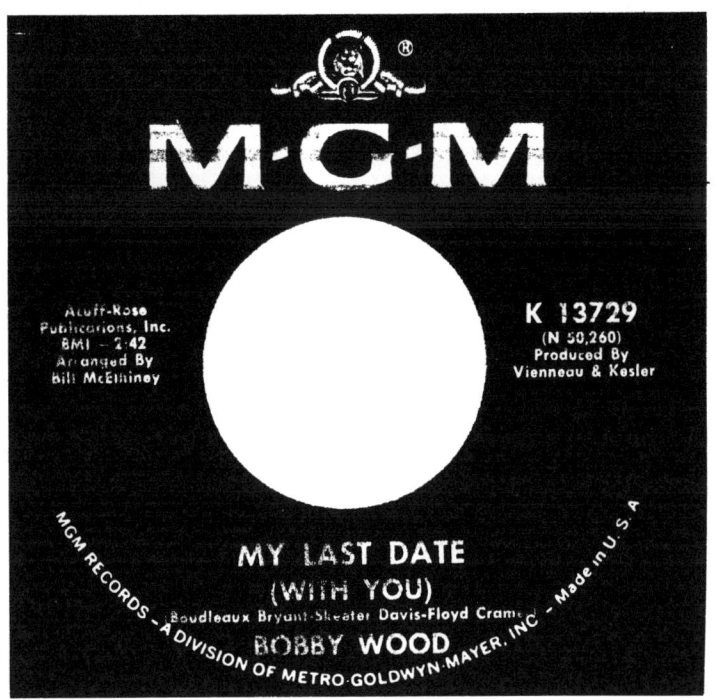

but Stan shopped the new master around and we finally got some interest over at a little label named Joy Records. "Fool" ended up doing pretty well, too. Got up in the 70s nationally, I believe, and at the top of many local charts. It was a regional hit a little at a time, hanging on for six months. The kids went crazy over it. Although the record had no promotion to speak of, it went from city to city, hitting high on the local charts wherever it went. When I left Joy, I went over to MGM Records, and those people put out "Break My Mind" and "Last Date," among others. But I still got little promotion. I did get to tour some with the Beach Boys and Jan and Dean, but I had an automobile accident in Ohio and got injured. I was out of it for six months. That just about did it for me. I never did like the road anyway, and I was enjoying playing on recording sessions about that time. So after the accident I just decided to hang it up as a vocalist. It proved to be a good decision because in the late '60s I was fortunate enough to get into the session thing strong with producer Chips Moman in Memphis at the American Studios. Chips wanted to put together a section of the best players he would find. I had played on "Little Red Riding Hood" by Sam the Sham and "Mr. Bojangles" by Jerry Jeff Walker. Then I played on many hits, including "The Eyes Of A New York Woman" and "Hooked On A Feeling" by B.J. Thomas, Neil Diamond's Memphis stuff, the album "Dusty In Memphis," and so many other big records. I haven't sang much ever since. In fact, the closest I came was when I wrote "Talking In Your Sleep" with Roger Cook. Roger and I fooled around and spent $5,000 on the demo, which I sang. He even put strings on it. Suddenly RCA heard it and sent me a contract. They wanted to release the demo as a record. I got to looking at the contract, though, with all that was involved with it, including appearances, and I said, "Now *wait* a minute." Then I heard that Crystal Gayle was cutting the song. I said to Roger, "Now that's the way it *should* be." Just let me play the piano.

Nashville, Tennessee; February, 1987.

Photograph: Bobby Wood during his MGM days in the mid-'60s.

DALE WRIGHT

In the mid-'50s I was a teenage disc jockey on WING in Dayton, Ohio. I worked there all during school. I once met a pretty blonde girl at a swimming pool from which we were broadcasting one day, and she said she had some friends who wanted to organize a band. I thought about it and later decided to help them. I had won contests singing classical music as a boy, so singing wasn't foreign to me. One night, during the late hours when I was on the air, we were running some long religious program and I had time to think. I sat down and wrote a song called "Walk With Me," about polio, because I was to do my first telethon in Dayton the next Sunday. I was only sixteen and scared to death, so I asked the band to go on the air with me and play. That way, I thought, I wouldn't have to talk. The band agreed to do it, so we recorded the song. We went on television and the kids went crazy. They tried to rip my clothes off. Girls brought bras back stage for me to autograph. A few days later, Harry Carlson of Fraternity Records in Cincinnati called and said, "Dale, I heard that you nearly caused a riot the other night." He asked me if I wanted to record the song for Fraternity, and I said, "But Mr. Carlson, it's a song about *polio*." Then he suggested that I change the lyrics to "walk with me down the aisle," and I did. The record eventually came out, and the band, the Rock Its, traveled around the area with me, playing at hops and other events. We sold 800 records at a Dayton record store in one day. That wasn't an uncommon thing in the '50s, if you had a hot record. In Lexington, Kentucky, where I've had a radio talk show for the last 17 years, the girls tore off our clothes. They stole my shoelaces, too. Later, we decided to try a second record, a song of mine that we had cut as a dub at the station. It was called "She's Neat." I took it to Mr. Carlson and he conferred with some people. "Dale," he said, taking me into his office, "that is the worst record anybody has ever brought in here." I told him "She's Neat" was a good song, though, and he finally let us rerecord it at the old King studio in Cincinnati. Mr. Carlson hated it anyway. He waited months to release it. Then, in late 1956, I believe, he sent the records out in the mail, hoping they would somehow get ignored by the radio people with all the new Christmas records coming out. I know that sounds odd, but that's the kind of guy he was. He said he would put our record out, and he was going to keep his word, even if he disliked

Dale Wright on the air as a high school disc jockey.

the record. To his surprise, though, it started hitting in St. Louis and other cities. Mr. Carlson couldn't believe what was happening. Neither could my band, the Wright Guys, who were listed as the Rock Its on the record. The Rock Its were replaced because they didn't want to join the musicians' union. They were really into country music, and I liked a lot of black music, especially Little Richard and Chuck Berry. I guess the sound came through, sort of a soulful rockabilly. On "She's Neat," we used an upright bass, but the bass lines recorded weakly, so Mr. Carlson took the tape to Nashville and overdubbed an electric bass with Elvis Presley's bass player. I've always regretted that decision. The sound was changed. I went on to cut fifteen records, and every one reached number one in some market. If I had had the money and proper backing I could have made it bigger, but all I had was a lot of friends with good taste and ideas. And, oh, incidentally: with my royalties from "She's Neat," I accompanied Mr. Carlson to a Cincinnati car dealership and bought the car of my dreams — a light blue Corvette, like the one driven on the television show *Route 66*. Yes, I certainly had a good time.

Nicholasville, Kentucky; October, 1986

Dale Wright, about 1964.

Left: publicity photograph of Dale Wright, from about 1960. Bottom: Wright in his Corvette, purchased with a royalty check.

Fraternity Records publicity photo of Dale Wright, late 1950s.

HE STILL WANTS TO
Rock Old Sputnik To

The
MOON

NELSON YOUNG

One afternoon in 1957, I was driving from Cincinnati to Hamilton, Ohio, to play at a club called the Blacksmith Shop. The announcer had been saying all day how the Russians had launched the first satellite, the Sputnik, and I guess my mind must have been on that event because I pulled over and starting writing a song – "Rock Ole Sputnik To The Moon." By the time I reached the club, I had the song finished, and we played it that day. Three weeks later, I cut the song for Lucky Records of Cincinnati, and I pushed the record all the way to Nashville, where I appeared on the Ralph Emory Show. I just can't believe all the attention that little record gets today. It wasn't a hit, as

Nelson Young and the Sandy Valley Boys on the set of a WKRC-TV show, 1960: Nelson Young, Don Boone, Danny Burton, Junior Boyer, Leon Boyer, Jim Wade, and Teddy (Bear) Brown. Portrait photograph of Nelson Young on previous page is from 1957, the year of "Rock Ole Sputnik To The Moon." Photographs courtesy Nelson Young.

hits go, but it was the first record about a satellite. We cut the song in the Rite Recording studio in Cincinnati. I played rhythm guitar on the session. In those days, our band, Nelson Young and the Sandy Valley Boys, played a little of everything — country, bluegrass — you name it. Then, when Elvis arrived in the mid-'50s, and, later, Carl Perkins and Jerry Lee Lewis, we had to add rockabilly. We had a ten-piece band. We were on television on *Cornhuskers Jamboree* on WCPO-TV, and, later, on other shows. We got all kinds of nightclub work then, so we split into various groups so we could get even more work. I finally took the band to Orlando, Florida, in 1963, and we eventually worked at Disney World. I've lived in the hills of North Carolina now for a few years, and I love it. I'm in my forty-third year in show business.

Grover, North Carolina; November, 1986

Nelson Young and the Sandy Valley Boys, 1960: (first row, left to right) Jay J. Johnson, Kathy Wood, Texas Slim; Jim Fee, Nelson Young, Herman Cress, and George Robinson. Young played fiddle and guitar in this band.

Bibliography

Dellar, Fred, and Thompson, Ray, *The Illustrated Encyclopedia of Country Music* (New York: Harmony Books, 1977)

Tobler, John, *The Buddy Holly Story* (New York: Beaufort Books, 1979)

Broven, John, *Rhythm and Blues In New Orleans* (Pelican Books: Gretna, 1978)

Muirhead, Bert, *The Record Producers File* (Dorset, England: Blandford Press, 1984)

Nash, Bruce M., *Whatever Happened To Blue Suede Shoes?* (New York: Grosset & Dunlap, 1978)

Greil, Marcus, *Mystery Train: Images of America in Rock 'n' Roll Music* (New York: E.P. Dutton & Co., 1976)

Hershey, Gerri, *Nowhere To Run: The Story of Soul Music* (New York: Penguin Books, 1985)

O'Shea, Shad, *Just For The Record* (Cincinnati: Positive Feedback Communications Press, 1986)

Shaw, Arnold, *The Rockin Fifties* (New York: Hawthorn Books, Inc., 1974)

Lydon, Michael, *Boogie Lightning* (New York: The Dial Press, 1974)

Index

A

Atkins, Chet, 47, 51
Avalon, Frankie, 12

B

Ballard, Hank, 66
Bare, Bobby, 204
Beatles, 25, 192
Belew, Carl, 32
Bennett, Boyd, 65, 72, 74-75
Bennett, Joe, 181
Black, Bill, 21, 77, 254
Blackboard Jungle, 20
Bland, Bobby, 52
Bond, Eddie, 205-206
Bowen, Jimmy, 26, 171, 177
Bradley, Owen, 47, 208
Brians, Robin Hood, 207-208
Brown, Roy, 20
Bruce, Edwin, 52
Burgess, Sonny, 209-212
Burlison, Paul, 213-214

C

Campbell, Cecil, 32
Campi, Ray, 12, 215-216
Carlisles, The, 66
Carlson, Harry, 204, 208
Cartey, Ric, 175
Carroll, Johnny, 217-218
Cash, Johnny, 32, 52, 155
Channel, Bruce, 65, 219
Chapel, Jean, 55, 190, 200
Clark, Dick, 12, 132
Clark, Roy, 180
Clay, Joe, 220-221
Clement, Jack, 53
Cochran, Eddie, 98, 167
Collins Kids, 178
Copas, Cowboy, 10, 32, 66, 119-124
Country boogie, 14
Craddock, Billy "Crash," 183-184
Crudup, Arthur, 21, 78
Curtis, Mac, 65, 222-225
Curtis, Sonny, 226-228

D

Daily, Pappy, 68
Dalhart, Vernon, 46
DeKnight, Jimmy, 21
Delmore Brothers, 15, 20, 66
DeShannon, Jackie, 198
Dickens, Little Jimmy, 17, 32
Dominoes, 15
Donner, Ral, 171

E

Everly Brothers, 174

F

Fabian, 12
Feathers, Charlie, 24, 65, 71, 229
Felts, Narvel, 230-233
Foley, Red, 14, 47
Fontana, D.J., 21, 115-118
Ford, Tennessee Ernie, 17
Freedman, Max, 21
Frizzell, Lefty, 20, 125
Fuller, Jerry, 26

G

Glenn, Glen, 235
Gilley, Mickey, 34
Gracie, Charlie, 172
Gunter, Sidney, 14-15

H

Haley, Bill, and Comets, 17, 20-21
Hamilton, George, IV, 166
Handy, W.C., 48
Harris, Wynonie, 20
Hart, Freddie, 32
Hawkins, Dale, 236-237
Hawkins, Ronnie, 182
Head, Roy, 34
Helm, Levon, 182
Herzog, E.T. Sr., 47
Holly, Buddy, 11, 76, 84-87, 164, 177
Honeycutt, Glenn, 238
Horton, Johnny, 32
Howlin' Wolf, 52
Hubbard, Orangie Ray, 240
Hunter, Ivory Joe, 16, 20
Husky, Ferlin, 33

I

Independents, 226, 231, 241-243, 246, 273
Inman, Autry, 178

J

Jackson, Bull Moose, 16
Jackson, Wanda, 25, 180, 186-191
James, Sonny, 175
Janes, Roland, 12, 135
Jeffrey, Willie, 23
Jones, George, 33, 68
Judd Records, 53
Justis, Bill, 53

K

Kerr, Anita, Singers, 47, 51, 208
Kesler, Stan, 24
King, B.B., 52
King, Pee Wee, 121
King, Sid, and Five Strings, 241-242
King Records, 15, 47, 65-70, 121, 140, 222
Knox, Buddy, 170-171, 177

L

LaBeef, Sleepy, 12, 33, 243
Lee, Dickey, 136, 144-150
Lewis, Jerry Lee, 10, 34, 103-105
Little Green Men, 24, 135
Lloyd, Jimmy, 25, 245-247
Lou, Bonnie, 65, 201-203
Loudermilk, John D., 34
Lowe, Jim, 188
Luman, Bob, 178

M

Mack, Lonnie, 108
Mack, Warner, 34
Maddox Brothers, 17, 65
Maddox, Rose, 17, 185, 186, 192-193
Martin, Janis, 189-190
Memphis Recording Service, 21
MGM Records, 32, 273
Midwestern Hayride, 47, 125
Mizell, Hank, 65
Moman, Chips, 48
Montgomery, Bob, 89
Moore, Merrill, 17
Moore, Scotty, 21, 77, 254
Morgan, Al, 16
Mullican, Moon, 15, 20, 65
Music Row, 45

N

Nashville Sound, 46
Nathan, Sidney, 65, 121
National Barn Dance, 16

O

Opry, Grand Ole, 76
Orbison, Roy, 52, 177
Owens, Buck, 180

P

Parsons, Bill, 204
Payne, Leon, 33
Penny, Joe, 65
Perkins, Carl, 24, 52, 76-77, 88-96
Phillips, Dewey, 145
Phillips, International, 53
Phillips, Judd, 53
Phillips, Sam, 21, 24, 50-54, 152
Pierce, Don, 68
Pierce, Webb, 20, 32
Pittman, Barbara, 185, 197
Poovey, Groovey Joe, 255-256
Presley, Elvis, 10-11, 21-22, 52, 78-83, 116, 153, 187
Price, Ray, 20
Pythian Temple, 213

R

Rambo, Bobby, 257
Raney, Wayne, 15-16, 32
Reed, Jerry, 34
Renfro Valley Jamboree, 47
Reno, Don, 32
Rice, Denzil "Dumpy," 9, 106-114
Rich, Charlie, 52
Richardson, J.P. (Big Bopper), 163-164
Riley, Billy Lee, 12, 24, 51, 134-138
Robbins, Marty, 173
Robertson, Robbie, 182
Robison, Carson, 32
Rodgers, Jimmie, 46
Roulette Records, 246
Ryan, Charlie, 16

S

Saddle, Rock and Rhythm Boys, 17
Scott, Ray, 261-262
Seals, Troy, 263
Self, Ronnie, 51, 162
Sharpe, Ray, 264
Simmons, Gene, 157-161
Singleton, Shelby S., Jr., 54
Skipper, Macy, 265
Smiley, Red, 32
Smith, Ray, 64

Smith, Warren, 33, 51, 270
Snow, Hank, 32
Stanley Brothers, 66
Starday Records, 15, 22, 33, 68, 122, 241
Starr, Ray (Ray Pennington), 139
Sun Records, 15, 20, 24, 50-57, 134, 145
Sun International Corp., 54

T

Taylor, Bill, 24
Taylor, Chip, 26
Tex, Joe, 66
Thompson, Hayden, 266-268
Trammell, Bobby Lee, 244, 269
Tubb, Ernest, 20, 47, 126
Tubb, Justin, 32
Twitty, Conway, 100-103

V

Van Story, Marcus, 270
Velvet, Jimmy, 180
Vic Records, 220
Vickery, Mack, 34
Vincent, Gene, 97-98, 257

W

Wayne, Thomas (Perkins), 53
Watkins, Bill, 271
Wilburn Brothers, 66
Williams, Hank, 14, 16, 19, 47, 125
Williams, Otis, 66
Wills, Bob, 16, 32
Wood, Bobby, 271-272
Wright, Dale, 273-277
WSM Radio, 46

Y

Yelvington, Malcomb, 135, 151-156
Young, Nelson, 278-281

SONG INDEX

Ain't Got Time To Be Unhappy, 178
Alabam, 122
Almost Paradise, 177
All-American Boy, 204
All I Have To Do Is Dream, 174
All Night Rock, 239
All Shook Up, 104
Arkansas Twist, 244, 269
Baby Let's Play House, 24
Ballad Of Two Brothers, 178
Believe What You Say, 176
Be-Bop Baby, 176
Be-Bop-A-Lula, 24, 97,
Bird Dog, 174
Birmingham Bounce, 14
Black Slacks, 181
Blue Jean Heart, 222
Blue Moon Of Kentucky, 12, 21
Blue Suede Shoes, 24-25, 76
Blues, Blues, Blues, 266

Boogie Woogie On A Saturday Night, 15
Bop-A-Lena, 126
Bop Pills, 265
Boppin' The Blues, 25
Breathless, 104
Butterfly, 172
Bye Bye Love, 174
Caterpillar, 215
Chantilly Lace, 164
Circle Rock, 32, 122
C'mon Everybody, 167
Cracker Jack, 221
Crazy, Man, Crazy, 20
Daddy-O, 66
Daydreaming, 252
Dis A Itty Bit, 208
Dixie Fried, 90
Don't Be Cruel, 22
Don't Cheat In Our Hometown, 141
Don't Destroy Me, 183
Down In The Alley, 182
Down To My Last I Forgive You, 249
Drinkin' Wine Spodee-O-Dee, 153
Duck Tail, 221
Dum Dum, 198
Early In The Morning, 86
Everybody's Movin', 235
Fairlane Rock, 266
Filipino Baby, 121
The First Kiss, 177
Fly Right Boogie, 17
Flying Saucers Rock 'n' Roll, 24, 51, 135, 261
Forty Days, 182
Fujiyama Mama, 187
Geraldine, 179
Gonna Find Me A Bluebird, 179
Gonna Rock 'n' Roll Tonight, 248
Gonna Shake This Shack Tonight, 241
Goodbye Kisses, 124
Good Rockin' Tonight, 20
Granddaddy's Rockin', 222
Great Balls of Fire, 104
Great Impostor, The, 198
Green Door, The, 168
Haunted House, 158, 253
Heartbreak Hotel, 22, 33
Hey, Baby! 219
Hey, Little Dreamboat, 17, 186
Hillbilly Boogie, 15
Hillbilly Fever, 17
Honey Bop, 187
Honey Don't, 92
Honey Love, 231
Hot Dog That Made Him Mad, 187
Hot Rod Lincoln, 258
Hound Dog, 22
Hula Love, 170
Hula Rock, 32
I Don't Know, 17
I Forgot To Remember To Forget, 24
I Need A Man, 194
I'll Be Around, 238
I'm Left, You're Right, She's Gone, 24
I'm Sorry, 162
It Doesn't Matter Anymore, 86
It's Only Make Believe, 100
I've Got A Rocket In My Pocket, 25, 245
Jailhouse Rock, 22
Jealous Heart, 16
Knock Three Times, 184
Last Date, 272
Let's Have A Party, 25, 187
Let's Think About Living, 178
Linda Lu, 264
Little John's Gone, 252
Little Miss Linda, 222

Love Me Tender, 234
Matchbox, 92
Maybe Baby, 86
Maybellene, 173
Mama, Mama, Mama, 266
Mary Lou, 182
Mona Lisa, 248
Motel Time Again, 127
Mule Skinner Blues, 46
My Kind Of Carrying On, 254
Mystery Train, 24
Now She Cares No More, 254
Ooby Dooby, 189
Party Doll, 170
Peggy Sue, 25, 86
Penny Loafers, 181
Pink Pedal Pushers, 25
Put Your Cat Clothes On, 90
Raining In My Heart, 186
Ramblin' Man, 140
Rave On, 86
Red Hot, 24, 135
Red Sails In The Sunset, 264
Rinky Dink, 101
Rock Around The Clock, 120
Rock Around With Ollie Vee, 226
Rock It, 33
Rock Love, 234
Rockin' Daddy, 205
Rockin' Love, 248
Rock Ole Sputnik To The Moon, 279
Rock The Joint, 20
Rock-Rockola, 17
Rocket 88, 20
Rockin' And Rollin', 32
Rockin' Little Angel, 53
Running Bear, 163
Seventeen, 66, 74
Shake, Baby, Shake, 269
Shake, Rattle, and Roll, 20
Shaking The Blues, 126
She's Neat, 273
Shirley Lee, 269
Shotgun Boogie, 17
Strange Little Girl, 32, 122
Sugaree, 25, 131
Summertime Blues, 167
Suzy-Q, 236
Sweet Love, 240
Teenage Boogie, 32
Ten Long Fingers, 255
Tennessee Waltz, The, 119
That's All Right Mama, 21, 222,
3,000 Miles, 231
Tobacco Road, 34, 166
Tootsie, 252
Tore Up, 243
Two Young Fools In Love, 195
Ubangi Stomp, 33, 53
Wake Up Little Susie, 174
White Lightning, 164
White Sport Coat (And A Pink Carnation), 173
Who Put The Squeeze On Eloise? 265
Where The Rio Del Rosa Flows, 246
Wild, Wild Women, 218
Wild, Wild Young Men, 192
Will You Willyum, 189
Wings Of A Dove, 33
Words Of Love, 86
You Are My Sunshine, 252
You Drive Me Crazy, 261
Young Love, 175

The author is grateful to Cheryl McNutt, Wayne Perry, Dave Travis, and Jim Rohrer for their help and encouragement.